T0374929

The publisher and the University of California Press Foundation gratefully acknowledge the generous support of the Atkinson Family Foundation Imprint in Higher Education.

The publisher and the University of California Press Foundation gratefully acknowledge the generous support of the Lawrence Grauman, Jr. Fund.

The publisher and the University of California Press Foundation gratefully acknowledge the generous support of the George Gund Foundation Imprint in African American Studies.

Education in Black and White

Education in Black and White

MYLES HORTON AND THE HIGHLANDER CENTER'S VISION FOR SOCIAL JUSTICE

Stephen Preskill

UNIVERSITY OF CALIFORNIA PRESS

University of California Press
Oakland, California

© 2021 by Stephen Preskill

Library of Congress Cataloging-in-Publication Data

Names: Preskill, Stephen, 1950– author.
Title: Education in black and white : Myles Horton and the Highlander
  Center's vision for social justice / Stephen Preskill.
Description: Oakland, California : University of California Press,
  [2021] | Includes bibliographical references and index.
Identifiers: LCCN 2020035403 (print) | LCCN 2020035404 (ebook)
ISBN 9780520302051 (cloth) | ISBN 9780520972315 (epub)
Subjects: LCSH: Horton, Myles, 1905-1990. | Highlander Folk School
  (Monteagle, Tenn.) | Highlander Research and Education Center
  (Knoxville, Tenn.) | School administrators—Tennessee—
  Monteagle—Biography. | Social justice and education. | Adult
  education—Social aspects—Tennessee.
Classification: LCC LA2317.H75 P74 2021 (print) | LCC LA2317
  .H75 (ebook) | DDC 371.20092 [B]—dc23
LC record available at https://lccn.loc.gov/2020035403
LC ebook record available at https://lccn.loc.gov/2020035404

Manufactured in the United States of America

29 28 27 26 25 24 23 22 21
10 9 8 7 6 5 4 3 2 1

Contents

Prologue: The Highlander Fire of 2019

On March 29, 2019, the main administrative building of the High-lander Research and Education Center in New Market, Tennessee, burned to the ground. Although no one was injured, valuable documents were reduced to ashes, and thousands of people with close ties to the center experienced profound feelings of loss and grief. Near the site of the burned-out building, arsonists had scrawled a crude white nationalist symbol on the parking lot pavement. As two writers put it, the fire wasn't just property loss: "It's as though a sanctuary was violated."[1] John Lewis, a congressman from Georgia who had his first interracial meal at Highlander and spent many eye-opening hours there as a student activist, pondered, in the wake of this act of hate, "What makes us feel threatened by a center that promotes peace and brotherhood for all humankind?"[2]

Although the fire must have left Highlander feeling battered, its official position was to stay strong and united: "This is a time for building our power. Now is a time to be vigilant. To love each other and support each other and to keep each other safe in turbulent times."[3] Highlander's co-director, Ash-Lee Woodard Henderson, commented that one of the center's sources of strength is "the wisdom of the elders we still have access to." In the wake of such a tragedy, it helps to know "that this is not the first storm we've weathered, which is why this moment isn't hopeless." The message was clear. The ability of the center to withstand such a violation is rooted, at least in part, in the memory of comrades and colleagues who, at a very young age, repeatedly absorbed the blows of racist bullies and somehow "survived those storms, too."[4]

One of the most prominent of those colleagues and elders was Myles Horton, who, in 1932, at the age of twenty-seven, co-founded the Highlander Folk School with twenty-six-year-old Don West. Horton would remain at Highlander in a variety of roles, mainly as director, for another fifty-eight years, until his death in 1990 at the age of 84. Throughout that period, he witnessed numerous attempts to destroy Highlander by threatening its staff, raiding its meetings, burning its buildings, and, finally, padlocking its grounds and confiscating its property for allegedly promoting communism. Although Horton and his colleagues were never communists, they did seek to usher in a new social order, one that would ensure justice, decency, and a meaningful voice for all, especially the poor, the downtrodden, and the oppressed. Even after Highlander was shut down by the state of Tennessee in 1961 on baseless charges, it rose again, stronger than ever, first in Knoxville and then, in 1971, in New Market, Tennessee, as the Highlander Research and Education Center. Over the years, as Horton and the staff learned to take nothing for granted, they became resigned to the fierce opposition that its egalitarian, anti-racist mission all too often inflamed. The Highlander fire of 2019 was another episode in a long line of attempts to intimidate the center into extinction, to prevent it from doing what it had always done best: bring people together to create a more democratic and hopeful future.

The Highlander fire, although devastating, had one positive effect. It reminded thousands, perhaps even millions, of people of Highlander's unremitting commitment to social justice and its remarkable capacity for resilience in the face of adversity. It also re-introduced them to Myles Horton, whose legacy of educating for democracy and forging a beloved community during Highlander's first half century continue to sustain the center with reservoirs of strength, inspiration, and hope.

Introduction

Not long after Myles Horton died in 1990, activist Anne Braden paid tribute to Horton for his commitment to doing "the impossible." As she saw it, establishing the Highlander Folk School in 1932 in the depths of the Great Depression and in a profoundly impoverished part of rural Tennessee epitomized the impossible. Just as improbably, Horton chose to make Highlander a center for adult learning where subjugated southern workers, both black and white, could meet in a spirit of equality and mutual respect. Few places in the world were as inhospitable to workers' rights and racial justice as the rural South in the 1930s. Jim Crow segregation engulfed the region, and workers who organized for higher wages and better working conditions risked being branded as Communists. Braden called it an impossible mission at an impossible time. Nor did she underestimate its perils: "One did not challenge the South's 'way of life' without risking one's own life in the process."[1]

"From the beginning," sociologist Aldon Morris affirmed, "Highlander was a rarity. In the midst of worker oppression, racism, and lynchings, Highlander unflinchingly communicated to the world that it was an island of decency that would never betray its humanitarian vision."[2] Somehow, despite the implausibility of their quest, Horton and his Highlander colleagues persisted. In time, the southern workers did gain greater control over their lives, in part due to Highlander's efforts, and after many years of trying to bring integrated groups together without success, Highlander finally became one of the few places in the South where blacks and whites could rely on encountering one another as equals. When Student Nonviolent Coordinating Committee (SNCC) leader John Lewis attended a Highlander workshop in 1960, the extent of the integration stunned him: "This was the first time in my life that I saw black people and white people not just sitting down together at long tables for shared meals, but also cleaning up together afterward, doing the dishes together, gathering together late into the night in deep discussion and sleeping in the same cabin dormitories."[3] To Anne Braden, Horton and his colleagues were able "to attempt the impossible because they were gripped by a vision of a new kind of society . . . in which there would be justice for all."[4]

As director of Highlander over the course of some forty years, Horton had a hand in fueling two of the twentieth century's greatest social movements: the crusade for organized labor and the freedom struggle for civil rights. Because of Highlander, thousands of people gained the determination and the skills to make change for the common good in their communities. At the heart of Highlander's educational approach stood its commitment to democracy, which Horton saw as much more than casting a ballot or majority rule. For him, it meant nothing less than carving out a "free space" for people to learn, play, and work together and to gain greater control over their collective lives.[5]

In his 1952 book *South of Freedom*, which examined life under Jim Crow, black journalist Carl Rowan identified a handful of white southerners actively working for racial justice. Horton was one of these. Rowan admired him for spearheading one of the few meeting places in the South that insisted on racial integration, and for being willing to denounce "racial segregation" as "the root and perpetrator of all the evils" plaguing the South.[6] Forty-eight years later, when

C-Span founder Brian Lamb asked philosopher and social activist Cornel West which white person in American history, male or female, "was most sympathetic to changing racial differences," West responded, without hesitation, "Myles Horton." He called Horton an "indescribably courageous and visionary white brother from Tennessee."[7] Later, West also said Horton was "one of the great existential democrats of the twentieth century in terms of understanding democracy as a way of life."[8]

In November 2016, leaders in the Black Lives Matter movement chose the Highlander Research and Education Center as the site for an important organizational gathering because they knew about Highlander's relentless commitment to social justice. They knew that Highlander had fearlessly taken the side of the disempowered and the dispossessed for over eighty years. And they knew that when the civil rights movement reached its height, Highlander remained one of the few places in the South that embraced freedom fighters like Rosa Parks, Septima Clark, Ella Baker, Dorothy Cotton, Andrew Young, and Dr. Martin Luther King. All came to Highlander to continue the struggle for human rights, and all aligned themselves with Highlander in promoting participatory democracy and social change from the bottom up. Highlander's legacy lives on in the hearts of some of America's most dedicated racial justice activists.[9]

I met Myles Horton just once, when he was a guest speaker in a community organizing class at Carleton College taught by Paul Wellstone, later the two-term U.S. senator from Minnesota. It was the mid-1980s and I was an assistant professor of education at Carleton, where I had gotten to know Wellstone fairly well. He knew of my interest in Highlander and so encouraged me to sit in. Wellstone's emphasis on fostering social change was a perfect opportunity for Horton to share his favorite yarns about his work at Highlander. None of the students had ever heard of Horton or Highlander, but they quickly warmed to his folksy manner and irrepressible sense of humor. He loved to laugh and did so a lot, mainly in response to his own jokes and anecdotes. I remember, too, the affectionate bantering between Horton and Wellstone. It was clear they knew each other well and had worked together many times as activists. But Horton wasn't all smiles. He became deadly serious when he talked about how much work needed to be done to make the United States an authentic democracy. He said that democracy wasn't working at all, not just in Appalachia, but throughout the country. And until people found the strength, confidence, and spirit of unity to take charge of their lives and their communities, change would not happen.

Horton's eyes were lively and his wit was sharp, but he also seemed to tire easily—he was over eighty at the time—and would soon be diagnosed with cancer. When he and I were alone together for a few minutes after the class was over, I asked him about his biggest influences. I mentioned John Dewey, but he said George S. Counts was much more important to him, because when he was young he was such a bold advocate for radical change. He said Karl Marx was also a key influence, because Marx gave him the tools for understanding what he was reading and what he was up against in opposing powerful interests that didn't seem to care much about people in need. He also asked me a lot of questions about what I hoped to accomplish as an educator. When I responded that part of my goal was to follow his example, he laughed, partly because he didn't see himself as a role model and partly because he doubted I could accomplish much as a professor at an elite college. When I brought up Wellstone, he smiled serenely and then added: "Paul Wellstone is one in a million. Few, if any, can do what he does in working-class communities and still hang on at a college like this." I nodded without saying anything, perhaps because we both knew how close Wellstone had come to losing his position at Carleton near the beginning of his career, and how much tension remained between him and many of his colleagues. I wanted our time together to go on indefinitely, but Horton was late for a meeting in the Twin Cities and he was pretty much talked out. When the campus visit was over, I watched Wellstone and Horton say goodbye to one another with a warm embrace. Horton waved and urged me to come to Highlander. I never did.

Horton was a Tennessee native, born and bred in the western part of the state. Although he later traveled a great deal, raising money and enlisting allies to keep Highlander alive, he remained in rural Tennessee for the rest of his life. When asked why he planted his roots so firmly in Tennessee, he called it the region he knew and loved best. He looked on Tennessee as the place where he could make the biggest difference in people's lives, because it was under his skin, inseparable from how he saw himself as a person and an activist. Years later, Horton observed that he never wanted to create a school for the United States as a whole. He wanted to open a school for a specific place with specific boundaries, a place known as Appalachia. "I was trying to think of a school for people I knew . . . the largest number of poor white people in the United States; people who had some semblance of a tradition and background. . . . I knew there was a certain distinctiveness that grew partially out of poverty and partially out of isolation, and partly out of the background of people who came here."[10]

My background could not have been more different from Horton's. I am the product of a well-to-do family that settled in a prosperous Chicago suburb in the early 1950s. My father worked as an executive for a successful electronics company and my mother, who had earned a law degree, stayed home to care for my two brothers and me. I had virtually no adversity in my life. I attended a public high school that in many ways was the equivalent of an elite private academy. And although I didn't end up attending Ivy League schools or accumulating a lot of money, I never really lacked for anything. I grew up in a lovely and peaceful community, but I felt no tie to it, leaving it for good almost as soon as I could. Throughout my life, I have enjoyed enormous advantages as a white male heterosexual professor who had very little sense of what it was like to be poor or black or female or gay in the oppressive atmosphere of post–World War II America. While I never quite qualified as part of the one percent, I benefited from an immensely privileged position in one of the world's most privileged societies and understood almost nothing about the adversity faced by so many others.

I first learned about Myles Horton many years ago, when I discovered a two-hour television interview conducted by Bill Moyers to commemorate the fiftieth anniversary of the school Horton had started back in 1932.[11] When I first viewed the Moyers interview, Horton's respect for ordinary people and his uncompromising commitment to creating a truly equitable society astonished me. Who was this man who believed so totally in the ability of the person next door, whoever she or he was, to become a leader and learn how to change the community's life for the better? When Moyers asked what idea set Highlander apart from other schools, Horton replied, somewhat haltingly, that Highlander "believed in people." In another context, Horton called Highlander a "faith venture," not because its directors had faith in a method or a clever approach, but owing to their faith in people, above all.[12] He went on to say that Highlander always put people ahead of institutions or structures and that this first principle of prioritizing people made powerful learning possible, allowing them to realize that the answers to their problems resided inside of them. They just needed encouragement and time to reflect on their experiences and a few strategies to bring those answers to the surface. As Horton put it in 1968, "We have felt that people, especially poor adults, who had been denied opportunities for full development had a capacity that was untapped and if you could find some way to get people turned on and give them confidence that they had something to say about their own lives they would come up with some creative answers and activities."[13] In order to live this philosophy, Highlander found that it needed to erase the line between teachers and students. While the staff or teachers might have more formal knowledge or book learning, Horton found that the so-called students often had "deeper insights into human relationships . . . [and] a better understanding of how to deal with people, like themselves."[14]

While watching that Horton video, I recalled my own experiences in schools as a bored, disengaged student. Because of my dissatisfaction with the education I had received, I started out as a middle school teacher who wanted to turn all that boredom around and singlehandedly rouse my students to life. Unfortunately, I failed more often than I succeeded, and I could feel myself often falling back on the very same didactic methods that had so often put me to sleep as a student. Somehow, I wanted to incorporate Horton's far more liberating approach into my own teaching practice, or, at the very least, come to understand it better.

At that time, the best source on Horton and Highlander was Frank Adams's 1975 book *Unearthing Seeds of Fire: The Idea of Highlander*, a work that continues to be required reading for those determined to know Highlander and Horton more deeply. As a close collaborator of Horton's and former Highlander staff member, Adams might have been inclined to overpraise the school, but I took heart from Adams's own up-front admission of bias. Furthermore, I was drawn to Adams's belief that "education must be born from the creative tension between how life is lived and how life might be lived in a free society."[15] Was that the underlying idea Horton and Adams had in mind? I tore into Adams searching for answers. As I read, I quickly recognized that "the idea of Highlander" encompassed many ideas. Encouraging people to gain greater control over their lives by keeping the focus on their actual experiences emerged as one key idea. Another involved resisting individualism and embracing group learning in a residential setting. Still another emphasized identifying with the needs of the poor, the marginalized, and the discriminated against, employing many modes of expression, including music, dance, and drama, to bring people closer together. Additionally, and perhaps most importantly, Highlander embraced applied learning, inspiring people to build on what they had gained from workshops to spark change back in their home communities.

You might say the late 1980s and the early 1990s were the golden age of Highlander and Horton scholarship. In those years, the first edition of John Glen's definitive study of Highlander appeared.[16] The expanded and revised edition came out eight years later.[17] Aimee Horton's groundbreaking 1971 dissertation about Highlander was published as a book in 1989.[18] A year later, two additional works that directly involved Horton himself were published. *The Long Haul*—the engaging autobiographical portrait that Horton produced with the collaboration of Judith and Herbert Kohl—was one.[19] The other was the talking book he published with Paulo Freire called *We Make the Road by Walking*.[20] All of these added enormously to my understanding of Horton's development as an educator and activist and to the role Highlander played in pushing for social change. The final book to which I am especially indebted is the volume that Dale Jacobs put together and published in 2003. The *Myles Horton Reader* makes many of Horton's most important writings and interviews available to the general public for the first time. In addition, Jacobs writes a superb introduction that ably synthesizes Horton's key ideas and actions.[21] Lesser known but also excellent is Stephen Schneider's comparatively recent book on Highlander and its rhetorical practices, *You Can't Padlock an Idea*.[22]

This book is an addition to that literature, but in no way a replacement for any of it. In fact, without these works, I could not have told this story as I have. I also make no pretense of producing an exhaustive or comprehensive account. At the same time, I hope I have delivered a version of Myles Horton's life that is interesting and accessible. This work stands more as a reminder of Horton's legacy and why his accomplishments and influence remain as relevant as ever. It is also a ringing reaffirmation of Horton's lessons about educating for democracy.

If I have tried to do anything differently from past chroniclers of Horton's life, it is in framing his story as an account of an educator, passionately committed to helping adults, mostly poor and forgotten, to wake up to their own historic agency. Ordinary people have always found ways to solve their problems outside the formal educational system, primarily through informal experimentation in the midst of "daily attempts to live with dignity while trying to obtain food, clothing, and shelter."[23] But they have done so in fits and starts, rarely as part of an organized and consistent reaction to discrimination and oppression. Downtrodden people have often needed an instigator like Horton to help them rediscover their own power to think collaboratively and bring about life-giving change. Whether in his role as gracious host, wise storyteller, aggressive questioner, loyal ally, or committed resource provider, Horton affirmed people's strengths as learners and as leaders and rekindled their commitment to forging a more responsive and decent society. Only in this light can he be accurately seen: as one of America's most effective and inspiring adult educators.

In a larger sense, because Horton always worked outside any recognized system of institutionalized education and sought to collaborate with all learners equally, "unhampered by the need to rank, examine or certify," he led a movement for popular education.[24] As Highlander archivist and change agent Sue Thrasher has said, "Popular education comes from the bottom-up, from the grassroots, from people's organizations, and movements for social change."[25] No diploma or credential was necessary for participation in a Highlander workshop. Curiosity, mutual respect, and commitment to building a more just society were the only expectations. As a popular educator,

Horton brought diverse groups together to share their experiences and to heighten their awareness of existing social conditions, to help them analyze those experiences and to gain insight into the injustices of existing conditions, and to strengthen their ability to go back to their communities to continue the process of overthrowing those conditions. For Horton, education at Highlander was thoroughly dialogical and unapologetically two-way, a process in which everyone, by definition, enjoyed opportunities to serve as teacher and learner, encouraging all those assembled to achieve a deeper, more critical, more truthful reading of the world. Like all education growing out of a genuine democratic impulse, Highlander's movement for popular education embraced "the same commitment to reflect on reality and to 'name' it, and finally to act in order to transform it."[26] Perhaps veteran adult educator Tom Heaney said it best: "The aim of popular education is to have voice," not in order to adapt to what is, but to claim what "ought to be."[27]

Popular education and deep democracy, as Horton lived and practiced them, continue to be the foundation for all meaningful social change today. But as in 1932, when Highlander first began, our current authoritarian moment feels like an impossible time to try to reinvigorate democratic education. To understand why Horton's approach remains more relevant and more urgent than ever within the twenty-first century, this book focuses on his story and how the strategies developed at Highlander served the interests of the poor, the marginalized, and the oppressed. It begins with Horton's boyhood, growing up poor in western Tennessee, and includes a few of the critical incidents that led to Highlander's establishment in 1932. It also chronicles how he gained influence as an advocate for organized labor, an activist for civil rights, a supporter of Appalachian self-empowerment, an architect of an international popular education network, and a champion for direct democracy, and why the example he set remains education's last best hope today.

1 *Beginnings*

LEARNING FROM FAMILY

The story of Myles Falls Horton begins with deep poverty. Born in 1905 in a rural part of Tennessee, about one hundred miles east of Memphis, Horton knew how it felt to go hungry, to have only a single change of clothes, and to see his parents struggle to make ends meet. Most of the time, his parents and he and his three younger siblings had enough food to eat, but there were no extras in their lives and little relief from their daily hardships. Yet Horton didn't think of his family as poor or working class. They were just an ordinary family with very little money.[1]

Horton's parents, Perry and Elsie, had gotten as far as the eighth grade in school, which at that time in Tennessee set them apart as "well educated" and qualified them to be public school teachers. They had met while teaching, enjoyed their work, and appreciated having positions with regular paychecks.[2] But not long after Horton's birth, they lost their eligibility to teach when new certification rules mandated that all teachers have at least one additional year of schooling beyond the eighth grade. For a while, Horton's father found steady work as a county clerk in Savannah, Tennessee, but that, too, eventually ended. To bring in enough money to keep the family fed, Horton's parents took any work they could find, selling insurance house to house, working in a northern Mississippi canning factory maintaining the company's records, repairing sewing machines—whatever came along. Later, as the Great Depression approached, with hard times hitting the rural South much earlier than other parts of the country, they had to scrape by working as sharecroppers and domestics. Over time, that uncertainty undermined their faith in an economy that failed to make full use of two extremely hard-working people. The radical historian Howard Zinn, in recalling his own conscientious mother and father, concluded sadly that they had little to show for their hard work. He "resented the smug statements of politicians, media commentators, corporate executives who talked of how in America if you worked hard you would become rich." He knew this was a lie because his parents "worked harder than anyone."[3] In the same way, despite working about as tirelessly as anyone can, Myles Horton's parents continued to come up nearly empty. The few photographs of them that exist show two humble people, quite thin and of modest stature. They are not smiling but they aren't grim either, just very determined, refusing to let all that adversity keep them down.

Because of their backgrounds, Horton's parents did not waver when it came to educating their children. Whenever the family moved, which occurred often to chase down possible employment, Horton's father made sure that the schools were decent and promptly removed his children from any school he deemed inadequate. Horton said that without his ever quite knowing why, education remained central to his family's life. His parents insisted "you should go to school as long as you needed to and that nothing should stand in the way of an education. You could do without meals, you could do without a lot of things, but not without schooling."[4] The family moved to the town of Humboldt when Horton turned fifteen, despite poor job prospects there, because Humboldt was one of the few towns in the area with a good high school. Later, when the family moved to Forked Deer River and jobs were even scarcer, Perry Horton did not start looking for a job until he conferred with the superintendent and felt confident that the local school met his son's educational needs.[5] In the end, all four of the Horton children graduated from high school at a time and in a place that made this achievement remarkable. At least two of them, Myles and his sister, Elsie Pearl, graduated from college.

Part of the problem that Horton's father encountered in landing steady employment stemmed from the fact that western Tennessee, particularly the area just east of Memphis, was especially slow in making the transition from agriculture to industrialization. Farming and sharecropping remained the most common ways to make a living well into the twentieth century and left most people poor. Coal miners, woodcutters, and textile workers didn't fare much better. None of these jobs paid much, nor could any of them be counted on for stable work, especially in the 1920s and 1930s. Savannah, Tennessee, where Horton and his family first lived, was a county seat in the southwest corner of the state whose population dropped fairly precipitously, from around a thousand people when Horton was born in 1905 to just over seven hundred by 1920. The decline was doubtless driven by the scarcity of jobs, though other factors probably contributed to the sense of precariousness, not least of which included an astronomically high infant mortality rate and frequent outbreaks of typhoid fever.[6]

The family's precarious financial situation touched Horton far less than did others' deprivation. His awareness of their troubles came largely through his mother's lived examples. She often served the family only half of the evening meal so she could bring food to their more disadvantaged neighbors. As Horton said, she needed "to share out of her poverty," to help those who were not only poor, but also sick and frail from lack of nutrition. On those nights, Horton went to bed with hunger pangs, which he must have resented to a degree. But he mainly felt respect for his mother and her commitment to making a difference. As he put it, "I knew it meant so much to her, and I wouldn't have wanted to hurt her feelings by complaining."[7]

Not surprisingly, Horton gradually developed an affinity for poor working people, not because there was anything noble about being poor; he hated poverty and spent most of his life trying to defeat it. Rather, he admired poor people for enduring adversity without complaining, while enriching their communities in so many other ways, as dedicated laborers and good neighbors. Like most people in Appalachia, Horton didn't run into many rich people, so he was largely ignorant of the luxuries they enjoyed. Occasionally, though, he would spy an absentee landholder or a coal mining executive riding around in a big automobile and wonder how some people could "work so hard and get so little, and for somebody else to have so much."[8]

Horton's paternal grandfather, Mordecai Pinkney, or "M.P." Horton, who often voiced his hatred for rich people, served as one of Horton's earliest teachers. Though lacking formal education, primarily because accessible schools were almost unheard of in the part of Tennessee where he grew up in the 1850s, M.P. Horton could perform complicated math calculations in his head, which he used with some success in buying and selling cattle. Horton said that when his grandfather looked at a cow he could "weigh it in his mind" and then multiply by the market rate per pound to get a surprisingly accurate estimate of the cow's value. Sometimes Horton would read the *Cattle Report* to his grandfather, who surprised his grandson with the retentiveness of his agile mind.[9]

In particular, Horton loved the stories his grandfather shared about his childhood, regularly using memorable epithets for the rich people he detested. He often spoke of the rich as if they were a different species, saying, "that's just for rich people," or "rich people are the only ones who do that." He never aspired to be rich because, as he saw it, the wealthy "lived off of somebody else," which signaled that they misunderstood the purpose of life and most likely "were go-ing to hell."[10]

The elder Horton instilled in his grandson a belief that poor peo-ple lived with dignity, simplicity, and humility; they didn't need to exploit others to make a living. Still, the privations that working peo-ple experienced were unacceptable. They needed "to live decently on the basis of their work" and were justified in resisting the hard-ships that the rich imposed.[11] With such a background, Horton soon came to regard the wage/labor system as inherently unfair. He never could shake the feeling that this unjust system was the root cause of most of society's ills. He resolved to devote his life to righting this in-justice through the best means he knew—helping people learn how to gain control of their situations to make their shared lives better.

Membership in the Cumberland Presbyterian Church (CPC) also shaped the Hortons' family life. A Kentucky and Tennessee offshoot of the more conservative Presbyterian church, the CPC had an informal-ity and accessibility that many country people appreciated. For one thing, services were conducted in colloquial English, not the lofty rhet-oric of the more traditional church. For another, the church encouraged women to be leaders and supported the ordination of female preachers. Some even referred to the CPC as "the people's church." The CPC also made modest efforts, thanks to people like Elsie Horton, to look out for the most disadvantaged members of the surrounding community. As Frank Adams noted, "The Hortons gave what they could of their scant supplies of food and clothing in times of need or emergency. This was the extent of a church member's responsibility."[12]

As Horton learned more about the church's beliefs, he grew wor-ried, confessing to his mother that he didn't see how he could con-tinue to be part of an institution that espoused things like predestina-tion and original sin. These ideas just didn't make sense to him. She dismissed his worries as mere details, just "preachers' talk." What mattered, she explained, "is that you've got to love your neighbor."

Reflecting on her stance much later, Horton recalled that his mother didn't say anything about God: "Love was a religion to her, that's what she practiced."[13]

For Horton, these teachings formed the basis for Highlander: "If you believe that people are of worth, you can't treat anybody inhumanely, and that means you not only have to love and respect people, but you have to think in terms of building a society that people can profit most from, and that kind of society has to work on the principle of equality."[14] Horton understood that some people might come across as mean or abusive or hateful and therefore didn't seem to merit that love and respect. He assumed, however, that these negative qualities resulted from the cruelties of an unjust and unequal society, not something intrinsic to the person. So although people might seem unloving and untrustworthy, they had to be treated as if they *were* loving and trustworthy. Love and trustworthiness had to be baked into the democratic process of relating to one another, until eventually, sometimes after a very long period of time, some of that love and trust could be reciprocated.

Still, when Horton was growing up in rural Tennessee, white people who were inclined to extend a hand to people in need rarely reached out to blacks. When it came to love and trust, African Americans simply did not count. Although Horton would eventually focus his attention on the problem of racial injustice, he remained ignorant of the discrimination faced by people of color throughout his boyhood because, like so many other white Tennesseans, he took much of that discrimination for granted. As Horton explained in an interview from 1959, the desire to help others in Tennessee's rural communities was not extended to blacks: "It was never in our culture or in our philosophy to accept Negroes," Horton conceded. In fact, it went even farther than that. The culture literally thought "Negroes were not people."[15]

Horton did know one black family quite well—Aunt Donnie and her grandson Bob. Aunt Donnie took care of the Horton children when they were very young, just as she had cared for his mother years before when she was little. She didn't live with the Hortons but would stay for extended periods and pretty much took over the household whenever Elsie became ill or was called away. As Cynthia Stokes Brown has said, Perry Horton's willingness to relinquish his favorite rocking chair to Aunt Donnie whenever she visited signified her special authority. As youngsters, Myles and Bob, roughly the same age, reveled in these visits because of the fun they had playing together. But as the two boys got older, the adults around them subtly discouraged their friendship, a change that saddened and confused Horton at the time. One day, Bob approached the Hortons' ramshackle house in a wagon filled with groceries. As he drove up close to the family's front door to empty his load, Aunt Donnie barked some scolding words that Horton never forgot: "Boy, don't you never come up to white folks' front door. Take that bag 'round back."[16] Decades later, as he recounted this story, Horton said "he could still see the tears that flowed down Bob's cheeks." Horton didn't fault Aunt Donnie; he knew she had to teach her grandson the lessons that could spell the difference between life and death in the Jim Crow South.[17]

GROWING UP

From an early age, reading held a special place in Myles Horton's life. He read anything he could get his hands on. Since his family lacked money to buy books, and no public libraries existed in the remote part of western Tennessee where he lived, he had to borrow books from neighbors, often going from house to house in search of any kind of reading material. He was indiscriminate, reading everything from encyclopedias to pornographic novels to Sears mail-order catalogues, building up skills that put him ahead of his peers. Eventually, reading became a meaningful part of his development, but at this early age, he simply liked the sound of words and the warm feelings that came over him as he pored over a text, even when he couldn't personally relate to its content.[18]

One summer, some relatives moved into town. They had a magnificent glass-covered bookcase stuffed with books. It was the grandest collection Horton had ever seen, and he knew he had to read them all. There were dictionaries and encyclopedias, medical texts and manuals about animal husbandry, but the strange titles didn't discourage him. At that point in his life, he hadn't even developed a concept of preferring one book to another. The books sitting there on those long, smooth, wooden shelves beckoned him, and so he devoured them, one right after another.[19]

At some point, Horton and his brother Delmas, also an avid reader, made an important discovery. They could order five books for a dollar from the Sears and Roebuck catalog, and if they didn't like the books that arrived, they could exchange them for no added cost. They claimed not to like any of the books they received, returning them in exchange for new ones, then expressing dissatisfaction with whatever the next shipment brought. Because Sears was so big, many months went by before the company finally discovered the boys' scheme. By that time, they had gained free access to hundreds of volumes of reading material that helped satisfy their penchant for print.[20]

Horton's parents greatly valued their son's passion for learning. They never doubted that he should attend high school. They found a decent secondary school in Humboldt that Horton could attend, some twenty miles or so from where the family was living. However, because walking was Horton's only mode of transportation, commuting would be impractical. He would have to live on his own and fend for himself. He stayed in a friend's garage apartment and did all his cooking over a Sterno can heater. His parents often visited on weekends, driving a team of mules that dragged a wagon filled with potatoes to supplement Horton's meager diet. He began to do odd jobs and eventually got steady work helping out in a grocery, which gave him income for essentials and solved his problem of trying to get by on a near-starvation diet.[21]

This was hardly the first time Horton had coped with hunger. Before going away to high school, Horton's prized possession and only real pleasure was a piglet that he had nurtured into a fat, gleaming adult hog, large enough and well fed enough to compete for a blue ribbon through the local 4-H Club. For the first time in his life, as Horton remembered, he would be getting recognition for a long-term project he had accomplished on his own. Unfortunately, as the time for the awards contest drew near, the family experienced an especially hard season that made food even scarcer than usual. They slaughtered the pig to feed the family.

After the family dined on the pig, Horton felt sorry for himself and wandered out into a clover field to lie down under a night sky blazing with stars. The moon and the stars seemed near enough for him to reach up and stir them around, and he started to cry. Hardly a minute had gone by, though, before he grabbed hold of himself and choked off the flow of tears. He even started to laugh out loud at what he suddenly saw as ridiculous behavior. What warranted such self-pity? Weren't his parents doing everything possible to support him? In that moment, he pledged not to feel sorry for himself ever again. But he also reflected on his dilemma and began to turn his thoughts from his parents and his personal feelings to a system that he increasingly saw as unfair. His parents weren't to blame, as he would say later. "I knew my Dad had hunted everywhere for jobs. He'd been laid off every job he had. He was doing the best he could, and my mother was making do with limited resources. They loved us but they were crippled. They were handicapped by this situation. And from that time on I never felt sorry for myself."[22]

Recollections of this little epiphany stayed with Horton as he proceeded through high school. Whenever he started to feel resentment toward the people who seemed to be responsible for denying him some simple pleasure because he lacked the resources to enjoy it, he would remind himself not to hold the individual accountable. The true culprit was an oppressive system that granted a few people a great deal of wealth while forcing the vast majority to eke out a meager living. For Horton, this shift in thinking meant that he could stop wasting his sympathy on himself and retain more of it for other people and the situations that kept them down.

Horton's inclination to trust his own instincts and critique the institutions he found himself connected to often got him into trouble. In school, he would put aside assigned texts to focus on content that he found more interesting and made little effort to conceal his preferences. One day, while in geography class, he thought he could outsmart the teacher by holding the oversized textbook in front of a travelogue about India that especially captivated him. Suspecting something was up, the teacher snuck up behind him and tapped him on the shoulder to deliver a few admonishing words. He politely put down the book and redirected his attention to the teacher's lecture, but soon returned to his far more absorbing adventure story.[23]

Horton told stories such as this throughout his life to convey his distaste for institutionalized education; these stories also reflected his mounting anger at the injustices he encountered. It was unjust that the state of Tennessee allocated so little money for public education. Equally unjust was the scarcity of secondary schools and the fact that teachers received such low salaries and so little support to further develop their skills. Overall, the inadequacy of public education in Tennessee struck Horton as a great injustice, especially when compared to the far better schools in the North, just a few hundred miles away. His anger did not lessen with time. With each passing year, as Horton encountered more and more of the indignities of an often backward and deeply discriminatory South, his rage grew. In the late 1930s, after suffering through a series of long leaves of absence from Highlander to recover from bouts of physical and emotional exhaustion, he realized that he had to find a way to dampen the intensity of that anger.[24]

He gradually learned that his anger was an important motivator for the kind of work he was trying to do, so he didn't want it to die out entirely. But he also couldn't afford to let it get out of hand. He learned to both appreciate and manage his anger, treating it as a constant, but not explosive, ally. The fire of his anger became "smoldering . . . subject to revving up and getting going" but also subdued, which made him better able to meet the needs of activism's long haul.[25] It was, as Jeanne Theoharis has recently said with respect to the Montgomery bus boycott, "Anger transformed into action." Like the boycott, Highlander's ability to create a center where blacks and whites could learn and agitate together grew out of "an accumulation of perseverance, anger, and relationships built over years."[26]

One of the most important outlets for that anger was Horton's voracious reading, which gradually evolved into one of his chief ways of making sense of the world. He still didn't have money for books, but he relied on wealthier classmates who agreed to lend him reading materials as long as, in return, he would interpret the content for them so they could pass their exams. Some of these transactions involved boring textbooks, but others included classic literature, like Shakespeare and Shelley, two authors who became lifelong favorites for Horton. Even in high school, formal education dismayed Horton. His classmates were learning to hate great literature because nothing mattered except passing exams; reading to excite the imagination or make sense of the world had no place for them. Once again, Horton did not fault his classmates; he condemned an unjust system that seemed to be designed to kill off "any possibility of students ever enjoying this literature."[27]

Despite Horton's frustration with formal schooling, he compiled a strong academic record—an accomplishment that when paired with his talent for football brought him a scholarship to Cumberland University, a small institution in central Tennessee affiliated with the CPC. Tennesseans rarely attended a four-year college in the 1920s, and students who had grown up in poverty, like Horton, almost never enjoyed this privilege. Without football, college would have been out of reach for him.

Because of its affiliation with the CPC, the church he had grown up in, Cumberland must have seemed like a good fit. Located in Lebanon, Tennessee, also home to a large woolen mill, Cumberland was established in 1842 and had a long history of serving relatively prosperous white males and perpetuating "Southern values." From the start, Horton did not hesitate to interrupt some of that privilege. Upon arriving, he organized a protest against the abusive hazing that aspiring fraternity brothers observed as a common rite of passage. It was the first of many acts of resistance that Horton would initiate against taken-for-granted but unjust institutional practices.[28]

Although Horton entered the university as a religious studies major, he quickly changed his major to English and spent a lot of his time in Cumberland's library catching up on literature that had gone unassigned in high school.[29] Horton also enjoyed football practice and was expected to spend a good deal of his time outside of class on the field. His tall, lanky build meant he had to get by on his wits rather than brawn. As a defensive tackle, he developed an aptitude for analyzing a situation quickly and then figuring out how to take advantage of it—a skill that would later come in handy as an activist on the cutting edge of social change. At games, he would give the opposing tackle a false sense of security that Horton was predictable and easy to handle. Then on crucial plays, he would use a new move, taking his opponent completely by surprise. His approach made him "famous for making tackles behind the line."[30]

He was an accomplished athlete at Cumberland, but his growing self-sufficiency and rapidly shifting interests led him to give up football in his senior year because the team's practices interfered with his independent reading and his campus organizing. The university threatened to expel him because he was breaking the terms of his scholarship, which apparently didn't faze Horton. The threat was never carried out, probably because faculty and peers alike thought highly of him. The same year in which he quit the football team and Cumberland threatened expulsion, the senior class elected him president.

PAYING THE BILLS

Throughout Horton's time as a student, having enough money for basic living expenses preoccupied him. When not reading, attending class, or going to football practice, he was usually busy with one odd job or another. He couldn't make ends meet without summer employment. In the summer of 1925, when he turned twenty, he worked in a box factory. It cost the company five cents to make each box, which it then sold, in turn, for fifteen cents. The workers produced thousands of boxes each week, receiving twenty-five cents an hour for their labor. The work was grueling in the hot factory, but Horton felt lucky to have any kind of job.

Alongside the plant stood the luxurious mansion where the factory owners lived. Next door sat a commodious barn, about which Horton often fantasized. He imagined gathering with other workers in the barn to play games, tell stories, and eat hearty meals, never having to worry about going hungry or running out of food. This fantasy got Horton thinking about rural Tennessee as a place that was defined by two kinds of people: "Those who own and those who work." Even though he envied his wealthy neighbors' lives of ease, he didn't aspire to become rich. He simply wanted his own life and the lives of people he worked with to be healthier, freer, more creative, and somewhat less precarious.[31]

That same summer of 1925, the famous Scopes trial was under way on the other side of the state in Dayton, Tennessee. It was a titanic battle between Clarence Darrow, the celebrated criminal defense lawyer, representing John Scopes and his right to teach Darwin's theory of evolution, and William Jennings Bryan, the Democratic Party's nominee for president three times over and a Christian fundamentalist who shunned Darwin and believed unquestioningly in a literal interpretation of the Bible. The confrontation between these two giants put Tennessee at the center of the world that summer. During breaks, the workers in the box factory talked about what journalist H.L. Mencken had labeled "The Monkey Trial." Some thought the trial a waste of time; others insisted Bryan's crusade was the work of the Lord. Horton, virtually alone, supported Scopes. At first he tried to defend Scopes, arguing for the right of free speech and the importance of teaching the latest scientific knowledge. He also loved to talk of what he had read about Darrow's brilliantly argued case. His coworkers would frown, turn away, or dismiss him with a profane word and long, drawn-out sighs. All his "jawing" increasingly exasperated them, so Horton eventually stopped talking about the trial altogether. He did not, however, stop reading about evolution or about the significance of what was transpiring in Dayton. Something was happening to him that summer in the box factory. He was moving away from the traditions, biases, and unreflective judgments of the culture that had shaped him. He was developing a mind of his own.[32]

CONFRONTING WHITE SUPREMACY

While representing Cumberland as a member of the state of Tennessee's student YMCA, Horton traveled to cities like Nashville and

Knoxville for the first time and experienced the cruelty of Jim Crow segregation up close. Once, while attending a gathering in Nashville, he invited a Chinese girl to accompany him at dinner, only to learn that no restaurant would admit them. During that same trip, he attempted to escort a black woman into a public library, but officials blocked the doorway, telling them interracial couples could not enter. What especially galled him and caused him such a "rude shock," he later said, were the limits imposed by white supremacy on his "own desire for expression." Though he would later analyze the situation more deeply, using an ethical and collective lens, his first reaction was personal: How dare the state limit his freedom.[33]

In these early years, Horton railed against segregation of any kind because he resisted any practice that excluded him, that put unwarranted limits on what he could do. As a mountaineer, he didn't like being excluded from people who weren't mountaineers. As a country person, he hated being excluded from city folk. As a poor person, he resented feeling excluded from a lot of things. As he put it years later, "I was excluded because I didn't have clothes . . . I was excluded because I didn't have money . . . I've been excluded for a lot of reasons . . . I don't like to be excluded."[34] Because of his upbringing, Horton knew that his anger couldn't stop with getting what he personally wanted. He had to fight for everyone who faced exclusion and hated it as much as he did.

Horton's work with the YMCA student group in college led to a position after he graduated in 1928 as the head of Tennessee's student YMCA. He traveled more than ever and grew increasingly troubled by the conflict between his belief in inclusion and the entrenched segregation of Tennessee. As the leader of the student YMCA, he decided to hold integrated meetings, even though they were outlawed by the state, risking punishment, perhaps even jail, to remain true to his beliefs.

On one occasion, he invited both black and white representatives of Tennessee's student YMCA to a banquet at a whites-only hotel in

Knoxville to launch the group's state-wide meeting. Believing even then that the best way to change people's minds was to immerse them in an experience, rather than ask for permission or warn them in advance, he brought 120 black and white participants into the banquet hall and invited them to eat. Startled by the setting but habituated to eat when food is presented, the students began sharing the dishes already spread out on the table. When the all-black hotel waiters objected, saying they could not continue to serve the integrated gathering, probably because they feared the reprisals of their white bosses, Horton assured them that it would be all right. He said, "We're paying you to serve us. We hired you to wait on us. If we get up and leave, you'll go home without any pay, and if we don't get any food, we'll get up and leave." Finally, the waiters relented and the integrated banquet went on. Although he could have been arrested for transgressing the segregation statutes of the state of Tennessee, Horton was willing to take the risk. As he put it, he "took the gamble of doing something about a moral problem instead of simply talking about it."[35]

Horton became increasingly preoccupied with the problem of racial discrimination. In 1929, he wrote a series of short stories about the indignities of everyday racism in Tennessee, likely drawing on his firsthand observations. In one story he portrayed a recently married, well-educated black couple patiently waiting for a Nashville commuter bus to fill up with white passengers, so that, according to Jim Crow laws, they could take the last remaining seats at the very back of the bus. They were anxious to make this trip because it was their honeymoon. The wife, a recent college graduate who had enjoyed a racially sheltered existence at her all-black school, "had almost forgotten what the world was like." Suddenly, a surge of white passengers jumped the line in front of the couple. They grabbed the last seats, including those in the back, leaving the couple stranded in the aisle. Spotting the husband's frown, one of the last white passengers said sympathetically, "Too bad, but this is the kind of world we live in and it will stay this way until we change it." The husband, lips quivering, responded, "Yes, this is the world we live in all right but some of *us* didn't quite make it."[36] The moral reflected the heart of Horton's developing vision for his school: to create an environment in which all, without exception, would help to make the world they lived in.

Most whites, though, even those who were disturbed by racial discrimination, did relatively little to push for change. A number of white volunteers for the student YMCA who opposed segregation would sit down privately with their black peers to explore strategies for uprooting Jim Crow, but out of "respect" for southern white traditions, would refuse to eat with them or to meet over coffee. Horton believed such compromises emboldened white supremacists by reinforcing their norms, serving only to perpetuate and even deepen existing prejudices. Besides, for Horton, talk without action would never bring about needed change. Sometimes actions needed to be bold, showing a willingness to directly confront the unquestioned conventions of the South. He knew successful change would require "action to be the main thrust."[37]

Horton's unrelenting insistence on direct action made him infamous. He was the stubborn Y employee who always insisted on interracial gatherings wherever he held a meeting. He didn't ask permission; he just did what he thought was right. As it turned out, he succeeded in holding integrated meetings, but his efforts mostly turned people off. When he resigned, after a frustrating year of being labeled a troublemaker and a rabble-rouser, the Y's officials admitted being relieved.[38]

For Horton, that year with the Y constituted another kind of coming of age. He fully realized the limits and harms of racism, not just for African Americans, but for everyone, including himself. As he put it in an interview many years later, "I made it an operating principle that no one should have their rights interfered with as long as they were minding their own business. . . . Somehow I had enough understanding to know that I couldn't have rights just for me . . . that there were no rights just for me alone."[39] He was realizing that his right to have a life of unlimited possibility and creativity depended on everyone else being guaranteed the same right. Whether they were black or white, male or female, city dweller or mountain hermit, if they did not get a chance to enjoy that same unlimited freedom that he cherished so deeply, his ability to live his own life to the fullest would also be in jeopardy.

AWAKENING TO WORKERS' OPPRESSION

While at Cumberland, Horton's growing commitment to racial equality overlapped with an increasingly keen interest in labor unions. As a youngster, he had listened to his father speak out against unions and at first wondered if they were a mistake. His father opposed them on principle; he feared that they threatened worker independence. But once Horton started working and saw how badly management exploited labor out of what appeared to be sheer greed, he began to look more closely at the advantages of getting workers organized. In a course on labor history, a young sociology professor encouraged him to write an ambitious paper about a tobacco farmers' cooperative in Kentucky that had been organized by a transplant from New York. He urged Horton to explore how this outsider used his skills and knowledge to get farmers to work together instead of competing against one another. The experience of writing the paper and the positive feedback Horton received from the professor spurred him on.[40]

In 1927, during the fall semester of his senior year, Horton encountered the wealthy mill owner John Edgerton for the first time. Edgerton, head of the Lebanon Woolen Mills and the most prominent businessman in Lebanon, Tennessee, had served as president of the conservative National Association of Manufacturers and had coerced the organization into actively opposing any move to improve workplace conditions for the rank and file. He was a proud member of the owner class who made no apologies for worker exploitation. Horton knew relatively little about the historic struggles between capital and labor at this time—he was only twenty-two years old—but when he heard Edgerton speak with contempt and condescension for workers during a special Labor Day celebration, his "blood just boiled."[41] Edgerton's dismissive attitude toward organized labor helped Horton to see that classism, like racism, was another form of prejudice he needed to combat.

In his speech to the Cumberland community, Edgerton argued that owners must retain total control over the workplace, that workers had no rights that owners were bound to respect. Edgerton saw advocates for the rights of workers as dangerous radicals, either as Communists or as funded by Communists. He especially despised proposals to reduce the work week from six days to five, fearing that more leisure would lead to degeneracy and greater radicalism. As he put it, "The common people had to be kept at their desks and machines, lest they rise up against their betters. . . . Nothing breeds radicalism more quickly than unhappiness unless it is leisure, and as long as the people are kept profitably and happily employed there is little danger from radicalism."[42]

Horton felt deeply violated by what he heard. It all sounded terribly backward and was profoundly insulting to people he knew, like his fellow workers at the box factory. As he recalled much later, hearing Edgerton's words "absolutely set me wild."[43] He was so upset that he "almost wanted to pull him off the platform and beat him up!"[44]

Horton, characteristically compelled to act when he saw injustice, paid at least one unannounced visit to Edgerton's woolen factory to speak with the workers as they exited the plant. He urged them not to put up with the low wages, long hours, dangerous machinery, and incessant racket that he had heard plagued the mill. They should organize, protest, demand that the mill be made fit for human beings. The workers, unused to such mobilizing efforts and wary of anything that might threaten their job security, mostly turned away from Horton or pretended not to hear him. Stunned that he had failed to stir up any followers, Horton returned to campus to another surprise: He was charged with insubordination. When Edgerton found out that Horton had visited his mill to attempt to influence his workers, he demanded the student be punished. While no real consequences ensued for Horton, university officials warned him not to return to the mill or he would face expulsion.[45]

Horton agreed to stay away and graduated the following spring, but he emerged from college a changed man. What he had experienced had radicalized him, exactly the thing Edgerton most feared. Horton understood that he needed a deeper, more systemic analysis of Tennessee's complex history to make sense of how its engrained hatreds and prejudices had shaped life in the state. He had also decided that conventional schools were neither designed nor equipped to make sense of injustice. People needed a new kind of school or gathering place to empower them and to reverse the conditions that kept everyday citizens permanently under the thumb of white supremacists and unsympathetic business owners. He started dreaming about this school. He imagined it as a place where everyone's participation actually mattered and where democracy truly lived.

2   *The Lessons of Ozone*

As Myles Horton turned twenty-one in the summer of 1926, he was completing his first year as a vacation Bible school teacher for the local Presbyterian church in Ozone, Tennessee, one of a number of sparsely populated towns dotting the Cumberland Plateau in the eastern part of the state. Although Horton had lost interest in organized religion, he continued to see church as inseparable from everyday life in rural Tennessee. Whether one believed in the precepts taught by the church or not, religion enjoyed a preeminent place in a community's affairs. Moreover, Horton admired the CPC for its plain-spoken theology, which his mother had boiled down to the simple phrase "love thy neighbor." But he hadn't taken the job to help children understand the Bible. He took it because he needed money to return to college the following fall. Though his church salary barely constituted a living wage, it beat working in a textile mill or a coal mine. He also identified with the adults who lived there, mostly poor and working-class people struggling, like him, to scrape by. The isolation and natural beauty of the surrounding mountains drew him, too. Positioned along the Cumberland Plateau, where some peaks stretch more than 1,500 feet above sea level, the town of Ozone had some of the finest views in the region. Low pay aside, it was a perfect job. Horton gained valuable teaching experience, the isolated location allowed him to commune with nature, and the solitude gave him the peace of mind he felt he needed to contemplate his future.

Horton also spent a good bit of time worrying, because Ozone's long-term prospects seemed so dim. The region's rural economy had been badly depressed for years. Industrial farming had destroyed formerly fertile land. Lumber companies had greedily slashed out most of the available timber. Jobs were scarce in the small textile mills that had begun to sprout in the nearby towns. The few coal mines that remained weren't hiring much or were paying subsistence-level wages, because coal mining had become increasingly unprofitable.

In addition, the burden of Tennessee's shameful racial history continued to limit development. While mining had once been an almost certain means of employment for Appalachians, the industry had embraced the widespread practice in the Jim Crow South of using prisoners as free labor. As a result, during the post-Reconstruction period, many mining jobs were reserved for black convicts who served as unpaid labor through Tennessee's prisoner lease system, which was tantamount to a new form of enslavement.[1] Most of these prisoners had been apprehended for "crimes" categorized as vagrancy or loitering; often these were activities as harmless as pausing on a street corner to strike up a conversation with a passerby. White supremacists' interest in using the law to maintain segregation thus directly served capitalists' interests as well, providing industry with a steady stream of free black labor. Tennessee's extremely weak union movement was largely powerless against this system, though in the early 1890s, poorly organized white miners had resorted to violence to unseat convict leasing practices, leading to some permanent changes. But new, more covert forms of convict leasing developed, continuing well into the twentieth century.[2] So gainful, steady employment in the mines was relatively rare, and those able to find regular work frequently faced early death from accidents or black lung disease, occupational hazards approaching epidemic proportions.

Given all of these challenges, that first summer at Ozone proved difficult for Horton. He still had not found a way to relieve the burdens of the local people. He taught the Bible and managed the various Sunday schools under his supervision, but he did so with diminishing enthusiasm. He got more satisfaction out of sharing his love of sports and Appalachian lore with the children. He taught them to swim and play football and introduced them to the songs and stories he recalled from community gatherings back home. But he had a feeling that he could and should do more, so he began conferring with community leaders to understand how to serve. In any case, he felt sure that the long Bible passages, the memorized verses, and the hymns offered minimal comfort to people who often went hungry, lacked steady employment, and felt defenseless against life-threatening illnesses. He had grown tired of the church's lessons because they did nothing to help people cope with the challenges of their everyday lives.[3]

As Bible school ended after that first summer, Horton's supervisors asked him to return the following year, even promising a few additional dollars to pay for some assistants. Horton accepted their offer, but would not, he decided, teach the Bible himself; he would train his assistants to do that. He looked forward to being freed up to get to know the community better and to extend a hand to people in need.[4]

THE REVEREND NIGHTINGALE

Horton's main mentor in thinking through the issues confronting the region was the minister of a Congregational church in nearby Crossville named Abram Nightingale. Reverend Nightingale had grown up in the North and had been ordained at Moody Bible Institute in Chicago. For ten years he served as a pastor on the Fort Berthold

Indian Reservation in North Dakota before heading south to accept a post at the Crossville church. Although a self-conscious outsider upon settling in Crossville, he resolved to know the town and its surroundings as well as any native. He did things that most preachers regarded as beneath them. He volunteered in hospitals, taking on any job that needed to be done, including emptying bedpans. He accompanied farmers into the fields or miners into the quarries to learn about their work firsthand. He maintained an open-door policy, not only for townspeople, but also for the parade of displaced people who passed through Crossville needing a hot meal or a warm bed. He welcomed people from a variety of faith traditions into his church and favored racial equality and integration, despite the backlash from an unsympathetic white community. During World War II, he publicly opposed the inhumane treatment of German and Italian prisoners of war assigned to Camp Crossville, not far from his church, even though this, too, triggered negative reactions from locals.[5]

A calm, unsentimental figure, Nightingale led a spartan existence. He ate little, slept sparingly, and read widely. He saved money by building his house with his own hands, and he loved sparking long, meandering discussions that lasted late into the night. Horton came to view him as a kind of saint, invigoratingly different from other clergymen he knew.[6] Indeed, Nightingale's example so impressed Horton that he soon adopted the reverend's philosophy of the Social Gospel and began to give serious consideration to attending Union Theological Seminary in New York City after graduating from college, to learn more about how to use Scripture to address social problems. Nightingale also encouraged Horton to read *Our Economic Morality and the Ethic of Jesus,* written by Harry Ward, one of Union's most radical faculty members and one of the nation's best-known proponents of this school of thought.[7]

Horton stayed with Nightingale for long stretches of time during those summers of teaching, often relying on Nightingale to supplement his meager diet. In addition to a square meal, he could count on the minister to give him a shirt to wear or a pair of socks to replace the ones that had long ago become worn out.[8] Nightingale also listened. He spent many hours sitting with Horton as he spun tales of teaching the children in the mountains and of growing increasingly disillusioned with his ineffectualness. Nightingale counseled Horton that he couldn't begin to make changes without getting to know the people and the issues troubling them. Besides, those actually living with those problems understood them best. If Horton really wanted to be of service, he should try calling a meeting to find out what was on people's minds.

COMMUNITY CONVERSATIONS AT OZONE

At the start of the second summer, Horton took Nightingale's advice, announcing his plan to host a meeting for parents of the Bible school students and other community members at the local Presbyterian church. Best known for its picturesque waterfall, Ozone was a very sparsely populated community, boasting little more than a tiny post office, a few scattered homes, and the church. People usually lived some distance from the town center, but Horton felt that its modest size made it the perfect spot for his "experiment."[9] He didn't say anything about the topic for the meeting; he himself didn't know what the focus would be. He publicized it as a chance for people to get to know one another better and to talk about some of the issues that concerned them.[10]

When only a few people appeared at the scheduled time, Horton couldn't help thinking that his plan had been a failure. But soon more families arrived, all on foot or by horseback, delayed by the long distances they had traveled on poorly maintained roads. Horton greeted them with a firm handshake and a warm smile as they passed through the church door. He made a point of thanking each attendee personally for going to the trouble of coming. His contagious laugh echoed throughout the old, cramped sanctuary.

Once everyone was settled, he informed the parents that Bible school was going well. He introduced his assistants, who shared examples of how much the children had learned. He also highlighted how comfortable the children had grown in the water because of the swimming lessons. He then invited the parents to speak up about any concerns they might have. For many of the parents, it was a strange request; they had no experience talking about themselves in a public meeting. Some parents mumbled a few words about the school and how much their kids enjoyed it, and others compared notes on how far they had traveled to attend the meeting, with at least one person claiming she had come a full ten miles on foot.[11] Little else was shared.

For a few moments, only the sound of people shifting in their seats filled the awkward silence. Horton waited patiently. He stood tall, his angular, rail-thin figure leaning reassuringly toward the audience. The grin on his long face underscored his ingratiating nature. He liked to be alone, but he also loved to gab with people about virtually anything—from the natural beauty of the mountains to the meaning of existence. He could have easily filled the silence for the whole evening by telling a story about growing up in western Tennessee or how, as a defensive tackle on Cumberland's overmatched football team, he had learned to outfox opposing players.

But the point of the meeting was to get the people to tell their stories, not for him to tell his. Finally, Horton cleared his throat and began to explain why he had brought everyone together: "You know, I know some of the problems here. I know some of you people are working in mines. Some of you are trying to make a living on farms. Some of you are going off and working in textile mills. Some of you are back home, suffering from what happened to you in the mines and in the textile mills." There was a growing suspicion that the bad working conditions often led to illness, and examples abounded of preventable accidents that required months of recovery without pay. Horton added, "It's getting pretty serious, pretty desperate. Let's talk about some of these problems that we have."[12]

First, someone mentioned the weather and its effect on the crops. Somebody else expressed worries about the economy. Agricultural prices were badly depressed, so most farmers and sharecroppers were hurting, many of them desperate for cash. On top of that, jobs for miners and woodcutters were increasingly scarce, and it was hard to want to work in a mill or factory where you had to be cooped up indoors for long hours for such low wages. One person brought up typhoid, then rampant in the area, wondering how to test wells that might be carrying it.[13]

An older woman spoke longingly of an earlier time, before the strip mining and the timber cutting, when the land had been gleaming and untouched. She wondered out loud, looking straight at Horton: "Could the once beautiful hillsides ever grow trees again?"[14] He listened and looked back and tried to smile reassuringly, but he had no real answer.

As with so many of the issues that were raised, he lacked a satisfying response. Even as he stood before the people gathered there, he wondered if he should pretend to have solutions to problems that eluded him. At first, he opted to evade the queries by responding sympathetically, without commenting further. Finally, Horton realized he couldn't deceive them any longer. He admitted he didn't call the meeting to supply answers.

"I don't know the answers," he recalled telling them, "and I don't have any technical competence" to find the answers. Fearing that his admission might strike some people as resignation, he sought to relieve some of the uncertainty by telling a simple story. When he was growing up, people would sometimes sit around talking casually about their problems and what could be done about them. It helped just to talk things out, to get different people to start thinking about those problems and how they had been approached in the past. "Somebody would say 'try this' or somebody else would add 'I heard about this.'" When people talked to each other like that, "a lot of ideas and knowledge would come out."[15] Horton proposed that the group give this a try. "Maybe what you know will help somebody else and what they've done [can] help you. Let's talk about what you know. You know this better than anybody else. You don't have any answers, but you know the problems."[16]

Somehow, Horton's pep talk broke the tension in the meeting, leading to a new, livelier stage in the discussion. One person explained how to apply for a job in the local mill; another cautioned people about the all-too-common practice of merchants intentionally undervaluing the weight of a harvest at market; still another shared news about a labor union planning to enlist new members. Horton joined the discussion, too, sharing that he had met a health official who knew a few things about staving off typhoid. But he was only one of many. They began to look to each other for answers, not just to him. Everyone was surprised by what happened because no one had "any terminology for this or any concepts" for making sense of it. But the discussion continued for a long time with no signs of fatigue or slackening interest. "Before the evening was over, people began to feel that from their peers they were getting a lot of answers." For Horton, this was a pivotal moment. As he said much later, "That was the beginning of this understanding that there's knowledge there that they didn't recognize."[17]

Horton had little experience reading the faces of these particular participants, so he couldn't decide at first whether or not to call a follow-up meeting. When he did extend a second invitation, an even larger and more vocal group showed up. This time, Horton brought along a knowledgeable county agent named Bob Lyons, whom he had met through Nightingale. Lyons gave the people information about how to organize co-ops and introduced a different resource person who offered to help them add privies to their land, as indoor plumbing was still at least a decade away in this part of rural Tennessee. The enthusiasm and knowledge of the parents especially surprised Lyons. He promised to return for subsequent gatherings.[18]

Horton felt relieved to have someone like Lyons on hand. His presence allowed Horton to listen more supportively, ask helpful follow-up questions, underscore important points, and, in general, deepen the spirit of engagement. Although listening did not come easily to Horton—he was inclined to be a storyteller—he had a way of listening, when he really wanted to, that "lifted people out of themselves." When he put his mind to listening, when he devoted every fiber of his being to absorbing what people were saying, they, "heard the sound of their own voices being taken seriously about issues of great import in their lives, usually for the first time ever." Horton may not have been fully aware of the quality of his listening, but there is little doubt that part of the secret to his success in such group settings grew out of his extraordinary ability to will himself to pay close attention to others.[19]

Although Horton couldn't explain exactly what aroused such intense involvement, he knew the meetings had value for people. They laughed, asked a lot of questions, and sat through long exchanges without complaining. Gradually, Horton developed a routine for getting the meetings started. He might open with a well-known tune that the entire gathering could sing together, or he'd ask an older resident to tell one of those familiar country stories that everyone knows but people never tire of hearing.[20] He'd try anything so that people once again warmed to the idea of talking through their problems and exploring possible solutions together.

In time, weekly meetings weren't enough to keep the community satisfied. As Horton said, "the word spread" so rapidly that we started having "one every night."[21] During the summer of 1927, attendance grew to almost eighty people. The numbers were so surprising that one Presbyterian Church official warned Horton to lie about his figures: "Say 20," the official suggested, because "nobody ever got that many people to a meeting in the mountains."[22]

Without experiencing the meetings firsthand, no one could comprehend the sense of relief people gained from talking openly about their lives and problems. They kept coming back because they seemed to need to talk to each other, to identify with one another's experiences, to gain the sense of community solidarity that can grow out of dialogue and mutual consultation. Knowing the answers to their questions was the least of it. "That was probably the greatest discovery I ever made," Horton observed. "You don't have to know the answers. You raise the questions, sharpen the questions, get people to discussing them. And we found that in that group of mountain people a lot of answers were available if they pooled their knowledge."[23] Just as important, the process bolstered confidence, making people feel more valued and hopeful than they had in a long time.

As Horton prepared to return for his senior year of college at the end of that second summer, the experience at Ozone continued to nag at him. The rich discussions the community enjoyed surely resulted in deeper learning and an increased sense of togetherness. At the same time, Horton confessed to himself that nothing substantive had occurred. The poverty that he confronted at the first meeting remained stubbornly resistant to change. The job situation was no less dire. The barren land was still fallow and ugly, just as it had been prior to the meetings. What difference had it made? He was so dissatisfied with his own efforts that when a group of Ozone citizens invited him to relocate permanently after graduation, this time just to lead community meetings, he was flabbergasted. They told him honestly that they didn't really like everything he did. Sometimes he misled them or rubbed people the wrong way, but, in the end, he gave the community a boost and a new reason to feel proud. In addition, a woman in Ozone who had heard about the effect of the community meetings on the townspeople proposed that her home, which was quite close to the big Ozone Falls, be the new site for future gatherings. She also offered free room and board as a further inducement to Horton. "I have a home here," she told him, "and this is the kind of thing I'd like to see done. I'd like to turn my home over to you to run this kind of program here."[24]

Despite the attraction of the remarkable offer, Horton said no. For one thing, he wasn't ready to settle down. He also knew he lacked the analytical skills to make sense of what had happened. At that time, he was still so conditioned by "the traditional way of doing things" that he couldn't quite discern how his approach departed from business as usual. As he put it, the whole experience rang a bell that was very low and "when it would start ringing I'd kind of cover it up so I wouldn't have to listen to it, because I didn't understand it." He knew he needed more time to think, to figure out how to turn a largely spontaneous initiative into something closer to a systematic and replicable program.[25] He would later contend that Ozone gave him the idea of Highlander, though it took him a long time to realize it.[26]

Even after he finished his last summer in Ozone, Horton continued to drop in on Reverend Nightingale. They talked for many hours about Horton's experiences, and what other activists, including Jane Addams in Chicago and Reinhold Niebuhr in Detroit, were doing to help communities respond to poverty and joblessness. Horton told Nightingale that Ozone felt like a turning point, not just for him personally, but also as a symbol of what it might take to shake up a community. For years, he placed an "O" in his journal next to all the experiences and encounters that reminded him of Ozone. But primarily, Ozone represented a specific place for Horton, and for him it was important "to think in terms of place." As he put it, "My mind's just more comfortable dealing with something I could see." He wrote that he needed to go on a quest, traveling across the state, the country, and even the world, to actually drop in on places that might inform his goal of planting more Ozones in Appalachia.[27]

During Horton's time as state secretary of the student YMCA, he visited most of the high schools and colleges in Tennessee. He scoured the state searching for an Ozone-like program, some kind of model that might help him build on what he had already learned. All he learned was that no such model existed, at least not in the state of Tennessee.[28] What he found instead, much to his frustration, were highly traditional vocational programs that neither prepared students to think critically or creatively nor helped them address their everyday problems. While he encountered a number of worthy university and college extension programs that taught people how to run a farm or to start a business, none of them set out to examine or analyze existing societal conditions.[29] Even worse, he found that the education establishment made few allowances for the special needs and unique perspectives of students from remote mountain locations like Ozone. He wanted something very different. He wanted to inspire learners, to get them to see the value of their own experiences. He also wanted to discover free spaces where nothing was off limits. He dreamed of an approach that was radically open, where it would be okay to bring people together from wildly diverse backgrounds to "talk about anything regardless of anything."[30]

Throughout what was an unsatisfying year after graduating from college, Reverend Nightingale continued to counsel Horton and to lend him books. He also brought him an application to attend Union Theological Seminary in New York City. Although Horton had his doubts at first about the value of attending Union, Nightingale ended up writing a long and glowing recommendation for Horton that clearly played a role in getting the young man admitted. According to Horton, the fact that he was from the Tennessee mountains also gave him an advantage, because places like Union didn't attract many people like him. He was, in a sense, Union's "token hillbilly."[31] In the end, Horton agreed that he should go. During one of their last meetings, Nightingale sought to put graduate education into a proper context for him. Union "won't give you any answers to your problems," he said. Advanced study couldn't solve the types of problems Horton was interested in anyway. But it would be a good place for getting exposure to a wide range of ideas. "And let's face it," the reverend concluded, "You need background. You just don't know enough." As Horton said many years later, Nightingale couldn't have been more right. In August of 1929, just two months before the most devastating stock market crash in American history triggered the Great Depression, Horton headed for New York City to attend classes at one of the world's great theological seminaries.[32]

3 *Graduate Education and Denmark's Folk Schools*

Union Theological Seminary enjoyed a reputation as one of the world's most renowned centers for the study of liberal Christianity when Myles Horton arrived in the fall of 1929. Founded by the Presbyterian Church in 1836, Union opened its doors to a wide variety of religious faiths from its beginning, and by the 1890s had declared its independence from the Presbyterian Church, welcoming students from all denominations. Rooted in progressive principles and dedicated to alleviating human suffering, it regarded itself as an elite alternative to more conservative institutions such as Princeton Theological Seminary. Union started its own settlement house in 1895 and from then on encouraged students to devote as much time to social activism as they did to academic study.[1]

The school's best-known professor in the 1920s, Harry F. Ward, a strong anti-war activist and trenchant critic of capitalism, had just published *Our Economic Morality and the Ethic of Jesus,* a controversial best seller that argued for putting moral principles ahead of corporate profits.[2] Reverend Nightingale had suggested that Horton read the book, and it so deeply affected him that one of its central passages appeared sixty years later in his autobiography:

A capitalist economy rests on the hypothesis that man is a creature who prefers material comforts to moral values, who would rather have an increase in goods than in the quality of existence. The only future it can offer man is one in which he will get more conveniences but less freedom, justice, and fellowship. . . . The ethic of Jesus rejects this estimate of human nature; insists, moreover, that the very making of it is the negation of personality, whose essence lies in the making of choices and whose development consists in preferring moral satisfactions to material.[3]

Ward helped establish the American Civil Liberties Union (ACLU) in 1920 as an emergency response to the so-called Palmer Raids, in which A. Mitchell Palmer, United States attorney general under Woodrow Wilson, rounded up and deported alleged radicals without regard for their constitutional rights. Ward served as ACLU's national chairman during its first twenty years before resigning in protest over its 1940 decision to purge Communists from leadership roles. He never forgave the ACLU for betraying its founding principles by trampling on the most basic right of all—the right to free speech.[4]

Ward was widely admired for his willingness to intervene in crisis situations and for exhorting his students to use their learning to support subjugated people.[5] When Reinhold Niebuhr, probably Union's most celebrated theologian of all time, once overheard some students comparing him to Ward, Niebuhr helped them identify the key difference. It "was simple. I didn't have as much guts as Harry Ward when it came to the realities of the social struggle."[6]

Reinhold Niebuhr

Though Horton enrolled at Union to study with Ward, they never developed much of a relationship. Ward traveled widely and, with the exception of first-rate scholars like James Dombrowski, who later helped Horton establish the Highlander Folk School, Ward had few advisees.[7] Instead, Reinhold Niebuhr rapidly became Horton's most formative influence. Niebuhr had just joined Union in 1929, after a decade serving a working-class congregation in Detroit. While in the Midwest, Niebuhr involved himself in the labor movement and spoke out often against racism. At Union, he began work on *Moral Man and Immoral Society,* an erudite study that became a best seller in 1932 for its penetrating critique of knee-jerk liberalism. Niebuhr famously drew a distinction between individual and group morality, between those who conscientiously practiced kindness and generosity in their private lives and the tendency of collectives to deteriorate into cruelty and selfishness. He argued that although individuals might be motivated by love and mutual concern, groups were inevitably embroiled in a power struggle in which they said or did whatever it took to consolidate their power.[8] It followed, he argued, that individual morality did not translate easily to social movements, and that schemes to remake society in the image of the moral self inevitably met with failure. For Niebuhr, there was no sure way to bring about a just society, and overweening optimism about what could be accomplished in pursuing social change invariably resulted in disappointment. Still, oppressive systems, such as capitalism or communism, which accentuated the herd-like tendencies of human beings, had to be subordinated to those aspects of "the democratic creed which transcend the interests of the commercial and industrial classes."[9] Horton called this complex dichotomy between the moral self and the immoral society "exactly my problem" and looked forward to working with Niebuhr to examine this issue systematically.[10]

Niebuhr also fearlessly challenged John Dewey, at the time America's most famous philosopher of democracy, for being what he called "a tepid apostle . . . of political gradualism."[11] He ridiculed Dewey's "inordinate faith in reason to bring about social change" and mocked Dewey for his "dangerous utopianism."[12] Niebuhr further argued that under some circumstances, moral ends necessitated coercive or even violent means. Horton sympathized with Niebuhr's hard realism, believing that the unseen violence of hunger, homelessness, and chronic unemployment preyed unmercifully on oppressed people. He too thought lesser forms of violence might be justifiable to alleviate the greater and more sustained violence that stems from extremes of wealth and poverty.[13]

When the two met, Niebuhr was attempting to form the Fellowship of Socialist Christians and recruited Horton as a natural ally. He also invited Horton to attend his advanced seminar, which he built around the lectures eventually incorporated into *Moral Man and Immoral Society*. Even well-prepared students who had far better educational foundations than Horton did braced themselves for a challenging course. Horton reluctantly participated but felt discouraged almost from the beginning. During a break in the second or third session of the class, as the students and their professor congregated in the courtyard a few steps from their classroom, Horton approached Niebuhr about his need to withdraw.

"I just have to tell you I'm going to drop out," Horton began. "I'm not going to go back in because I can't understand anything you're saying. I'm not going to waste my time listening to you without understanding, because I can go over to the library and read something I can understand." When Niebuhr objected, Horton repeated, "I don't know what you're talking about at all."[14]

Niebuhr turned to the other students around them, many of whom held advanced degrees. He asked a friend and fellow pastor first. "Horton here says he can't understand what I'm talking about. How about you? Am I getting through to you?" The embarrassed pastor shook his head: "It's really hard going for me too." Niebuhr proceeded to survey the other students in the class. Each one, without exception, admitted that they couldn't say with confidence that they fully understood Niebuhr's lectures.[15]

Niebuhr took these confessions as a sign: Horton had to stay in the class as the resident truth teller, the one student he could count on to speak up when the lectures became impenetrable. As the semester wore on, Niebuhr often turned to Horton, especially when introducing dense content, for what he called an understanding check. Right in the middle of class, Niebuhr would lean toward Horton and ask, "Myles, do you understand what I'm talking about?" If Horton nodded, then he could proceed with confidence. As Horton recalled, "The others were ashamed to say they didn't understand. I had no pride. I was there to learn and wasn't even worried about grades or credit. All I wanted was to understand, to know."[16]

Undoubtedly, Horton's honesty and Niebuhr's appreciation for his forthrightness drew them closer together. Throughout his life, Horton's willingness to tell the whole truth, even when doing so brought unwelcome attention, deepened his reputation for integrity. Whether talking to a Tennessee sharecropper or an icon like Dr. Martin Luther King, Horton told his side of the story with raw, unvarnished honesty. Niebuhr revered this habit and soon became one of Horton's chief advisors. Niebuhr listened attentively, though with limited comprehension, to Horton's dreams of a mountain school where the people themselves could work out the answers to their own problems. For Horton, unlike Niebuhr, "theory was valued only as a prelude to action."[17] Given that difference, Horton never quite understood why Niebuhr supported his goals so strongly. Additionally, Niebuhr didn't really grasp Horton's emphasis on supporting people so they could learn from their personal experiences, drawing on their inherent wisdom to address pressing problems, and doing all of this with a minimum of help from outside experts. Many years later, as Horton reflected on his time at Union, he singled out Niebuhr for believing in him and not giving up on him. "He was the one person who had confidence in my ability to work this thing out," Horton recalled. He always remained "really sympathetic to my ideas."[18]

In a sense, Niebuhr, with all his erudition and influence, represented what Horton's own education lacked. What Niebuhr expounded upon so brilliantly as a teacher and scholar, coupled with the connections he had forged with distinguished scholars from all over the world, drove Horton to keep learning, to gain some measure of access to this set of theoretical understandings that might prove useful to him in the realm of action: "If I hadn't gone to Union, my world would be much smaller. I wouldn't have gotten to know faculty and student social activists and become involved in all the issues I didn't know existed before I left Tennessee."[19]

The Education Critics

Aside from Niebuhr, three additional faculty, all of whom were affiliated with Columbia University, strongly influenced Horton. John Dewey, who, despite Niebuhr's critique, received wide acclaim as America's leading public intellectual, left a lasting mark on Horton's practice. The others, George S. Counts and Eduard Lindeman, enjoyed reputations as two of the most widely read radical educational theorists of the period.

The year that Horton enrolled at Union, Dewey turned seventy. An immensely prolific author who had already produced dozens of books on every conceivable philosophic subject, Dewey continued to influence scholars and to shape public opinion. He became well known for his criticisms of traditional schooling and his advocacy of a more open, democratic, and learn-by-doing approach to education. Horton had no special relationship with Dewey, the way he did with Niebuhr, but Horton was stimulated by Dewey and inspired by his social optimism. "Dewey permeated the whole atmosphere at this time," Horton later observed. The political dimensions of Dewey's educational thought also proved influential; in particular, Horton came to share Dewey's belief that one of progressive education's primary aims must be to actively "take part in correcting unfair privilege and unfair deprivation, not to perpetuate them."[20]

Out of all of Dewey's teachings, his philosophy of experience probably had the greatest impact on Horton. Whether he had read Dewey accurately or not, Horton used Dewey to argue that all education grows out of an analysis of experience. By valuing those experiences, revisiting those experiences, and reflecting critically on those experiences, true learning can happen. Horton was also drawn to Dewey's refusal to accept premature conclusions, to keep options open, and to recognize that whatever one believed right now functioned as provisional knowledge, subject to revision based on new evidence and new experience. Like Dewey and the other pragmatists, Horton also felt that the most profound and lasting learning happened in groups whose deepening understanding formed the basis for collective action.

A few years after Highlander's opening, an article appeared calling Horton a disciple of Dewey. Somewhat embarrassed that unfriendly critics might misuse this information, Horton wrote to Dewey explaining that he did not really think of himself as a disciple. He added, "I'm grateful for the things I've learned from you, and I'm delighted to say that I've learned these things from you, but . . . I take sole responsibility for my ideas. And they're my ideas and I don't want you to be embarrassed by criticisms of me that imply you approve of my thoughts or actions." Dewey responded ruefully, "I'm delighted that you don't claim to be a disciple. My enemies are bad, but my disciples are worse."[21]

When Horton met George S. Counts, Counts had not yet delivered his blistering 1932 address before the Progressive Education Association, "Dare the School Build a New Social Order?," but within the community of Columbia University and its Teachers College, Counts's ideas were well known. Subsequently published as an influential pamphlet, "Dare the School" called on teachers to condemn capitalism as a failing system and to teach their students that a new, more equitable way to organize production must be put in its place. Counts insisted that the Great Depression handed teachers a new responsibility not only to get students to think for themselves, but to advocate for the adoption of specific systems and programs that served the interests of people in need. To spur change quickly, Counts urged teachers to make these ideas an important part of the curriculum and to freely impose them on their students. Counts not only approved of such indoctrination; he called it essential to combat the deepening economic crisis of the Great Depression. Besides, he argued, schools already imposed certain ways of thinking simply by never challenging the existing social order.[22] While Horton never fully supported Counts's call for indoctrination, Counts's fervor attracted him. He was drawn to Counts's passionate desire to do something decisive to relieve suffering and redistribute wealth. Horton agreed with Counts about not making a fetish of educational neutrality, especially in a time of national crisis. They both opposed education's timidity in dealing with controversial issues and favored teaching those things, however contested, to stimulate consideration of dramatically different alternatives.

Horton's initial attraction to Eduard Lindeman, the celebrated author of *The Meaning of Adult Education,* grew in part from the similarity of their perspectives. Lindeman had traveled extensively through Denmark and found much to admire in the Danish folk school tradition, which reflected many principles Horton held to be important for adult learning. By the time Lindeman came to Columbia in 1926, he had already accumulated a lot of practical experience working with groups of adults in a wide variety of community settings. On the strength of his accessible writing style and compelling arguments, he became the period's leading theorist on adult education. Following Dewey, his close colleague, he argued that adult learning at its best *is* life itself, not preparation for life. Education should rid itself of artificiality and strive to be just as real and consequential as everyday experience. Lindeman also argued for adult education's universality, where highly participatory, group-based learning would become the norm. For Lindeman, narrowness in adult learning had no place. Its purpose was "to put meaning into the whole of life." Accordingly, he felt adult education should keep the focus on situations and problems to which everyone could relate, rather than spotlighting specific vocations or academic specialties.[23]

Horton saw Lindeman as a "fresh breeze" who helped him make sense of adult education and gave him a way to promote group interaction that might alleviate "some of the problems of working with poor southerners."[24] Lindeman's emphasis on experiences and situations resonated with Horton's, likely giving Horton new confidence about the viability of an Ozone-like community school. Undoubtedly, Lindeman's commitment to democratic discussion and the value of using many methods and strategies to foreground people's voices and personal stories left an indelible mark on Horton's approaches.[25]

When not poring over class assignments, Horton roamed the streets of New York, working at whatever odd jobs he could find or volunteering for a variety of causes. He regularly visited a wide range of churches, synagogues, and mosques, attended worker education classes, showed up at union halls and strike rallies, and spent long hours "listening and discussing politics at Union Square, where Communists, anarchists and socialists gathered." He called it "a big smorgasbord of ideas and activities" that opened him up to the world and allowed him to "learn all the things he could and test them against my beliefs and figure out if they would be useful when I went back to Tennessee."[26]

One of his first New York experiences taught him to appreciate the depth of the emotions underlying the struggle for self-determination. While wearing a maroon sweatshirt from his days playing football for

Cumberland University, Horton attended a May Day parade without really knowing the significance of the celebration. Suddenly, a mounted policeman came from out of nowhere and walloped him over the head with a club, yelling "Goddamn Bolshevik!" The policeman had mistaken a college sweatshirt for Communist propaganda. As Horton recalled, "I hurried back to my books to find out what a Bolshevik was."[27] The attack contributed to his radicalization, making his search for answers by drawing on a mixture of theory and experience more urgent than ever.

At the end of the academic year in the spring of 1930, Horton prepared to move on. Niebuhr had suggested that Horton go next to the University of Chicago to work with sociologist Robert Park, who had become prominent in academic circles for his theories about conflict and social change. Niebuhr also hoped that Horton would get to know the legendary Jane Addams, longtime director of Chicago's Hull House.

LEARNING IN CHICAGO

Robert Park

Horton set out for Chicago in the fall of 1930. Uninterested, as usual, in attaining a degree or accumulating university credits, he nevertheless committed wholeheartedly to learning from his new mentor. In particular, Park showed him how to analyze social situations by making fuller use of both direct involvement and firsthand observation to understand the dynamics of social conflict.[28] Social movements happened when large numbers of ordinary people became dissatisfied enough with current conditions to speak out against them or to take actions to disrupt them.[29] Their dissatisfaction needed an avenue for expression, which could then be translated into changes to the system. Park's understanding of democracy also reflected Horton's own growing convictions. In a letter to Horace Cayton, a prominent

African American sociologist, Park wrote: "Democracy is not something that some people in a country can have and others not have, something to be shared and divided like a pie—some getting a small and some getting a large piece. Democracy is an integral thing. If any part of the country doesn't have it, the rest of the country doesn't have it."[30]

While Horton and Park were aligned philosophically in many ways, Park, like Niebuhr, did not fully understand Horton's vision. Park's focus was on researching the origins of social conflicts and learning how to resolve them. Horton, on the other hand, was interested in the practical applications of conflict and how it could be exploited to make deep, lasting change. He thought that conflict often resulted in decisions and actions that could form the basis for subsequent reflection, leading to even more effective agitation. As Horton developed his community school ideas, he adapted Park's theoretical understandings, imagining a place where people would hash out competing perspectives about social conflict to explore an issue's complications and contradictions. Through these activities, Horton believed they would gain new insights and create a shared understanding of what to do next.[31] In fact, many of Highlander's early interventions involved starting a small co-op, organizing a protest, or supporting a strike—anything that could then become the basis for a deeper and more systematic analysis of the underlying conflicts blocking change.[32]

Jane Addams

As Niebuhr had hoped, Horton also managed to forge a relationship with Jane Addams. At the peak of her career, between 1905 and 1915, her accomplishments as social worker, union activist, pacifist, educator, and best-selling author had made her, in historian Allen F. Davis's words, "the most famous woman in America."[33] She co-founded Hull House without fanfare in 1889, originally as a center where the educated and wealthy took on the task of "civilizing" new arrivals to the country. But Addams never stopped learning, and she listened closely to the people around her, including those she served. As a result, Hull House soon transformed itself. It emerged as a center for political activism and social change, often spearheaded by the very people—the poor and newly arrived immigrants—Addams had originally intended to "civilize." Addams later said she gained far more from the people of the local community than she was ever able to give them.[34]

Near the end of Addams's long career, during the early fall of 1930, Horton joined other students from the University of Chicago to pay her a visit at Hull House. They found her at the same Near West Side location where she had opened her settlement house back in 1889, but by 1930 Hull House had become part of a great complex of buildings and community programs that dominated the still diverse neighborhood. As the students gathered around a long seminar table set up in the main building, sipping tea and enjoying snacks, they took turns showering Addams with compliments and tributes. Horton, never one for idolatry, refrained from praise, choosing instead to concentrate on Hull House's origins. "Well, I'm not really interested in what's going on here now," he said, "but I'm terribly interested in how the place got started, the early struggles, and how you dealt with the problem when you were put in jail and what happened when you were branded as Communists."[35]

A profound silence followed. Addams had responded to every other student, often with wide-eyed enthusiasm, but she had nothing to say in response to Horton. He wondered if he had been too frank, and perhaps had even hurt her feelings. He remained quiet for the remainder of the visit.

When the meeting ended and everyone got up to leave, a staff person informed Horton that "Miss Addams wants you to come over and talk to her privately." Joining her alone at the corner of the large table where everyone had been sitting just moments before, Horton readied himself for a scolding. Addams, more intrigued than angry, asked Horton about his brash statement. He answered honestly that his words reflected what he cared about most: the problems and possibilities of social conflict and the often hazardous work of fighting for equality. As he spoke, his idea for creating a rural mountain school for southern radicals also tumbled out. Addams got excited and seized on the notion that what Horton had in mind was "a rural settlement house." But Horton, who would not have appreciated Hull House's expensive furnishings and fancy place settings, answered, "No, no, if it could be like you had at the beginning here, fine, but I don't want it to be like it is now." Addams laughed, inviting Horton to return for a longer talk.[36]

Among the things he learned from her during subsequent visits was the role organizations might play in empowering individuals. Horton knew people needed organizations to help keep them focused and working together toward a single worthwhile goal, but he feared organizations' tendency to become inflexible and burdensome.[37] As a leader in the student YMCA at Cumberland University, he regretted that unaffiliated students who lacked insider status were not allowed to make vital and creative contributions, in part because of organizational constraints. Addams's group had combatted similar issues by encouraging a high level of neighborhood input; the day-to-day operations of Hull House largely rested in the hands of community members themselves, who enthusiastically welcomed and acculturated recent arrivals.

That approach to organizing also reflected Addams's view of democracy. When Horton once asked what democracy meant to her, she said, "It means people have the right to make decisions. If there's a group of people sitting around a country store and there's a problem they're talking about, there are two ways to do it. They can go out and get some official to tell them what to do, or they can talk it out and discuss it themselves. Democracy is if they did it themselves." That notion reinforced the direction of Horton's own thinking.[38]

But the process of democratization was not as easy and problem free as that. Addams's commitment to democracy and to ensuring that immigrants and other marginalized people had control over their own destinies got her into trouble again and again. Her views on women's rights, labor unions, and opposition to most, if not all, international conflicts branded her a dangerous radical. For taking such strong stances, she withstood threats, vilification, and targeting by hate groups. Horton took heart from the fact that Addams "did not let these attacks get under her skin" or let them "impede her mission at Hull House." To Horton, Addams was the most persistent and resourceful activist he encountered in those early days. As he expressed it, "She put her intelligence to use as well as anyone."[39]

Once Highlander was established, Horton and his colleagues took Addams's practice of community control to heart by giving full control of residential workshops to the groups that gathered for them. As Horton said, the participants "ran everything from the minute they got there until the time they left. We insisted they do it. . . . For example, we were interested in cooperatives, to get people together, and instead of talking about it, we'd say, set one up and run it from the beginning, organize it and run it, keep the records, go broke, whatever happens. . . . We leave decision making to the people involved."[40]

TRAVELING TO DENMARK

Robert Park appreciated Horton, saying publicly that he wasn't the smartest sociology student he ever had, "but he was the damned most notorious," inviting his other University of Chicago sociology students to emulate Horton's feisty spirit.[41] The spontaneous radical edge that Horton brought to meetings and classes clearly appealed to

Park, making Horton valuable, just as he had been to Niebuhr, as a tell-it-like-it-is graduate student. Park implored Horton to stay for a doctorate and to serve as his research assistant.

Unfortunately for Park, Horton was eager for new adventures. He had begun studying Danish in preparation for a trip to visit Denmark's folk schools, which had become famous as open centers for adult learning. These schools had a long tradition of being more flexible and less traditional than other educational institutions, and Horton wanted to experience them firsthand. Thinking ahead, Horton had lived frugally and had saved enough money from a series of odd jobs to make the trip. He had been especially fortunate to snag a well-paid position as a research assistant to a Chicago psychiatrist only a few months before setting off for Denmark.[42]

Bishop Nikolai Grundtvig, who founded the Danish folk school movement in the mid-nineteenth century, hoped to liberate schools from the lifelessness of conventional education, introducing young people to learning experiences that shunned rote learning, formal examinations, and esoteric theorizing. In a "school for life," the focus would be on understanding common everyday problems and using people's collective intelligence to find meaning and promote well-being. Horton had to see for himself what these "schools for life" looked like.

In Copenhagen, Horton stayed with a family and continued to strengthen his Danish at a nearby high school. When he had gained enough confidence in the language, he began to visit folk schools to catch the spirit of their approach.[43] While he found the visits instructive, he was also dismayed, feeling the schools he saw might have lost their way. Informal interaction between teachers and students rarely occurred, and classroom discussion was uninspired. Horton noted a listlessness, a surprisingly pervasive complacency.

He wondered whether there might be a way to recapture some of the original spirit that had defined these schools and made them famous. He decided to launch a series of interviews with retired teachers and elderly ex-pupils to learn what they thought had set the original folk schools apart.[44] One of his first questions focused on what the original folk schools had meant by "the Living Word," a central idea in all the literature about the movement. He learned that the concept originally envisioned the creation of holistic educational environments synthesizing physical, spiritual, intellectual, and emotional ways of being. Though not evident in his site visits, the vision was inspiring. He later noted, "I found the totalness of the concept shockingly and refreshingly nonacademic and was reminded of the holistic philosophy of the Hopi Indians in America."[45]

One of the most important discoveries Horton made during his interviews related to what he praised as Grundtvig's notion "that people found their identity not within themselves, but in relationship with each other," reinforcing the value of all forms of group process.[46] Grundtvig also believed that "through songs and poetry students could grasp truths that might otherwise escape them." Hailing from the hill country of Tennessee, where spontaneous musical performances augmented every meaningful occasion, Horton's experiences resonated with Grundtvig's conviction that "singing in unison was an effective way of inspiring people and bringing them closer together."[47] For Grundtvig, these activities were not frills. Poems and songs "carried messages of hope and joy" that enlightened and enlivened people, giving them the confidence to take action, "to shape the emerging democratic society."[48] Highlander's subsequent emphasis on music and group singing grew directly out of Grundtvig's powerful influence.

As Horton absorbed the principles of the early Danish folk schools, he generated a list of their most salient practices, many of which later helped him define Highlander's culture. First, the folk schools had embraced the practice of students and teachers living together in a residential setting away from the pressing concerns of the outside world, where they could put democracy into practice by governing themselves. Second, the focus on general, non-vocational adult education in which all learned to think together more deeply about relevant life issues meant a great deal to both Grundtvig and Horton. As Lindeman had also taught, they believed adult education should be for everyone, regardless of position or profession or wealth, avoiding specializations and hard-to-understand jargon. Third, each community member should be seen not only as a student, but as a teacher, leader, and catalyst whose commitment to action would contribute to the common good.[49]

All these practices demanded different conceptions of what it meant to teach. The unique role of the teacher in folk schools was clarified by Joseph K. Hart in his 1927 work documenting the Danish schools. He likened the job of the teacher to that of the farmer: "He does not make *life;* he makes the conditions under which life springs into being."[50] The more deeply Horton understood the world of Danish folk schools, the more he realized how important it was to give people a direct, lived experience that enlivens them, that breathes new life into them.

Additionally, Horton was thrilled with what the director of one of the more successful schools told him: "We try to evoke among our students a picture of reality not as we have met it in our surroundings, but as we ourselves would have formed it if we could—a picture of reality as it ought to be."[51] This idea of helping people gain a picture of how things ought to be, despite the impediments of injustice and suffering, would emerge as one of Horton's favorite themes.

Many years later, one of Horton's longtime colleagues and admirers, Alice Cobb, would recall the speech in which he introduced "the ought to be" as a central concept in the social justice struggle. She called this notion a "freedom to dream," praising Horton for creating a school where dreams could be imagined and people could gather "to use all of [their] resources to realize that dream, and then to hand the dream along." She was grateful that there "might be one place, that is free . . . and dedicated to freeing other people . . . and whose service is represented in freer persons living all over the imprisoned South."[52]

As stimulating as his sojourn to Denmark had been, however, Horton arrived at the end of his journey somewhat disappointed. He had found no clear-cut, unproblematic model to draw upon. He had learned a great deal, but he would still have to devise an approach of his own that would meet the unique needs of Appalachia. He would have to plant the seeds he had gathered back in his native land to see what grew. It would be a rich, complex, often disorienting amalgam of all that he had been through, constantly renewed by an open, moving spirit of adventure and improvisation.

COMMITTING TO HIGHLANDER

On Christmas night in 1931, sitting at a desk in his cramped Copenhagen room, he scribbled a few words in his journal hinting that it was time to go home. He now realized that nothing he could study or observe would yield the long-sought-after blueprint for his special school. As he put it, "You can go to school all your life, you'll never figure it out because you are trying to get an answer that can only come from the people in the life situation."[53] It was time to return to Appalachia. His journal that night specified, with surprising clarity, how his school might be organized. It should be

> a school where young men and women can come for a minimum of three months and be inspired by personalities expressing themselves through teaching (history, literature), song and music, arts, weaving, etc., and by life lived together. These people should be from the South if possible. Negroes should be among the students. Some students should be from mountain schools, others from factories. Such

a school should be a stopping place for traveling liberals and a meeting place for southern radicals. In the years to come the whole mountain side should be covered with visitors who come from all around to have [sic] singing or to hear a speaker with a message.[54]

In early 1932, after returning from Denmark, Horton invited Niebuhr to co-author the original fundraising announcement for Highlander, even before the school had a name. In the announcement the school is called "The Southern Mountains School." The lengthy letter, which accentuated the "need for training radical labor leaders," also explained: "The objective in general is to enable those who otherwise would have no educational advantages whatsoever to learn enough about themselves and society, to have something on which to base their decisions and actions whether in their own community or into an industrial situation in which they have been thrown."[55] The letter and Niebuhr's other lobbying work proved effective. When the school opened in November 1932, about $1,300 had been raised, a considerable sum, especially given the hard economic times.[56]

The Highlander Folk School would go through many changes over the years, but it always remained true to Horton's journal entry in one crucial respect—that the only answers worth having are the ones that come from the people who are themselves grappling with the challenges of everyday life. Highlander never wavered from this central idea. Indeed, its greatest successes were always in response to what people, based on a rigorous analysis of their own experiences, claimed they needed most.

4 *Highlander's Beginnings*

On November 1, 1932, in the tiny and isolated town of Summerfield, Tennessee, the Highlander Folk School opened its doors. Perched on the southern tip of the Cumberland Mountains, about fifty miles northwest of Chattanooga, Summerfield could hardly have been more obscure. To this day it cannot be found on most maps, which is why Highlander is usually identified with the somewhat larger town of Monteagle, about two miles away. Few took notice when Myles Horton and Don West, two twenty-something activists intent on helping the local populace gain greater control over their collective lives, moved into the grandest house in the region. One longtime resident of Summerfield remarked that it was a particularly quiet and unceremonial beginning.[1] Hulan Glyn Thomas, an early documenter of Highlander's history, playfully underscored the ordinariness of the school's debut: "The usual pomp and circumstance attending the opening of a new school were not present that day in 1932. There was no brass band from the local American Legion or Loyal Order of Elks; there were no smiling public officials present to participate in the dedication ceremony; nor was there a festive crowd to applaud the patronizing utterances of the community fathers."[2] In fact, the school's modest launch was entirely consistent with the contribution Highlander hoped to make: blending into the community while foregrounding the strengths of the ordinary but feisty people who lived there.

Only a few months earlier, Georgia native Don West had learned that Dr. Lilian Johnson was looking for someone to take over her estate in Summerfield, where she had resided for seventeen years coordinating a variety of activities designed to uplift the local community.[3] A veteran educator with a Ph.D. in history from Cornell University, she had also served as president of Ohio's Western College for Women. Johnson settled in Summerfield in 1915 to revitalize the community's depressed economy and pursue a very different kind of educational project. Under the auspices of a company she had created called Kinco, short for Kindred Company / Kinder Company, Johnson had set out to promote the benefits of cooperative agriculture, jump-start a transition to a less profit-driven local economy, and support experiments in progressive education. From the beginning, she had her heart set on creating a "country Hull House" that "would lead to independence and sustainability for local farmers while stimulating growth in schools, health care, and transportation."[4] For many years, she also served on the local school board. Unfortunately, Kinco enjoyed only limited success, and so after years of effort, Johnson resolved to step aside and lease her home to a younger and more energetic successor. West, a recent graduate from Vanderbilt University, was eager to begin his own adult learning center; he seemed an attractive candidate.

The circle of radicals and progressives in the South was small, so word of West's plans soon reached Horton. He connected with West, who was attending a YMCA summer conference in Blue Ridge, North Carolina. They had much in common, including having visited Denmark to learn about its fabled folk schools. After the conference was over, West and Horton traveled together for a few days while Horton considered possible sites for his own school.[5] They spent a lot of time feeling each other out, sharing views on adult education and scouting locations in North Carolina and Kentucky. When nothing they saw struck Horton as promising, West agreed to show Horton the Johnson estate in Summerfield. The substantial two-story house, sitting on a grass plateau overlooking the Cumberland Mountains, had enough room to accommodate a small staff as well as a few students and featured a long, inviting porch and a large living room where Dr. Johnson held regular public meetings. Horton liked what he saw and asked if he could join West as a partner. West agreed.[6]

In many ways the two co-founders were a study in contrasts. West was very tall, plain, quiet, and deadly serious. His ideals meant the world to him, and when they were challenged he was reluctant to compromise. He was also steady as a rock. Horton was committed, too, at times just bursting with righteous anger, but also more pragmatic and easygoing than West. He loved to talk, and he quickly became known as someone who seemed to have a story for every occasion, which he often punctuated with a loud, drawn-out guffaw. He was also known for being a tireless worker. Sometimes, though, he pushed himself to an exhaustion so debilitating that an extended period of bed rest was the only way for him to get back on his feet. As he got older, he would learn to take occasional holidays to prevent these periodic breakdowns.[7]

Despite their differences, Horton and West shared a desire to establish a gathering place where small groups of ordinary citizens could meet to "learn how to take their place intelligently in the changing world."[8] Both were products of poor, rural families who found a way to go to college and then enrolled as graduate students at leading universities. While Horton attended classes at Union and the University of Chicago, West studied at Vanderbilt with the charismatic Social Gospel proponent and activist Alva W. Taylor, who was, in a sense, West's Reinhold Niebuhr. West described Taylor as "a great spirit . . . who was completely dedicated to human welfare.

He had the knack," West added, "for challenging and stimulating students to get into the things that really mattered."[9]

But as much as they valued their university experiences and the mentorship of their favorite professors, these two men also shared an impatience with the academic formalities and narrow specialties of higher learning. They pined for something much more open and creative and more applicable to the everyday lives of the poor people they wanted to help. Influenced by the Danish folk schools that they had both visited, West and Horton dreamed of creating an adult learning center that would be responsive to the concerns of the local community. They were thus delighted when Dr. Johnson agreed to give them the right to use her estate for free for one year. She was also willing to consider extending the arrangement once she had an opportunity to assess their progress.

With the help of West's pregnant wife Connie and two friends of Horton's from Union, John B. Thompson and his sister Dorothy, who joined them later, the school slowly got under way. Horton and West first gave the school a name. "Highlander" reflected the school's location on the edge of the Cumberland Mountains and the custom of calling the inhabitants of these mountains "highlanders." The words "folk school," borrowed directly from the Danish movement that West and Horton so admired, underscored the goal of fostering "pride in culture among the people of the Appalachian South."[10] They carved this new name on a piece of discarded wood and placed it over the property's front gate. They also created stationery that declared the Highlander Folk School's purpose: "To educate rural and industrial leaders for a new social order."[11]

The five staff members, soon joined by the Wests' infant, huddled together in Dr. Johnson's house during most of that initial tumultuous year in which money and materials were always in short supply. Although Horton had raised sufficient funds, mostly with the help of his northern university contacts, to get the school started, the bulk of it went to transportation, upkeep of the house, books, and dozens of unforeseen expenses. There was little to spare. The staff subsisted almost exclusively on beans and wheat. Wheat sprinkled with a little milk sufficed for breakfast; beans complemented with more beans constituted lunch and dinner. As Don West later said, those few months were "slim pickin's."[12] John Thompson, recalling the first year, commented, "We nearly starved, literally."[13] By October 1933, some eleven months after the school's founding, prospects were grim. The school's official cash balance for that month was $5.57.[14]

But lack of money was hardly the only problem. The greatest challenge entailed generating interest in an institution that bore no resemblance to the schools most people knew. Few Cumberlanders had ever heard of a school that exclusively catered to adults (later, a nursery school was added for a short while) or knew what to make of one that shunned credits, grades, and diplomas. Furthermore, they had no conception of education benefiting the community as a whole. Education meant "reading, writing, arithmetic or doing a little something else."[15] Horton and West were thus tasked with recruiting students to an institution that seemed provisional and uncertain and made little sense to the community it hoped to serve. Even Lilian Johnson, an experienced experimental educator, was taken aback by the decision of her tenants to create a residential school "without courses or a planned curriculum where intelligence would be nourished without a diploma to certify its validity."[16]

In the beginning, the two gangly southerners regularly wandered into the tiny town of Summerfield or nearby Monteagle to meet people and attempt to stir up interest in their school. They tried not to be outwardly anxious and made awkward small talk before asking the inevitable question about coming to Highlander. But with few exceptions, the response was a silent shrug or a fully voiced "Not interested!"[17] They visited neighboring towns to hold community meetings in people's homes and to find out what most worried the local populace, as

Horton had done in Ozone. In this way, they hoped to drum up interest in the school. But the residents of these isolated mountain hollows eyed Horton and West with suspicion. They were put off by their big words and their strange talk of the need for a socialist revolution. Others, especially those who were prominent in the community, attacked Highlander as having communist leanings and an appetite for brewing trouble. Within weeks of Highlander's opening, both West and Horton had been labeled dangerous Reds and were summarily barred from holding public meetings in the local school's facilities.[18]

As they set out to help people develop solutions to their problems, the two young educators conceded that they risked alienating much of the local community by talking up the cause of radical change or trying to convince people to work for a new social order. It also didn't take long before they realized that the Great Depression had hit Summerfield and the surrounding region of Grundy County with especially brutal force. The most immediate problem wasn't capitalism or exploitation of labor but the gloomy persistence of raw hunger and spirit-killing destitution.

Between 1933 and 1935, an astounding 72 percent of Grundy County residents received government relief. In the town of Summerfield itself, economic activity had come to a virtual halt. One small mining company continued to operate, but all work was parceled out on a strictly part-time basis. Most stores had shut their doors, and no other industry remained. Three small churches and an elementary school constituted the town center. Most people lived in shanties with no electricity or plumbing; many did not have outhouses. Weather-beaten faces, looking old before their time, predominated.[19] A life of hard labor and mounting stress made chronic illness and early death all too common. At a time when average life expectancy was around sixty, few males in Grundy County made it beyond fifty years of age.[20]

When Horton began to tour Grundy County, he saw young children with bloated stomachs and oozing sores, adolescents whose growth had been badly stunted, and adults who complained of chronic headaches and persistent fatigue. Having found evidence of debilitating hunger and widespread social despondency everywhere they traveled, the Highlander staff started canned food drives, launched community gardens, organized farm co-ops, and gave away what food they could to stave off the worst and most immediate effects of hunger. They immersed themselves as well in a kind of impromptu union organizing to put pressure on employers to hire able-bodied, out-of-work laborers, if only temporarily, because for those who had fallen into despair, even a few cents might be enough to get them back on their feet.

Recalling those first two or three months, Horton admitted that Highlander projected disorganization and uncertainty. The school was hardly the confidence builder it needed to be, owed in part to Horton's fondness for not making a fetish of being too "well organized." But Highlander could do little more, at that early stage of its development and under those crisis conditions, than directly serve the needs of the community. By distributing food, securing medical care for ailing families, and campaigning for higher wages and the right to form unions, Highlander found its footing, winning the trust of many local inhabitants and slowly attracting more interested participants. As Horton said, despite all the challenges and missteps, "The thing that made Highlander work is that we had a *commitment*. All of us had a commitment to make it work in terms of the people's interest, not in terms of ours."[21] But the work proved perilous. A decision to support workers being cruelly exploited by unsympathetic owners could lead to a life-threatening backlash. Just such a situation arose in Wilder, Tennessee, only a few weeks after Highlander opened its doors.

ADVOCATING FOR WORKERS

In the early 1930s, the owners of the Fentress Coal and Coke Company not only controlled the production of coal in Wilder, Tennessee, a small mining town about a hundred miles north of Highlander; they had a fierce grip on the town itself. As one historian has put it, the company "owned the town and treated the miners as virtual slaves."[22] It had chosen to cut wages so savagely that families of miners grew weak from hunger, malnutrition, and chronic illness. Apparently, all of this was in retaliation for the fact that the Wilder miners, under the leadership of a miner named Barney Graham, had quietly organized a local of the national United Mine Workers and had successfully negotiated a contract in 1931 to avert a steep pay cut. When that contract expired in the middle of 1932, Fentress announced a 20 percent pay reduction and began to lay off union members. Out of sheer desperation, the local finally went on strike. The owners, enraged by the rebellion, retaliated by shutting off the heat in the workers' company-owned hovels and removing their front doors, despite the approach of winter. A few workers were thrown out into the cold. The company store was ordered not to sell food to the starving miners and their families, and most merchants were pressured not to extend the strikers credit.[23] The devastated workers remained steadfast, largely because of their undaunted union leader, Barney Graham. As Horton quickly learned, "Nothing the company did seemed to break the striker's morale, in part because of Graham," whose courage and commitment achieved legendary status.[24] Before long, Wilder was a war-torn area, with owners and workers alike responsible for mounting violence. Horton brought food, raised money, recruited activists like Socialist Party leader and U.S. presidential candidate Norman Thomas to exhort the Wilder workers, and wrote editorials for many of the local newspapers to gain sympathy for the strike.[25] Horton and his Highlander colleague John

Thompson hauled supplies to the strikers every Saturday, even though they did so at great risk to themselves. Thompson especially remembered the suffering he witnessed: "I will never forget the long line of gaunt, haggard, brave people who lined up to receive the scant rations we handed out to last them a week. Each family got a pound of dried beans, a half-pound of coffee, two tins of canned milk (if they had a baby), half a pound of sugar. These rations saved many lives, but meanwhile many babies had died of starvation."[26]

On November 24, 1932, Thanksgiving Day, Myles Horton broke bread with Barney Graham and his family at their unheated homestead. Horton had spent the previous few days recruiting new students for his school and gathering up as much information as he could about conditions in Wilder. The menu included turnips and sweet potato pie. Horton couldn't help noticing, as Barney spoke hopefully about his expectations of ultimately winning the strike, that this "feast" "used up the last flour in the house."[27] After dinner, as he awaited a bus to return to Highlander, Horton was approached by a captain in the National Guard who arrested him for "coming over here, getting information and going back and teaching it." Horton was jailed overnight and released the next day with the command to exit the vicinity. He did so, commenting much later that although he would be jailed many times over the years, this was the only instance when "I was ever arrested where the charge was accurate. That's exactly what I was doing."[28]

Not long after that Thanksgiving dinner, Horton learned that the mining company so feared Barney Graham's ability to sway public opinion that it had hired professional killers to murder the union leader. Horton knew the threats were real and warned Graham, in vain. Graham's commitment to the people of his community was total. He simply would not be deterred. Ever fearless and unconcerned about his own welfare, Graham refused to temper his actions or make himself less visible.

On April 30, 1933, two hit men gunned Graham down in front of the mining company's general store. The killers claimed self-defense, but no one believed them. As many as a dozen bullets were lodged in Graham's body, including four in his back, and for three hours his lifeless figure, oozing blood, was left untended by order of the Fentress company's hired guards.[29] One thousand people attended his funeral a few days later. Although violence continued to flare and the strike dragged on, further resistance became futile.

For Highlander, the strike experience was transformative. Horton learned firsthand the value of publicity, networking, and outreach, and of the need to monitor every new development during a crisis by staying in close touch with those engaged in the situation. He also learned that in a crisis situation like the one in Wilder, Highlander was largely powerless to influence the outcome. The school could support the strikers with food and try to gain the sympathy of the local populace by keeping the newspapers informed of events, but this was a time for action, not education. Yet Horton also realized that the strike had presented Highlander with an opportunity to gain the trust of workers who might later decide to become involved at the school. In that way, the Wilder strike set the stage for Highlander's new emphasis: working with local people and educating them to advance a sustainable and effective labor movement.[30]

In another sense, Barney Graham's murder demonstrated to Horton in the most visceral way possible just what Highlander was up against in endeavoring to combat injustice and counteract the effects of corporate heartlessness. The extremes that the mine owners resorted to seemed to be less about protecting their fiscal interests and far more about asserting their raw power over the weak and the vulnerable. Graham's murder "just killed me," Horton remembered. "If I hadn't already been a radical, that would have made me a radical right then."[31] The lesson was clear. Without unions, without some way of putting pressure on owners, workers would always be exploited. For Horton, then, the union movement was nothing less than a movement for advancing the cause of what ought to be.

BUCK AND ALICE KESTER

One of the people Myles Horton came to admire as Highlander struggled to establish itself was Howard Kester, who worked for the Fellowship of Reconciliation, an interfaith peace and justice organization.[32] During the Wilder strike, Kester and his wife Alice did more than anyone to support the starving, long-suffering workers. In one interview, Horton mentions that he never knew Kester well, but that everyone saw him as a kind of role model because he was so fearless in combatting both racism and the excesses of capitalism. In fact, for a time Kester saw the two as linked and became convinced that the war against racism could not be won without capitalism undergoing significant reforms. As Horton put it, Kester "was one of the most exciting people because of his beliefs." He was outspoken about the need to change society and did not think that the southern way of life was sustainable as long as segregation persisted.[33]

Kester was born in Martinsville, Virginia, and was brought up in an environment similar to Horton's, in which the traditions of the South, including its racial customs, were rarely questioned. Bitterly dissatisfied with the status quo, Kester soon began searching for answers. He attended Lynchburg College, a small Christian college in the Blue Ridge Mountains, where he developed a reputation for being not only a strong student, but also an engaged, inquisitive activist. As tough mentally as he appeared to be physically, he had acquired the nickname "Buck" as a member of his high school football team's immovable offensive line. In all of his subsequent interactions with friends, family, and fellow activists, he was known exclusively as Buck. Later, his college yearbook would describe Buck Kester as "fearless. An idealist with revolutionary tendencies, and with a code that brooks no compromise."[34]

As a graduate student at Vanderbilt University's School of Religion, Kester studied with Alva Taylor, the radical professor who would influence a whole generation of activists, including Don West. Taylor's fervent belief that Christianity must be translated into an agenda for humane social change resonated deeply with Kester's own commitments. In attempting to encapsulate the spirit of his Christian radicalism, Taylor wrote: "When science gives the technique and the Church gives the social passion, we will possess power to make the world over into the kingdom of God."[35]

Despite his increasing radicalism, Kester had not yet had a firsthand experience in which he was a witness or a participant in a labor dispute. That changed dramatically when he and his wife went to Wilder in December 1932, about the same time that Horton was making contact with strike leaders there. Aware that local miners had gone out on strike to protest a savage wage cut and that the mine owners had chosen to hire non-union labor to replace the striking workers, Buck and Alice journeyed to Wilder to assess the situation for themselves. By then, Tennessee's governor had called in the National Guard to maintain control, and sympathetic progressives were singling out the crisis to demonstrate capitalism's underlying cruelty. When the Kesters arrived in Wilder and witnessed the devastation that had befallen starving workers and their helpless families, they felt traumatized. Nothing in their past compared to what they saw—an entire community "virtually reduced to peonage."[36]

Later, the Kesters reported all of this to the state Fellowship of Reconciliation group in Nashville, which led to the founding of the Wilder Emergency Relief Committee. The Kesters "converted their dining room into a warehouse and soon had boxes of donated goods piled almost to the ceiling."[37] By spring 1933, they had helped more than three hundred families, never growing accustomed to the destruction the cruel mine owners had created by throwing their workers into poverty. The Wilder strike turned the Kesters into social radicals. Buck's faith in education and moral suasion had given way to seeing the need for a true class struggle, one that at times might even demand violence.[38]

At Wilder, Buck had become an intimate of Barney Graham's. Although Graham had little formal education, he read widely and analyzed social situations brilliantly. His reassuring presence had caused downtrodden workers to follow him faithfully and to believe that a fair resolution was possible. He was convinced that the strike could go on indefinitely and management would finally show some decency toward its employees. Graham's idealistic convictions spoke to Buck.

After Graham was murdered, the Kesters stayed at his home to comfort his widow and children. Once again, they were shocked by the destitution the family endured. The food cupboards were bare and there was no bed to sleep on. The Kesters "spent the night in two straight-backed chairs."[39] At Graham's funeral, Buck delivered the eulogy, praising Graham for his leadership and decency. Buck called Graham "a symbol of unselfish devotion to the cause of working people."[40]

The Kesters enacted what social gospel radicalism espoused. Though their upbringings were typical of the South at the time—both sets of parents ultimately disowned them for their work and beliefs— they were shaped by a string of harrowing experiences, coupled with exposure to radical educators like Alva Taylor, whose ideas fortified their resistance to the prevailing social order. Over time, they learned to use every tool at their disposal to combat injustice. As Myles Horton and Don West attempted to get Highlander off the ground, they took heart from Buck and Alice's ongoing struggle against terrible odds.[41]

SUPPORT FOR THE BUGWOOD CUTTERS

As if the Wilder strike were not enough to test Highlander's mettle, a crisis much closer to home soon came to consume the energies of the school. In 1933, the Tennessee Products Corporation had refused to pay more than 75 cents a day to workers in Grundy County who cut bugwood, the low-grade, otherwise useless wood pulp that the company used to produce distilled alcohol. Workers increasingly grew disgruntled; one, Henry Thomas, who had been a well-paid logger during more prosperous times, called some of his fellow woodcutters together and announced, "It takes a sharp axe, a strong back and a weak mind to cut bugwood at seventy-five cents a day. Let's strike!"[42] Rejected by the big unions they asked to represent them and more outraged than ever at the company's "compromise" of a five-cent-a-day wage increase, the woodcutters sought out the support of Highlander, which helped them form the Cumberland Mountain Workers' and Unemployed League. In no time at all, picket lines had been set up along the outskirts of nearby forests, preventing the introduction of scabs and the cutting of more wood. At least one Tennessee Products administrator attacked the league for staging an illegal strike, but the workers, who had spent time at Highlander, refused to be cowed. Highlander had taught them a few things, including that under section 7-A of the National Industrial Recovery Act, they were guaranteed the right to collective bargaining and to strike when the bargaining process broke down.[43]

With Highlander's guidance, the woodcutters proposed a significant wage increase, including pay by the cord and assurances that the company would not resort to fraud in measuring the amount of wood actually cut, then a common practice.[44] When the company refused to compromise, the workers wrote a series of letters, with Highlander's help, to U.S. Secretary of Labor Frances Perkins, requesting federal intervention. In one letter, the workers concluded that even though they were desperate to work, in the face of such injustice, they had "decided to try to live on blackberries and air until they [could] get a living wage."[45] Secretary Perkins remained unresponsive for weeks, so the workers sent her follow-up letters with references to "starving children" in their midst, to the fact that they had been "patient, much too patient" awaiting her reply, and to growing doubt about "what rights workers really have under our present form of government."[46] Most disappointing of all, when Horton led the workers on a trip to Washington, at considerable expense, to meet with Secretary Perkins in person, she refused to see them, claiming she had an important meeting with industrialists from which she could not break away. When the workers proposed remaining in the capital until their travel funds ran out, they were told by one of her aides that the secretary "could not be expected to give her attention to every delegation of workers that came to Washington."[47]

In the end, the strike and the effort to organize the bugwood cutters proved a dismal failure. But most accounts also affirm that Highlander and the workers in Grundy County learned a great deal from these experiences. Thirty years later, Henry Thomas, the woodcutter who had first called for the strike, told historian Frank Adams from his home in Summerfield: "People were in pretty bad shape. But at Highlander we learned how to handle our daily problems, to do by organizing, by showing our power and our strength. The most important thing the people ever learned from Highlander was what we learned then—how we could help ourselves."[48]

5 Building a More Stable Highlander

After its precarious first year of existence, Highlander's future became much more assured. As the 1930s progressed and the union movement gathered force, Highlander was able to establish strong connections with the newly formed Committee of Industrial Organization, later known as the Congress of Industrial Organizations (CIO). With its emphasis on organizing unskilled workers, including many in the South who had no one to advocate for them, the CIO rose rapidly as a strong, gritty national union that bargained tenaciously and was unafraid to back long strikes to secure better wages and working conditions. Highlander was named the South's first official CIO training center, and CIO workers started to come to Highlander regularly in 1937. Later, the CIO, which became increasingly conservative with every passing year, would unite with the more moderate American Federation of Labor (AFL), but from the mid-1930s to the mid-1940s it represented the vanguard of progressive unionism and a stable source of activism and revenue for Highlander.

In addition, Lilian Johnson had been pleased enough with the progress the school had made to extend its rights to her house and land for another five years. She saw Highlander's first year as a test of its commitment and effectiveness in working closely with challenged communities. As far as she was concerned, Highlander was passing this test very capably, making it likely that her alliance with Highlander would prove to be a long one. During the two decades that followed, as the school transitioned from a focus on labor unions to an emphasis on civil rights, Johnson's confidence in the school only grew. Indeed, she claimed that her own development as a person and leader paralleled Highlander's. Her association with the school helped her "to overcome barriers that had limited her effectiveness."[1] By exposing Johnson to people of different classes and races, Highlander helped her see beneath people's appearances and learn to give them the benefit of the doubt. Her later work as an eighty-something civil rights activist would be deeply informed by her association with the school.[2]

The Departure of Don West

In the middle of that first difficult year, as Highlander set about building up its staff, Don West decided to leave. In many ways, losing him was a setback. Not only was West an experienced educator, dedicated activist, and passionate communicator, he was an accomplished poet whose love for Appalachian customs and indigenous music set the stage for Highlander's famed cultural program. But West was also restless. Unlikely to stay anywhere for too long, he wanted to return to his native Appalachian Georgia to start a school he could call his own. Horton also probably hastened the departure of Don and his family. In a letter West wrote after he left, he claimed Horton badmouthed the Wests behind their backs, "hogging credit" for Highlander because of his fundraising ability, and created a nearly intolerable atmosphere for Connie West once she had had her baby. While caring for an infant under the dire circumstances must have required considerable sacrifices from everyone, Connie claimed that Horton did and said things once the baby was born that made the entire experience extremely unpleasant. She felt Horton's "abuse and insinuations" had contributed as much as anything to driving the Wests away from the school.[3]

The schism between these two men also had roots in their conflicting social philosophies. They were both idealistic, committed radical activists seeking to create a new social order, but Horton was less ideological and more conciliatory, West less compromising. West was inclined to flirt with communism, Horton likely to avoid alliances that felt doctrinaire or rigid. As West's biographer notes, the personal rift between the two widened as a result of "West's impatience with Horton's pragmatism as well as the pace of social change."[4] West's disillusionment may also have had more to do with his hatred for capitalism and its devastating effects on the mountaineers he loved: "The truth is that West, much more radical in his social analysis, had concluded that Horton's measured vision of social change was inadequate to meet the challenge of the hour. A man in a hurry, Don West was already moving toward a more active expression of Marxism than his partner could accept."[5]

James Dombrowski

James Dombrowski, who had helped to plan the school when he and Horton were students at Union Theological Seminary, was finishing his Ph.D. on American democratic socialism just as West was leaving Highlander. Horton and Dombrowski had always envisioned working together at the school they had planned. With West's departure, Dombrowski's arrival filled a critical gap.

Despite his pragmatic nature, Horton held anarchist tendencies and a distaste for structures of any kind: "I was kind of scared of structures, scared of organizations, because most of the organizations and structures I was familiar with in this country were oppressive."[6] Horton wanted an institution with a minimal amount of structure, just enough to avoid discord, yet not so rigid that it interfered with people's capacity to think and act creatively. Still, Horton recognized the school needed more organization, which Dombrowski brought. He liked to make things orderly, and he quickly brought a disciplined spirit to the school that lent it much-needed stability.[7] Dombrowski "did the solid work of coalescing the whole thing. He was the head of the school. He did the administrative chores, wrote promotions, raised funds, wrote the newsletter. . . . He brought people together who, while working on their own programs, provided support for the working-class struggle and for Highlander. I had the ideas; he had the vision and the strategy."[8]

Dombrowski had developed his skills through a life committed to service and learning. He attended Emory University as an undergraduate and eventually found his way to Union Theological Seminary after spending time at Berkeley, Harvard, and Columbia. A good eight years older than Horton, Dombrowski had been a foot soldier in the trenches of France during World War I. In 1931, he received Union's Traveling Fellow award, a highly prestigious honor that would have allowed him to pursue his studies anywhere in the world; his loyalty to Harry Ward, though, kept him in New York.

Under Ward's direction, Dombrowski focused his dissertation on an experimental utopian community, the Christian Commonwealth Colony, near Columbus, Georgia. Although it lasted only forty-four months, the colony won fame as one of the first attempts in America to create a community premised on the idea that society's wrongs could be reversed through the practice of Christian brotherhood and love, or, as one resident put it, by following "unselfish socialism."[9] But from the beginning, the colony suffered from inadequate financing and poor administration. The processes for joining the community were so lax that many settlers did not understand what the colony stood for, which compromised the community's sense of shared purpose. Within less than four years, the vague notions about brotherhood and love proved insufficient to sustain the colony.

The reasons for the colony's failure probably figured prominently in Dombrowski's thinking about Highlander. The school's ultimate sustainability would depend on hard-nosed accounting and highly disciplined administration. And he knew he could provide these valuable assets to the school. The staff appreciated his efforts, too. Shortly after arriving at Highlander, Dombrowski acquired the moniker "Skipper" in recognition of his quiet but effective management style. As Frank Adams has said, he "laid the school's administrative foundation," using his organizational ability for the first time in his life "for a cause he fully believed in."[10]

Dombrowski also successfully raised funds for the school. He turned a seemingly thankless task into a meaningful, even sacred activity, declaring, "I always felt that I was doing a person a favor when I asked for a hundred dollars or ten dollars." As Dombrowski saw it, that contribution would help redistribute wealth in an unjust economic system, whether to feed hungry workers, develop union leaders, or promote cooperative agriculture.[11]

Above all, Dombrowski personified the enthusiastic Christian radical who didn't hesitate to envision Highlander as an example of the Kingdom of God on earth. Horton had impressed Dombrowski with one of his favorite themes, that Highlander represented "a microcosm of what society ought to be." Dombrowski stayed at Highlander for almost ten years, in spite of the day-to-day problems and incessant outside harassment; he never stopped trying to make Horton's towering ideal the everyday reality.[12]

Zilla Hawes

Zilla Hawes also joined the staff in Highlander's second year. She brought strong connections to the union movement to the school, along with a passion for social change and unwavering belief in the value of places like Highlander. To people who knew her, Hawes was a brave revolutionary, "committed to a huge and [seemingly] impossible mission."[13] No matter how many times greedy corporations or racist police departments beat her down, she remained confident that great things happened when people pulled together. Some likened her to a whirlwind, a woman of "such vibrant and virile intensity" others could sometimes "feel like inarticulate clods."[14]

Born Elizabeth Day Hawes, but always known as Zilla or Zil, she grew up in a comfortable middle-class family, was educated in a series of public and private schools in the northeast, and eventually graduated from Vassar College in 1929. Her Vassar years had little impact on her social or political consciousness, but the time she spent immediately after graduation at the John C. Campbell Folk School in Brasstown, North Carolina, an adult vocational learning center based on Danish folk school principles, proved life changing. Hawes learned how to bring practical education directly to the local community at Campbell and eventually accepted the job of interviewing men and women living in remote sections of rural North Carolina to document their life histories. Later, she copied down many of the traditional tunes they sang as they went about their work. She learned a great deal about the honesty and straightforwardness of the people in remote North Carolina and also just "how hard it was to hew any kind of life out of those hills."[15]

While working as an organizer and member of the Socialist Party, she also took classes at Brookwood Labor College in Katonah, New York, for a year, focusing on labor journalism, labor history, and labor economics. After arriving at Highlander in the fall of 1933, she brought her academic studies, her work as an organizer for the Amalgamated Workers of America in Knoxville, and her experience as a strike coordinator together to lead a popular course on labor history. Highlander was not even a year old and in disarray when Hawes arrived, but she found its idealistic spirit irresistible. There weren't a lot of students going to Highlander at that point, so Hawes and Horton got to know each other well while cruising the hills and hollows near Summerfield in her broken-down car, which she had dubbed the "Mother Jones," as they tried to stir up interest in the school.[16]

In October 1934, Hawes, Horton, Dombrowski, and the other two full-time staff members at the time, Rupert Hampton and Malcolm Chisholm, who was known as Mack, signed a state charter of incorporation, which officially certified the school as a recognized institution of adult education. The chartering of Highlander, almost two years after its "unceremonial" opening, would constitute its official launch and presented the school with a more substantial reason for celebration. A tax exemption, still in the works, would be expedited by the charter and help establish the school as a true nonprofit, entitled to all the advantages accruing to charitable organizations. These five also formed the school's first board of directors.[17] Hampton, who had also arrived from Union Theological Seminary, was an accomplished musician, an early organizer of Highlander's cultural program, and a supporter of Highlander's ambitious cooperative movement.[18] He would be a mainstay of the staff throughout the 1930s. Mack Chisholm, an Alabaman with a strong literary background, would soon leave the school to serve with other Americans in the Spanish Civil War, where, sadly, he died opposing Franco's fascists.[19]

In recalling the early days of Highlander, Hawes appreciated how the staff used conflict to accelerate student learning. Sometimes, though, a focus on conflict for educational purposes could spill over into staff meetings and staff relationships. For instance, sharp disagreements could erupt over whom to admit to Highlander residential workshops. Were Communists welcome? Students advocating violence? Tensions also arose regarding Highlander's role in supporting ongoing labor unrest. Some believed that in a crisis, all educational work should be dropped to serve the needs of the union. Certainly,

Hawes believed this. For a time, so did Horton, who wrote to Jim Dombrowski in 1933 that the most effective way for "students to understand present social order is to throw them into conflict situations where the real nature of our society is projected in all its ugliness."[20] Others questioned the wisdom of using conflict as a means to awaken individuals, especially if taken to an extreme. Horton also had second thoughts as his organizing experiences started to feel less rewarding than his educational work.

The unresolved philosophical division came to a head in February 1937, when Hawes, serving as a lead organizer for the Amalgamated Clothing Workers of America, in the midst of a strike in Cleveland, Tennessee, sent an urgent message to Highlander staff asking for immediate support. To her disappointment, there was no response at all until it was too late to intervene effectively. It struck her as such a breach of trust that she almost resigned from Highlander. In a letter to the staff, she chastised her colleagues for not responding to her plea to join the strike, adding, "My confidence in Highlander as a responsible labor school is severely impaired."[21] She went on to say that a labor school of any kind, but especially one aspiring to gain respect within the movement, should be prepared to respond to any emergency and give students firsthand experiences of actual strike conditions: "Without this proved competency," she concluded, "I can see no validity to workers education."[22]

Although Dombrowski and Horton sympathized, and Dombrowski, in particular, offered apologies for the "blunder" of not responding promptly to Hawes's pleas, both men questioned whether worker education would gain its respectability primarily from crisis intervention.[23] They knew that responding to every crisis would risk destroying the continuity and long-term value of sustained leadership development, both through Highlander residencies and extension programs. More fundamentally, Horton had experienced organizing at Wilder. He would soon be immersed in a long period of organizing for CIO unions in North Carolina and South Carolina, again developing a distaste for organizing, especially in short-term crises. In a way, the tension between Hawes and Horton would set the stage for Highlander's next evolution, one which affirmed the value of organizing and field experiences but also represented a decided tilt toward deep learning, where critical reflection and collective enlightenment took precedence over enduring long, drawn-out strikes and vying for short-term victories.[24]

ORGANIZING VERSUS EDUCATION

Between 1935 and 1937, Highlander became one of the key places in the South where shop stewards and others who supervised rank-and-file workers learned how to build teams, improve communications, and ensure that the rights of union members were protected. As Highlander's trainings strengthened the union movement, the hostility that owners directed at unions, and by extension, Highlander, became increasingly intense and widespread. Threats of violence were constant. At the behest of companies, heavily armed police officers harassed union members and intimidated organizers. Even proposals for small increases in wages or negligible changes in working conditions were fiercely opposed. Witnessing the strength of the resistance to labor unions made Horton wonder whether he should remain at Highlander as an educator at all or be in the field as an on-the-ground labor organizer.

During this same period, Horton agreed to serve as lead strike organizer for textile workers in Lumberton, North Carolina, about five hundred miles east of Highlander. He knew that the workers would face a strike of at least two or three months, and it would be his job to keep the rank and file committed throughout that grueling period. Once the strike began, he used every trick he knew. During the day he would maintain a strict picket line that no strikebreaker was permitted to cross, but if the state police were said to be approaching, he would put attractive women and lively musicians in place of the picket line to make it seem the gathering was just a pleasant way to pass the time. Later, when that tactic grew ineffective, Horton instituted a twenty-four-hour picket line, which frustrated and exhausted the overworked troopers.[25]

Each night, after a long day of walking the picket line, Horton would tell and retell an endless stream of stories designed to keep the workers charged up. He cracked topical jokes, with company owners as the butt of his punch lines. He read newspaper stories from a variety of dailies, most of which heaped criticism on the strikers. But as he read, he painstakingly pointed out all the ways the newspapers had gotten the story wrong or had intentionally distorted it to give the owners a public relations advantage. He would invite the crowd to take careful note of what actually happened at their meeting and then to compare their own eyewitness accounts to the biased report found in the next day's newspaper.[26] He also served as a master of ceremonies, introducing a string of singers, musicians, dancers, and comedians to keep strikers entertained. And he stirred people up with inspirational speeches that drew on his extensive knowledge of labor history, spinning tales in which workers were pitted against owners, with workers almost always prevailing in the end.

One night in his hotel room, as he reflected on his effect on the crowds, Horton was overtaken with a feeling of power. He was both exhilarated and aghast. Some nights his knack for storytelling and passionate speech making held two thousand people spellbound. He knew he had a gift for narrative, but this inherently dramatic setting seemed to be the ultimate test of his ability to weave engaging yarns out of nothing. Sitting alone in his hotel room, he came to the realization that he was becoming addicted to the rush of pleasure that came over him every time he realized he could control the crowd and get them to do virtually anything he wanted. In a word, the temptations of demagoguery were getting the better of him, even though the hoped-for goals were both desired and mutual. In the end, this ability to manipulate people he was supposed to serve frightened him more than it pleased him. Intentionally or not, such power, he feared, could be terribly abused.[27]

Once the Lumberton strike was over, Horton resolved to deemphasize organizing and return to Highlander primarily as an educator. He disliked organizing's emphasis on results at the expense of learning and collective long-term growth. And he hated the ways in which he had to manipulate people to get things done. If he had to choose between getting things done and helping people learn over time, he would opt for the often slow but far more satisfying process of deepening understanding and broadening knowledge.

Horton had always respected the work of Saul Alinsky, one of the twentieth century's most successful organizers, but he had growing reservations about Alinsky's win-at-all-costs attitude. As Horton saw it, Alinsky's pursuit of the immediate objective always took precedence over education. Horton recognized that short-term objectives were necessary to advance the struggle, but increasingly he preferred educating through the struggles that people faced "to develop and radicalize people . . . to let the goal go and develop the people." By subordinating deep learning to short-term, piecemeal reform, Horton feared diminishing the possibility of bringing about long-term structural change. "If it's just limited reform, I would hesitate, because I don't think valuable learning comes out of winning little victories, unless they are calculated steps toward the large goal and will lead to structural reforms."[28] In an interview that he participated in near the end of his life, Horton further explained the difference between organizing and educating: "The purpose of Highlander is not to solve problems but to use problems and crises as the basis for educating people about a democratic society. To make them want more and make them understand they can do more."[29]

The Lumberton experience also taught Horton to distrust a certain kind of charismatic leader, those larger-than-life figures who
take control of a situation, bending it to their own purposes. He
feared their skills could easily be used to mislead and even deceive
followers, all for an outcome that too often benefited them more than
the people they were supposedly trying to lead. Huey Long, who
ruled Louisiana in the early 1930s before being assassinated in
1935, was an especially instructive contemporary example of how
rapidly rising charismatic leaders could turn into dangerous dema-
gogues. Posing as a New York City reporter, Horton interviewed
Long at the height of his power as dictator of Louisiana, and in a brief
four-page article, exposed his simplistic program, knee-jerk brutali-
ties, and proto-Hitler attitudes.[30] Later, Horton would express concern about Dr. Martin Luther King's far more benign form of charismatic leadership, especially because it prevented other, less magnetic
leaders from exerting influence on the civil rights movement. Pivotal
black leaders like Ella Baker and Septima Clark made similar claims.
Baker, in particular, who worked closely with King as the first head of
the Southern Christian Leadership Conference between 1957 and
1960, feared that many less magnetic but able leaders were bound to
be neglected and even lost to the movement because of the focus on
King's charisma. Her respect for the movement's rich complexity
caused her to believe that it was simply unwise and ineffective to allow one "magic man" to become the symbol of a struggle so diverse
and varied.[31] Septima Clark, who later worked at Highlander, once
wrote a letter to Dr. King asking him to allow others to assume leadership roles during marches and other movement events so that they
could have first-hand experiences with leading. When King read
the letter to his staff, everyone laughed. They took it for granted that
the only person fit to play the role of leader was King himself; to
suggest otherwise was somehow tantamount to "looking down on
Dr. King."[32]

Eventually Horton decided that on the whole, Dr. King's strengths as a force for good and for advancing civil rights outweighed his liabilities. Horton knew there was a role for charisma and making a difference through the power of one's personality, but he still "had a problem with it." When Dr. King's assassination left a gaping leadership hole in the civil rights movement, a hole no one was prepared to fill, Horton saw it as evidence of the dilemmas of charismatic leadership.[33]

A CIRCLE OF LEARNERS ON AN ISLAND OF DECENCY

By the early to mid-1940s, as Highlander gained influence and experience, Horton became a more careful and thoughtful articulator of the school's educational philosophy, finding ways to put his approach into a few well-honed words. He had found that one of Highlander's most important functions during a residential workshop or when running an extension program was to create "islands of decency," places where every participant enjoyed the entire community's respect and appreciation and in which the dignity of all was upheld.[34] Two inviolable democratic principles prevailed—freedom to speak and freedom from discrimination. To exclude any point of view by cutting a discussion short or privileging one person's view over another diminished democracy and prevented the group from getting the benefit of a potentially transformative opinion. As Horton put it, "All objections have to be heard, all disagreements allowed to come out in the open. You have to make decisions that everyone can live with. The decisions have to be on that level—universal."[35]

Workshops arose from the felt problems of the participants who, because of their potential as leaders, had been invited to Highlander to address a specific topic, such as school integration or union organizing or toxic waste. Just as important, workshops were premised on the assumption that "people have within themselves the potential, intelligence, courage and ability to solve their own problems." Highlander staff played a role in stimulating participants, exhorting them to probe their experiences more deeply, but the main thing was to immerse people in an environment where they could think hard together and pool their knowledge, making the most of one another's insights and perspectives.[36]

More than anything, Highlander created a microcosm of an integrated, democratic society. So in addition to discussion of shared problems, workshops included music and drama, long walks and square dancing, plenty of good food, rest periods, and stimulating conversation. This immersive experience might last two months, two weeks, or a long weekend. Regardless of the duration, the goal was to treat everyone well, to give them a peak experience with a powerful community of peers that would heighten their sense of agency and augment their ability to bring about change back home.

The "circle of learners" idea constituted Highlander's central practice and most telling symbol. It described, literally, how people at a residential workshop organized themselves—in a ring of rocking chairs—and embodied the school's fierce commitment to nonhierarchical discussion, group deliberation, and concerted collective action. Participants formed a circle so that everyone could see one another, feel included in the learning process, and "share what they know as equals." The circle broke the stratified patterns found virtually everywhere else in society and affirmed the idea that all have an opportunity to learn together, especially as members of a community of learners.[37] The circle also signified interdependence, the value of "groups working together, not only with their own neighbors but with all kinds of people . . . who have something in common." At the same time, the circle discouraged the deeply bred and pervasive impulse to advance oneself as an individual "at the expense of other people."[38] Group solidarity and developing a cooperative spirit were essential. As Horton put it in a 1977 interview, "you've got to get rid of individualism as a philosophy of life" in order to make the most of people working together.[39]

The signature practice in the Highlander circle was dialogue, where people with different experiences and different knowledge bases—but with the same potential to enlighten and stretch the group's thinking—communicated with one another as equals. "It's a bottoms-up operation instead of a top-down operation" where "everybody's on the same level trying to come up together," Horton explained. Dialogue was impossible without mutual respect, which was based on respect for each person's lived experiences, "'cause that's what a person is."[40]

When it came to Horton's responsibility in the circle, he saw himself carrying out multiple roles. One was as convener, the person who invited the participants and had thought through how to bring together the best possible mix of attendees. A second was as participant in the circle, with the same expectations as anyone else to hear, speak, and respect others. He also had a third role, that of trust builder and knowledge holder. He fully believed that every person had "experiences worth learning from" and that those experiences could productively form the basis for important group reflection and learning. Most others lacked this faith, especially if they were new to Highlander, or harbored doubts about the value of their experience and knowledge. In most cases, authority figures and the system as a whole had signaled to people that they didn't know anything or have anything of value to share. They had been told they weren't the experts or the ones in charge or the insiders worth listening to. Part of the point of the circle was to undo these feelings of worthlessness that had built up over time, to bolster people's confidence about the value of their knowledge, and to motivate them to share relevant incidents from their lives.[41] Gradually, as more and more people shared, group members developed the courage to analyze their experiences more closely and more critically, digging out lessons that weren't just personal but had a bearing on how the gathering as a whole perceived the problems it had tasked itself to address.

Once Horton had established his credibility as a fellow learner who was there to help people find solutions to their problems without dominating the process, he had an additional role to play: that of an informed, experienced observer with a trove of revealing stories and valuable lessons to share. Since Highlander served people on the cutting edge of social change, Horton knew he had experiences that would prove valuable to the circle of learners. But he had to wait to earn the right to share them, and they never took precedence over what others wished to contribute.

One of Horton's chief commitments as a facilitator of democratic discourse involved close listening. Horton loved to talk, to tell stories, to offer his view of what needed to be done. It was hard for him to sit back and just listen. At the same time, he knew his penchant for talking could limit others' participation, a potentially fatal blow to building a democracy. Horton's friend and collaborator Frank Adams noted, "Listening was not easy for him. His mouth [was] open in most of my memories of him." But when he finally closed his mouth, Horton could be a profound listener. When Horton made the effort to fully absorb someone's words, "People heard the sound of their own voices being taken seriously about issues of great import in their lives, usually for the first time ever."[42] Alice Wine, a resident of Johns Island, South Carolina, who learned to read and successfully registered to vote thanks to a Highlander-inspired citizenship school, said that the kind of deep listening Horton practiced "made the tongue work." You talked in spite of yourself, about your problems, both private and public, and before long, others facing similar challenges joined you in brainstorming solutions.[43]

Horton's way of listening was only the beginning of a process that eventually involved everyone. First, he modeled close listening in the large circle. Then people moved into small groups so they could practice close listening with each other. Next, he encouraged people to "listen" closely for the problems they all held in common. Individuals couldn't accomplish much on their own, Horton reasoned. But the more they listened to each other for the common experiences that bound them together, the more "they had a chance to devise some way to overcome" the oppression they faced.[44]

Another way to think about this process was in terms of a pie that represented a holistic 360-degree view of the problem under consideration. Each person who came to a workshop brought a small piece of the total pie. That piece stood for their important but still limited range of experience. As those pieces of experience got shared and were absorbed and digested by the group, a clearer picture of the whole situation came into view that each of the participants could now see more clearly. A fellow who visited from North Carolina found it helpful to think about a Highlander workshop in just this way: "I had a little piece of that pie," he began. "And Joe, here, he had a little slice, somebody else had a little slice. And Myles told us about some other people that had a little slice. . . . So now we got the whole pie and now I know everything. I got the whole pie, and I'm going to take the whole pie back home instead of [just] my little slice."[45]

Being respectful of everyone's slice of experience in the circle of learners helped defeat hierarchical assumptions that some participants brought with them, as Dr. Frederick Patterson, outgoing president of Tuskegee Institute, learned so memorably at a Highlander workshop in 1954, not long before the Supreme Court handed down its decision in the *Brown v. Board of Education* case. The workshop included a smattering of academics and scholars, and it also comprised a large number of sharecroppers and people with only rudimentary literacy skills. At first Patterson felt uncomfortable, unsure how to interact with individuals who seemed so limited educationally. Then he heard an illiterate sharecropper from West Tennessee speak with great eloquence and power about human nature and the things that draw people together. He was awestruck and wondered where this man had acquired such profound ideas. Suddenly, it dawned on Patterson that the man was speaking from his experiences, that he knew things the president of Tuskegee couldn't possibly know: "While I was learning to be president of Tuskegee, he was learning to live. When I was learning to be an academician, he was learning how to deal with his neighbors. So he had rich experiences that I was denied. And I was beginning to wonder what I could give to him—I knew what he could give to me."[46]

6 Zilphia Horton and Highlander's "Singing Army"

THINKING FOR HERSELF

Among centers for adult learning in the United States, Highlander was unique in its emphasis on song. No person did more to put music at the center of Highlander's way of life than Zilphia Mae Johnson Horton. Born in Spadra, Arkansas, on April 14, 1910, Zilphia grew up in a decidedly turbulent household. During her childhood, her family moved nineteen times. Her father, Robert Guy Johnson, a prospector and miner, was always on the lookout for a lucky strike or get-rich-quick scheme. He moved his family to Idaho twice and to multiple locations in Arkansas in search of that once-in-a-lifetime windfall. To bring stability to her life, Zilphia was sent to live with her grandmother for a number of years before the family settled down in Paris, Arkansas. She was fortunate to master the piano under her grandmother's tutelage.[1]

For Zilphia, Paris became home, the place where she attended high school and landed her first full-time job, when her father accepted an attractive position as superintendent of the Paris Purity Coal Company. Known as the coal capital of Arkansas, Paris promised enough wealth to satisfy Johnson.[2] Inclined to be conservative in most areas of his life, he became downright reactionary as a supervisor of mine workers, regarding all forms of organized labor as un-American. He was also a strict disciplinarian and harsh taskmaster whose relationship with his children could never be described as warm. Nevertheless, Johnson won Zilphia's respect for being a hard-nosed critical thinker. She remembered him as the person who taught her to be a "doubter," an independent thinker who "learned to approach any new experience with a challenging and open mind." Zilphia experienced the first of many admonitions to think for herself when she was six. She had already seen a popular traveling show in town but asked to see it again. When her father asked her why, she answered, "All the other girls go." Zilphia never forgot his firm response: "Remember this—no matter if every single person in this town goes to the show, if that's your reason, then you have no reason. You'll never amount to anything if you do things because other people do them."[3] She took his advice to heart and became a lifelong skeptic, the sort of person who refused to accept things blindly.

Johnson's work necessarily exposed Zilphia to the violence that accompanied labor struggles during that period. Despite her father's antipathy for the workers' plight, Zilphia was sympathetic to the dismal working conditions that most laborers faced. Even when her father derided members of the Industrial Workers of the World (IWW), a radical union, for never being satisfied with anything, she remained intensely interested in the IWW's goals.[4] She wanted to know more about the roots of their commitments and why they fought so uncompromisingly for their rights as workers.

After graduating in 1931 from the College of the Ozarks in nearby Clarksville, Arkansas, as an award-winning music student who received accolades for both her piano playing and singing, Zilphia returned to Paris to live with her parents, accepting a teaching position in the local schools. After her return home, she also became inspired by Claude Williams, a radical Presbyterian preacher and union organizer.

Arriving in Paris in 1930 with his wife Joyce, Williams gained notoriety almost immediately for his controversial ideas about how to attract people to his church. He wanted religion to be enjoyable, something that people connected to their real lives. He bought a pool table and encouraged card playing and checkers competitions, anything diverting to lure people into the church. Once there, he tried to win them over to a life that followed the teachings of Jesus. He sponsored a Sunday charity baseball game and called recreation a sacred activity: "Play is divine instinct," he said, "found in birds, babies and lower animals and is not immoral."[5] His ability to bridge the secular world and the spiritual realm had a wide appeal, especially for young people and those who had not found a church to call home.

Some of Williams's moves struck many local people as extreme. He reached out to all-black churches, delivering a series of sermons that attacked racism. He invited African Americans to his home and on those occasions openly condemned segregation.[6] He supported local miners who organized for better wages and working conditions. He directed attention to the devastation workers suffered because of low pay and company store prices, jeopardizing the health and well-being of their families. When workers struck for better conditions, he journeyed from village to village to condemn management's greed.[7] Of course, management at that time included Zilphia's father. Guy Johnson considered Williams an archenemy, who, like the IWW members he hated, would never be satisfied with anything.

Zilphia, on the other hand, loved Williams's defense of the underdog and became a kind of disciple. She attended his church regularly and even took charge of his highly successful youth group. She profoundly admired Williams's creative updating of traditional hymns to address current labor and race issues. His pervasive use of song had a deep impact on her and others, influencing her to make music a key part of her activism.[8]

In November 1934, over three hundred activists converged on Paris to attend a conference that Williams had organized with the support of Myles Horton "to face together the problem of creating a just society." Proposals came forward to establish old age pensions for all workers, supplemented by workman's compensation and social insurance. Taking great pride in the extent of the conference's racial integration, Williams wrote in his diary, "Negroes and whites participated on same program" and "sat and mingled together in audience," and even ate together without self-consciousness.[9] As historians Eric Gellman and Jarod Roll have said, "In the weeks following the conference, Williams increasingly had 'revolution' on his mind. His diary entries for this period include almost daily references to conversations he had about communism, socialism, and dialectical materialism." He believed nothing short of social upheaval would address the problems people faced.[10]

Zilphia's connection to the man many now called "the preacher" increasingly enraged her father. Not surprisingly, Williams also despised Johnson, whom he cast as an especially tyrannical member of Paris's ruling class. By early 1935, as Williams's radical zeal reached new heights and Zilphia's admiration for Williams showed no signs of abating, Guy Johnson issued an ultimatum: As long as Zilphia allied herself with Williams, she could not live in their family home. When Zilphia refused to change, her father evicted her.

Friends of Zilphia's, including Williams himself and activists like Howard Kester and Ralph Tefferteller, whom she had met through Williams, urged her to go to Highlander. Kester's advice, in particular, proved both sound and prescient. He wrote that by going to Highlander she would gain important grounding in the fundamentals of economics and labor history, while working in a place where "life is simple but exhilarating and stimulating." He added that at Highlander she could "make a genuine contribution." She determined to leave Paris and move to Highlander, making a far more fateful decision than she could possibly have realized. It would shape the rest of her all-too-short life.[11]

FINDING A HOME AT HIGHLANDER

Zilphia arrived at Highlander in early February 1935, at the age of twenty-four. From the start, she believed that giving people the opportunity to sing easy, familiar melodies together built a group's morale and sense of solidarity.[12] Her musical expertise "perfectly met Highlander's cultural needs," and her interest in drama and commitment to helping the underdog contributed to the good fit.[13] In addition, her vivacious demeanor, ready smile, and outgoing manner made her a welcome addition to the school's rather dour community of educators. Horton later joked that he didn't connect with Zilphia immediately; it took at least a full week before he realized he was falling in love with her. Less than a month later, on March 6th, they married.[14]

From the start, they enjoyed a deep and loving union. Not long after their marriage, Horton wrote adoringly to his bride: "I love you officially and unofficially, morning, noon, and night, asleep or awake; and in every mood or position that I find myself in or can imagine myself to be in."[15] In another early letter, he closed by acknowledging that his devotion to Zilphia had to be tempered by the recognition that the hard work of social change must go on: "My life, after all, is not made up of loving you even though my zest for life is. There is work to be done on tomorrow's class."[16]

In the first years of their partnership, they lived simply, in a one-room cabin a considerable distance from the main house, where all large gatherings occurred. Because they were in the public eye so much of the time, they savored opportunities to enjoy one another's company in solitude, which occurred all too infrequently. Their relatively primitive surroundings also provided relief from their public duties. They took baths in the nearby river, received their only heat from a roaring fireplace, and maintained a hefty supply of wood through their own exertions. As Frank Adams has said, all of these activities "furnished physical exercise for a couple who spent most of their lives at tasks of the mind."[17] Only when their two children arrived, Thorsten in 1943 and Charis in 1945, did the Hortons move, reluctantly, to a home closer to the center of Highlander activities, one equipped with indoor plumbing, central heating, and a badly needed telephone to maintain communication with the outside world.

Before marrying, Horton and Zilphia had many discussions about the challenges of forging a partnership between two committed and ambitious activists dedicated to "radical social change." To make it work, they would have to see their union as "a marriage of equals" committed to enriching each other's lives "through being and working together."[18] It must have been hard, given the conservative cultural milieu in which they were immersed, to maintain this spirit of equality consistently, but more often than not, Horton made good on his agreement to treat his spouse as his equal. For her part, Zilphia always strove to be her own person. Although many activists influenced her, she never functioned as a "passive disciple" to anyone, including Horton.[19] Almost immediately, she independently reshaped Highlander's music program and greatly expanded the drama program. By 1938, she enjoyed acknowledgment as the leader of Highlander's rapidly growing cultural program, receiving acclaim as an indispensable member of the school's teaching staff.

SOCIAL JUSTICE THESPIAN

After spending an internship in New York City in 1935–1936 learning how to use theater to deepen exploration of social issues, Zilphia became a kind of social justice thespian. She worked with hundreds of

Highlander students composing and performing lively, fast-moving labor dramas. As with singing, she sought to make the experience of performing dramas as simple and uncomplicated as possible. She did not ask participants to memorize lines or speak in artificial ways. Sets, curtains, and costumes mattered little in their productions. She focused on using dramatics to put Highlander participants in conflict situations that felt real, giving students an authentic experience of walking a picket line or negotiating a contract. As she put it, "Students should be faced with the same conditions at the school as they would be in their home situations."[20] Performing scenes about labor activism as it was actually experienced not only deepened students' understanding, it also helped audiences identify more strongly with the conflicts that often arose between management and rank-and-file workers.

Zilphia Horton rarely lectured. Learning happened through real-life improvisations, which grew out of the raw materials of actual experiences. Whenever possible, she kept the focus of the scenes on inherently dramatic subject matter such as a strike, an encounter with management, or a worker filing a grievance. The plays posed and addressed problems as the action unfolded or, if left unresolved, problems would be debated during a post-performance discussion. She often linked her drama class to the Union Problems class. Because students had already extensively discussed real-life union experiences, improvisational sketches could further contextualize and deepen participants' exploration of common workplace tensions. As John Glen put it, "Under Zilphia's direction, the emphasis of the dramatics program shifted away from educating those who observed the plays to educating those who participated in them."[21]

Zilphia developed two simple criteria for evaluating the drama classes. Activities had to be practical enough to "take back to their home organizations and put into use,"[22] and they needed to challenge conventional thinking by putting learners in situations that introduced dilemmas or complexities that confounded what many thought they already knew. As each drama class proceeded and new improvisations emerged, Zilphia marveled at how successfully her theatrical situations forced learners to respond creatively and to learn to formulate difficult on-the-spot decisions. To outsiders, the drama program might have seemed like a frill or an interesting extra, but Zilphia made it absolutely central to the process of preparing activists for challenging and unpredictable leadership roles.

Over time, Highlander gained fame for its labor dramas. Many of these skits, which began as improvisations and were never intended to be converted into written scripts, eventually made their way into print and enjoyed wide circulation. Whether improvisations achieved notoriety as published scripts depended on the evaluations of the students themselves. They subjected each performance to a careful analysis that tallied up its strengths and weaknesses. Groups of interested students further analyzed those performances thought to have merit, and those that passed muster underwent additional scrutiny before being put into print.[23] Zilla Hawes wrote one of the earliest plays that Highlander produced, setting the pattern for others. Called "Mopping Up," it was a simple story about workers' reactions to an authoritarian boss who refused to fix a defective ventilation system. Like many that followed it, the piece highlighted the role of collective resistance in responding to abusive managers, an especially important idea since unions played such a crucial role in promoting worker solidarity and resisting management's unreasonable dictates.[24]

Highlander eventually printed dozens of original plays about union experiences, all of which attempted to teach important lessons and enlivened some part of the workshop experience for union leaders. Additionally, they were sometimes produced for the benefit of the local community, as an alternative form of entertainment and to raise Highlander's visibility in Grundy County. The best of these plays made a contribution to the process of preparing emerging leaders for the uncertainties and perils of labor organizing in the 1930s and 1940s.

John L. Lewis, the legendary president of the United Mine Workers, called Highlander "a singing army" because of the way the school used music to inspire confidence and bring people together.[25] Ralph Tefferteller, who helped lead Highlander's cultural program before Zilphia arrived, praised her love of music, her uplifting spirit, and her vital contributions to the Highlander experience: "If ever there was a person who could invigorate and move a group of adults with musical participation, she was the prime example. . . . It was just such a joy to be part of it with her and to sit in any group and to see how they would respond. She had an infectious type of presentation that enveloped you and drew you in. You weren't on the outside as a spectator—you became wholeheartedly involved with the moment."[26]

Zilphia never gained the renown her husband enjoyed, but few activists at Highlander remained as faithful as she to the principles that the school lived by. She loved to be around people, getting to know them more intimately by drawing them out and learning about the stories, traditions, and songs that mattered to them. Her lovely, unpretentious alto voice could draw people into the choral singing she loved to lead.[27] A talented musician, she could play almost any song she heard on piano, accordion, or a wide assortment of stringed instruments. But her talent for singing and playing multiple instruments hardly explained her unique contribution to the school. Zilphia used music to invite people into the shared experience of the Highlander community.

As Zilphia began to emerge as the school's music director, singing became an essential element of any workshop, earning Highlander the reputation for being a "singing school." Horton called her "the moving spirit in shaping the singing and music program."[28] Just as she rejected traditional top-down methods of teaching, she spurned the elitism that prompted many trained musicians to choose complex, hard-to-sing songs. She wasn't interested in music for passive listening or songs that were composed to be silently savored. She preferred songs that supported the full participation of everyone, seeking out tunes that could be adapted and sung anywhere, whether on a picket line, in a union hall, or to energize a workshop.[29] Although she might sing solo to familiarize people with new melodies and lyrics, she never focused on her own musical performance. She wanted others to sing in unison, giving them something to share that might draw them closer together.

Like Horton, Zilphia began by honoring people's experiences by learning as much about them as she could. She then turned to song, especially folk songs, to build on and connect what she had heard. She wanted the songs that people sang together to be enjoyable, but even more, she sought the deeper enjoyment that comes from collaborating with others on something larger than oneself. She used songs about everyday things, "work, hopes, joys and sorrows," to reinforce pride in cultural heritage, to deepen understanding of the histories and traditions of others, and to help people recognize the common underlying themes that often bridged their different worlds. As she put it, "Music has been too generally thought of as an art form for leisure time, performed and enjoyed by and for the chosen few. . . . The folk song grows out of reality. It is this stark reality and genuineness which gives the folk song vitality and strength."[30] Folk songs, in particular, she believed, held great power to foster a sense of unity among people from vastly different backgrounds and cultures.[31]

In the 1948 edition of an adult education journal from Canada called *Food for Thought*, Zilphia published an article recounting a moving example of deep musical enjoyment she and Horton experienced while holding a workshop for a small group of poor black farmers launching a community co-op.[32] The workshop was scheduled to be held in an old garage with a dirt floor and no seats. While a few of the farmers and Horton tidied up the space and turned some old boards into a makeshift grandstand, Zilphia went across the street to the house of their host to wait. As she entered, a gleeful young child asked Zilphia to play "tinpan" piano, referencing the popular music of the time. Zilphia sat down at the family's beat-up upright piano and picked out some familiar songs. Her playing attracted so many eager listeners that soon the little room was jammed with people. Then "they requested a boogie and their faces broke into broad grins when I actually played one. A beautiful, radiant six-year-old Negro girl began to dance. The people began to clap and this kept up until the house was fairly rocking and the farmer came over and asked us to bring the crowd to the meeting."[33]

The actual meeting, like most Highlander workshops, began with singing familiar songs such as "Home on the Range." She then invited participants to sing spirituals they knew, including one with the line "Just like a tree that's planted by the water, we shall not be moved." The farmers were inspired to improvise some new lyrics about their co-op, which allowed "them to sing about themselves with a beautiful, familiar spiritual as the tune."[34]

Zilphia then shifted to an unfamiliar song that everyone soon was singing "as though the words were their own." Zilphia was convinced the informal singing and dancing that occurred just prior to the meeting primed everyone for more exuberant participation: "They learned the new songs quickly and transferred the same spirit and enthusiasm from the boogie across the road." By the end of the meeting, which had included a lengthy discussion about prejudice and more songs led by two farmers playing banjo and fiddle, there were multiple requests for additional workshops. To Zilphia, the music accomplished three goals: it enlivened the group, helped to unify it, and "underlined its purpose." Subsequent workshops could build on this day's success by reaffirming that music "is not separate from living," but a path "to a better way of life."[35]

Zilphia's approach was inviting and lively, energizing participants to achieve levels of engagement that took many of them by surprise. She quickly established trust with strangers because of her generous, outgoing spirit. The music drew people together, but so did her smile, her lack of pretentiousness, and her commitment to joyfully embracing the moment. Aleine Austin, a labor activist who first came to Highlander in 1942, said that while Horton was for the mind, "Zilphia was for the soul."[36] She had a way of using music to help people "get to their innermost feelings about what they were doing and living for."[37]

Unlike some of her contemporaries, such as musicologist Alan Lomax, who sought "authentic and distinctive music of a particular place," Zilphia welcomed songs from everywhere and in so doing "gave music back to the people who created it, hoping they would find new uses for it."[38] For Zilphia, music was not a respite from activism or a diverting break from the struggle for social justice; music was an indispensable part of inspiring social change, a way to give people new hope that their shared collective efforts might bear fruit. She uncritically welcomed any song someone shared, knowing that in some way it was part of the person's experience. Regarding songs as a window into a person's conflicts and struggles, she was eager to learn how the songs people loved had inspired them or helped them cope during difficult times. For her, songs could be a vehicle for analyzing people's problems, for getting them to see that their troubles were not one-of-a-kind events but part of a pattern of injustice endured by many. She masterfully found ways to adapt songs so that a new lyric or revised melody might more closely mirror their specific struggles, often adding words that introduced themes and ideas to challenge the status quo.[39]

You've Got to Move: Stories of Change in the South, the film about the Highlander experience that Lucy Phenix and Veronica Solver made in the early 1980s, opens with words that Zilphia faithfully lived by: "Dream of people all together singing, each singing a way to self, to realms on realms within, all singing their way on out of self, singing through to unity. There comes a moment, a turning, when people stop thinking about what has happened to them and start thinking about what they are going to make happen."[40] This passage beautifully captures what Zilphia knew: the power of song could move people from a focus on the individual to a focus on the many, from self-interest to community interest. Her songbook selections in the volumes she compiled were widely used at workshops and on picket lines all over the country to promote this all-important sense of group identity.[41]

"WE SHALL OVERCOME"

Zilphia's best-known contribution to the history of protest music is doubtless her influence on the song "We Shall Overcome." According to Pete Seeger, in 1945 or 1946 a group of striking tobacco workers, most of whom were African American, sang a song known as "I Will Overcome." Some of the workers from the tobacco union brought the song to a Highlander workshop in 1947, and Zilphia immediately recognized its power to move people. She changed the word "I" to "we" to reinforce the idea that the effort to overcome must be a collective struggle. She also adjusted the melody to make it easier to sing. That same year, she taught the song to Seeger, who published it in his newsletter "People's Songs." Later, the word "shall" supplanted the word "will." Many claim this change was Seeger's idea, but he recalled Septima Clark always preferred "shall" because it "opened up the voice"; perhaps she also preferred the call to action conjured up by the word "shall" over the simple intention of "will."[42]

For many years thereafter, Zilphia regularly featured the song in workshops. It became a kind of Highlander anthem but was not the iconic song it is today until Guy Carawan, who co-directed Highlander's cultural program for many years, began using it, first at Highlander's twenty-fifth anniversary celebration in 1957, and then with the Student Nonviolent Coordinating Committee activists in the early 1960s.[43] Although no other song that Zilphia worked on achieved such worldwide fame, her involvement with "We Shall Overcome" typified her commitment to adapting songs to enhance their protest value.

Fittingly, this song supported the black freedom movement for many years, with the majority of its royalties going to a "We Shall Overcome" fund administered by Highlander Center.[44]

Tragically, Zilphia Horton died in April 1956, just three days before her forty-sixth birthday, when she swallowed some typewriter cleaning fluid that she mistook for a glass of water. At first, the ill effects seemed relatively minor, but her health quickly deteriorated, and she succumbed to the poison within a few days. Zilphia's passing was a terrible shock to thousands of people, unleashing an outpouring of grief. Hundreds of friends and former students shared their memories of her singing, her leadership, and her kindness. Many especially recalled her ability to animate any gathering with her exuberance and lively demeanor. Her friend and colleague Aleine Austin spoke of her incomparable spirit, her ability to cross boundaries, to make connections, and to have fun. Without her, Aleine observed, Highlander "would have been a dry place." Guy Carawan, who was credited, along with his wife Candie, as having carried on Zilphia's legacy, said that "she was not here to tell her story." Her job was to help others tell theirs. She was the warm, embracing person "who made you feel welcome and at home. That was a lot of Zilphia's energy and spirit."[45]

Horton himself died in 1990, thirty-four years after Zilphia's death. The memorial ceremony for Horton included remembrances of Zilphia as well. A special fund was created that honored both of them: the Myles and Zilphia Horton Fund for Education and Social Change. There were many references to Zilphia's enduring legacy during the ceremony, and Highlander has continued to recognize Zilphia's work by creating the Zilphia Horton Cultural Organizing Residency Project and Institute, which connects cultural workers to a wide variety of community associations working with marginalized populations.[46] It is hard to imagine a more fitting tribute.

7   Racial Equality within the Union Movement

From Highlander's beginnings in 1932, full inclusion of all people, regardless of race, religion or gender, ranked as a first principle. When Horton had completed his investigation of Danish folk education at the end of 1931 and dreamed of a school where a diverse group of students would learn and work and play together, he visualized blacks and whites meeting with each other as equals. Yet when the school began in nearly all-white Grundy County, where Jim Crow discrimination fiercely held sway, these good intentions could not, at first, be lived out. For one thing, the state of Tennessee treated all interaction between blacks and whites as anathema and had created a complicated and redundant legal structure to maintain the complete separation of the races. They could not go to school together, could not travel together, could not eat or sleep together, and, above all, were forbidden to marry. Additionally, to millions of unsympathetic white southerners, integrationists who advocated for dismantling white supremacy were automatically considered dangerous subversives who must be rooted out using any means necessary, including violence. Put simply, the deeply entrenched prejudice of the larger society endangered the life of anyone seeking to abolish racial discrimination.

The very tenacity of racism in the South and the ways in which it interfered with progress in so many other areas made fighting against it, however covertly, a Highlander priority. Even when circumstances necessitated compromise, the commitment to undoing racism remained strong. Police raids, bomb threats, and even premeditated murder might threaten the community, but the school persisted toward its vision: true integration in which students of color became full participants in the life of Highlander.

TOWARD INTEGRATION

That sense of growing inclusiveness is most vividly illustrated by the school's residential program for industrial workers during its peak years between 1942 and 1947. During this period, Highlander sought to build "a broad-based, racially integrated and politically active southern labor movement and to foster a greater appreciation for the contribution workers' education could make to it."[1]

When Highlander opened in 1932, neither black nor white union members had shown much interest in attending integrated workshops. Whites still clung to segregationist practices and preferred the strict separation they knew best. African Americans refused to participate, both because of the pervasive humiliation that accompanied white rituals of non-acceptance and out of fear of all-too-frequent white violence. Horton later bluntly reflected, "We couldn't find many blacks who would take the chance of getting lynched."[2] In 1933, Horton reached out to historically black Knoxville College to invite students to Highlander workshops, but sociology professor J. Herman Daves answered warily, "At the time we know of no student or graduate of our school who would be a good candidate or would be desirous of enrolling with you."[3] Yet a year or so later, Professor Daves, who had just written a book about the black community in Knoxville modeled on W. E. B. Du Bois's groundbreaking study on the African American community in Philadelphia, decided to test the waters himself. His brief visit confirmed that Highlander's caution and Daves's initial reluctance to have his school participate had been entirely warranted: When the people of Grundy County learned of the plan to have an African American scholar address an all-white audience, a few local residents threatened to blow up the school with dynamite. The talk took place, but armed guards circled the grounds to maintain safety.[4]

By the following year, the climate had eased somewhat, allowing for a very limited form of desegregation. The distinguished sociologist and subsequent president of Fisk University, Charles Johnson, delivered the first of many lectures at Highlander without precipitating a major racial incident. In the years that followed, black speakers at Highlander became relatively commonplace. In a letter dated May 1940, Horton described Highlander's methods for introducing African American guest speakers into its workshops, which included something he called "natural exposure." By this, he meant treating all black visitors with the same respect as white visitors, without drawing attention to any group or individual. It was a step toward full integration: "When they come to the school as speakers or as casual visitors, the same consideration and courtesy is shown them as is shown other visitors, but no fuss is made about their presence. Eating and sleeping arrangements follow the routine of all guests."[5] When asked how he got black and white participants to eat together at Highlander, he answered matter-of-factly: "First, the food is prepared. Second, it's put on the table. Third, we ring the bell."[6]

On other fronts, while organizing textile unions in the late 1930s, Highlander made sure that blacks received the same pay increases and fringe benefits as whites, at a time when such agreements were rare. And Highlander successfully expanded a series of highly effective off-site extension programs, strictly for African American workers, that met in segregated locations throughout the South.[7]

Still, despite these efforts, the school continued to fall short of its dream of achieving full integration.

Finally, in 1942 Highlander officially declared its intention to end all forms of racial discrimination and to integrate future residencies.[8] Even so, it wasn't until 1944 that the United Auto Workers (UAW) agreed to host a desegregated residential workshop at Highlander, which marked the first interracial union gathering ever to be held in the South. Despite the desire to integrate boldly and without compromise, Highlander reluctantly announced that its plans for an interracial workshop would not go forward until all white participants had been informed, presumably to avoid ruffling the feathers of any unsuspecting white person in a region still fraught with racial tension. In the end, only three black participants joined fifty-three whites at the UAW meeting in June.[9] Although only a modest accomplishment, the experience gave Highlander new confidence. At last the school could say it was beginning to realize one of its founding principles. Highlander's annual report for 1944 expressed it simply: "This session was historic because, for the first time, Negro and white delegates studied, worked and played together at a Southern school."[10]

More integrated workshops followed during the summer of 1944, and soon Highlander became known as the only place in the South where blacks and whites could gather together to study and strategize for social change. By the end of 1944, Highlander was not only "the most important labor education center in the South"; it was unique for practicing racial integration.[11]

BOB JONES SPEAKS HIS MIND

Because the 1944 UAW meeting marked an important milestone for the school, interest grew in hearing from black union representatives who had helped break the color line. One of the first to speak out was Bob Jones, a young African American committeeman from

Memphis, Tennessee, who served as a member of the UAW and agreed to be interviewed by a Highlander staff member near the end of 1945 about his experiences at this first integrated workshop.

The interview began with an icebreaker about Jones's favorite courses. He hesitated before naming parliamentary procedure, law, public speaking, and labor history as his top picks, noting that they all just seemed "to hook up together." But the content from the labor history course especially energized him. Learning about black laborers who had been members of early unions and suffered discouragement and humiliation at every turn gave him a context for understanding the inhumane treatment he himself had faced prior to affiliating with the UAW. In Jones's case, his previous foreman had done everything possible to get him to quit by giving him all the dirtiest and most thankless jobs. But he had held on and finally secured a position as a metal cleaner, in which, with the union's support, he had received fair treatment ever since.[12]

One of the sessions Jones enjoyed most from the time he spent at Highlander emphasized the value of cooperatives. He wanted to start a union food co-op back home that the workers could run themselves, so they could get a better selection of food and keep prices reasonable. But whether that ever happened or not, he expressed gratitude for his Highlander experience and for the UAW: "The union is the only salvation for me and the other Negroes in the South. It means better working conditions, security, and everything good. When I first joined, I had an idea that there were people who didn't feel about Negroes like those I'd been brought up with in Memphis. And when I came to Highlander I became fully convinced there were such people. Here it's a matter of giving the [union] a chance to carry out its constitution."[13] As the interview wound to a close, Jones recalled a book he had recently read entitled *A Faith to Free the People*. He praised the UAW and Highlander for teaching that faith, adding, "There's more religion in this union than in the average church."[14]

As plans proceeded for the 1945 month-long convening of the Southern CIO School, anticipated to be the largest group ever to gather at Highlander, organizers feared discord, since racial discrimination was again on the rise. Some union officials expected a number of the white members to object strongly to integration, leading to racial hostility that could put future progress at risk. In the end, two black participants joined the twenty-four whites who attended, which was a much smaller group overall than expected. Nothing dramatic occurred, but two white representatives left defiantly, unwilling to accept any form of racial integration. Later that year, another much smaller, racially mixed group of UAW members met at Highlander. This time no racial disruptions occurred, despite the fact that more than a fourth of the attendees were black.[15]

At the convening of the 1946 Southern CIO School, five white participants spoke out against integration and threatened to leave. Highlander staff reluctantly worked out a compromise in which blacks and whites ate at separate tables and a few whites had access to separate sleeping quarters. Still, classroom activities carried on without racial separation, and all committees were composed of both black and white representatives.[16] Horton and other Highlander staff often claimed their interracial gatherings met with little or no resistance, but evidence exists that among whites, opposition to interracial education remained surprisingly vehement.[17]

These first efforts to integrate the residencies produced considerable tension. Fortunately, the residency terms for the CIO gatherings stretched from four to six weeks, giving people time to ease into a routine that allowed relations between the two groups to improve gradually. In most cases, by the end of a term, racial incidents were rare, and interracial friendships occasionally blossomed. Getting there, though, could be tough. One African American female participant who had endured repeated insults at the hands of whites confronted Horton, complaining bitterly he had not done nearly enough to protect her from their bullying. Horton listened sympathetically, but he also found reason to be optimistic about the long-term impact of prolonged interaction. He reportedly told her, "If segregation is to end in the South and the nation, people as strong as yourself will have to find the means to end it. That you feel free enough to assail a white man at a white school is cause for renewed hope."[18]

Though Horton understood the disproportionate burden black people faced in fostering racial equality, he believed the onus of responsibility was on whites. As the perpetuators of racism, Horton affirmed, whites had a duty to take concerted action to end it. As long as whites dominated interactions between the races, with blacks assuming a subordinate role, blacks could not possibly trust whites to respond positively to a friendly gesture, and they risked seeming "uppity" or aggressive if they took the lead. Given the racial dynamics of white supremacy, whites had to make the first move to ensure a positive interaction. In preparation for a Southern Farmers Union meeting, Horton wrote that sympathetic whites should take the lead in relating to black people and strategically place themselves at tables to facilitate relationship building and the holding of productive interracial conversations.[19] For the most part, these efforts proved successful. Many black representatives, not previously part of an interracial group, marveled at the respectful treatment they received at Highlander, which allowed them to relax and to get much more out of their experience there. At least one participant in the 1945 UAW summer term saw no hint of racial discrimination and summed up the experience as a triumph for Highlander and the union.[20]

Sometimes, Highlander's commitment to letting participants solve their own problems worked wonders in blunting white racism. During a fall 1946 meeting, a few whites once again objected to the integrated meals and sleeping areas. The offer of segregated facilities quieted the objections, but proved far less effective in softening white resistance than the independent decision by two concerned white participants from Memphis to hold informal discussions on race relations. Highlander staff followed their lead, making interracial cooperation a recurring theme in their classes and featuring the topic in a number of evening programs. The result was a group spirit across the integrated participants that exceeded anything yet achieved in Highlander's history.[21]

The fourth annual Southern CIO School held in 1947 enjoyed a similar group spirit and proved the most integrated yet, even though fewer than half of the fifty expected students actually showed up. Issues of universal brotherhood and racial harmony again dominated many of the discussions and activities and contributed to the students' sense of creative accomplishment. One student wrote a song that reflected these themes, and another, heartened by his first interracial experience, "concluded that people of all colors and religions should unite to solve their common problems."[22] Unfortunately, just prior to this workshop the CIO leadership forced one of Highlander's housekeepers, an avowed Communist, to resign as a condition of hosting the workshop at Highlander, an indication that the once radical union was distancing itself more and more from left-wing organizations and causes.[23] In fact, unfounded but persistent concerns that Highlander was little more than a Communist front prompted the CIO to weaken its connections to the school. Virtually all of the rumors about Highlander's Communist ties arose directly from the school's unyielding commitment to racial equality.

THE PACKINGHOUSE WORKERS

As Highlander transitioned from an almost exclusive emphasis on union organizing and labor education toward civil rights and racial integration, its efforts to democratize unions and to make them more racially inclusive had delivered only spotty success. As a result, Horton and the Highlander board decided the time had come to put all their efforts into the cause of advancing racial justice. Still, when the president of the United Packinghouse Workers Association (UPWA) approached Horton with the idea of his becoming director of education for the union in 1951, he was intrigued. In the late 1940s and early 1950s, the union movement, in both the South and North, had grown markedly more conservative, cautious, and bureaucratic, partly to avoid being red-baited by anti-Communist McCarthyites, and partly because union bosses with authoritarian tendencies increasingly controlled labor negotiations. Not surprisingly, support dried up, even in the CIO's most progressive unions, for the worker-centered methods that Highlander favored. The UPWA, which had represented workers in the meatpacking industry since 1937, had remained a refreshing exception.[24]

The UPWA also had a reputation for refusing to compromise on its strict non-discrimination policy. Horton believed that few unions equaled the UPWA's commitment to recruiting black members; by 1951, it had already accomplished a great deal to integrate its ranks. UPWA leaders had attempted to build a racially diverse labor force, with no racial differentiation regarding workplace benefits.[25] They stood behind the principle of equal pay for equal work, without regard for race or gender, a unique position at the time.[26] Horton also admired the UPWA because the union had chosen not to add an anti-Communist amendment to its constitution or to require employees to sign loyalty oaths, despite the pressure to do so in the face of McCarthyism.[27] Ralph Helstein, the UPWA's international president since 1946, who had previously been the union's chief counsel and remained a strong civil rights activist, proved the driving force behind all the positions of the UPWA that aligned with Highlander's principles.

Helstein thought Highlander's democratic approach to leadership development offered just what the union needed. Helstein loved

Horton's ability to make people feel valued, often for the first time in their lives, by impressing upon them that their rights to free speech and equal treatment were inviolable. Helstein also appreciated Horton's way of seeing the potential in people. "The great thing about Myles," Helstein said, was that he "never saw people as they were, he saw people as they could be. . . . He got people to do things that they didn't think they could do."[28]

Helstein also persuaded many staffers and workers to engage more actively in community-wide efforts to dismantle segregation. He took the position that the union not only had a responsibility to desegregate the workplace, but also to make inroads into the world outside the plant. Beyond serving as an economic instrument, the union "also had to be a social instrument to bring about change and progress."[29] To resolve what Helstein saw as a historic conflict between business unionism and social unionism, the UPWA needed to follow through on its non-discrimination commitments by advancing them everywhere: at home, in the schools, in religious institutions, and in neighborhood centers: "You have to be worried about what goes on in your city as well as in the plant, because people are not just workers of a plant, they're citizens of a community. It's important that we deal with these issues of discrimination no matter where they're found."[30]

Following Helstein's lead, many UPWA workers dropped in on segregated taverns and restaurants and department stores to put pressure on owners to change their policies. When these tactics failed, they imposed boycotts. In Chicago, the lunch counter of a well-known department store, Goldblatt's, remained segregated until workers affiliated with the UPWA sat in, demanding that lunch be served to all comers, regardless of race.[31]

Unfortunately, the Packinghouse Workers' quest to create an authentic interracial union was not as successful as Helstein had dreamed. In 1950, John Hope II, a social scientist at Fisk University, conducted a survey on race relations in the UPWA and found that in many cases African American workers could not access good-paying, higher-skilled jobs, and that discrimination against them was far more widespread than earlier estimates: "More than 30 percent of white members objected to working with a Black in the same job classification, and 90 percent of Southern whites supported segregated eating facilities."[32] Perhaps most devastating of all, Hope wrote, was that "union initiatives to confront discrimination in local communities were dangerously weak."[33] The survey's results led to a more ambitious anti-discrimination policy and the creation of a new Anti-Discrimination Department within the UPWA. The decision to bring in Myles Horton as education director also followed the release of the disappointing survey findings.

MYLES HORTON AS UPWA EDUCATION DIRECTOR

Upon assuming the position, Horton made it clear that he didn't plan to impose a particular program or sit in a room with his staff cooking up a lot of bright ideas. What he wanted to do aligned with the work he had done for close to twenty years at Highlander. First, he sought to learn from the workers, "to find out what people want and need" so he could "understand their dreams and struggles and help them to find a way to get what they . . . deserve."[34] In formal communications, Horton explained that his department existed "to see to it that leaders are developed and that a maximum of union education takes place on the job, in the union, and in the community; and that education is not something apart from the union program as a whole."[35] Predictably, Horton opted to keep himself and his staff in the background, providing supports for workers to educate themselves. He also favored a problem-based educational approach, with learning activities growing out of the actual needs of the workers.

In his conception of labor education, Horton drew a distinction between a "drip" system of training, which he rejected, and a "percolator" approach to worker development, which he endorsed. He condemned the tendency of most union administrators to seize control of the educational process, only gradually letting ideas "drip" down from the upper echelons to permeate the thinking of the lowly rank and file. Under the "percolator" style of education, union heads did not own or initiate all the worthy ideas; ideas could "percolate" up from anyone, regardless of their role. The percolator metaphor affirmed that good ideas often originate with those who are the least noticed or listened to in organizations. Horton sought to create an education program that would help the union discover and develop emerging leaders by empowering lower level workers, giving them the freedom to create more open, democratic, and percolator-friendly learning environments.[36]

Despite these good intentions and strong support from President Helstein, Horton ran into trouble almost from the start. UPWA Vice President and Personnel Director A. T. Stephens, a proud traditionalist who believed in top-down administration and "drip" approaches to education, feared any education program that was not inextricably linked to the established chain of command. Under the plan that Horton and Helstein had agreed to, Horton had hired a five-person staff that reported to him directly, with no oversight from Stephens. Additionally, Horton's charge to create new opportunities for self-education and self-empowerment struck Stephens as vague and dangerously isolated from the rest of the union's functions. Stephens also detested Horton's notion that this self-education process empowered the rank and file. Stephens thought that putting too much power into the hands of the ordinary worker was a recipe for disaster.[37]

Because Stephens hated any change that he saw as an erosion of his authority, he moved quickly to curb Horton's influence. First, he shortened an important training session for Horton's staff from four weeks to two. He followed up by temporarily reassigning two of Horton's staff members to organizing drives that had nothing to do with their educational work.[38]

Even so, at least at first, Horton's program continued to grow and receive favorable evaluations. In a surprisingly short period of time, Horton's innovations helped the UPWA increase the number of blacks, Mexican Americans, and women in leadership positions and eliminate many of the all-white departments that had dominated and encumbered the UPWA's administrative structure.[39] With the organization more committed than ever to addressing persistent discrimination, these historically oppressed groups felt emboldened to file complaints and demand prompt action in writing.[40] For a person like Stephens, who wanted to control everything from the top, Horton's vision of collective empowerment was becoming much too successful.[41]

Fearful about the speed of these changes and intent on eliminating Horton's role once and for all, Stephens wrote to Helstein, questioning the need for a separate education department. On the same day, he informed Horton "that Stephens' own staff . . . would be better able to serve the rank and file" than Horton's staff, citing statistics of decreasing educational activity. To Stephens, fewer formal trainings or professional development opportunities signified less productivity, a good reason, in his view, to cut Horton's department. Horton defended his approach by asserting that the whole point was to get workers "to do things for themselves" and to get local leaders to assume ownership of their own affairs. For Stephens, such initiatives threatened his source of power.[42]

Stephens's allies in the UPWA who strongly opposed its non-discrimination policy took advantage of longstanding lies that Horton was a Communist. Rumors started to circulate that in hiring Horton, the UPWA was allowing Reds to gain control of the union. By increasing doubt about the purposes of Horton's efforts, those upholding the traditional white power structure were able to delay efforts to integrate the remaining all-white departments.[43]

Unsurprisingly, the rumors led to pressure to make changes, so Stephens had the cover to reorganize the education department at the end of 1952 without any input from Horton. Stephens put his own staff, directly answerable to him, in charge, replacing the educational staff Horton had so carefully recruited. Stephens said the reorganization allowed for a "shift from straight education to program implementation," effectively eliminating all the democratic innovations Horton prized, including discussion circles, worker-generated goals, and self-directed learning.[44]

Whatever hope remained for some kind of compromise between Horton and Stephens came crashing down when Horton was reduced to asking permission to attend a March 1953 UPWA educational meeting held at Highlander, of all places. Horton also was appalled to learn that Stephens's restructured educational program embraced a thoroughly top-down orientation. At the end of the gathering, Horton submitted his resignation.[45]

Helstein was devastated by this turn of events but also felt powerless in the face of Stephens's ability to manipulate the situation for his own benefit. Horton's resignation thus marked the end of Highlander's involvement with unions and completed its shift away from labor education. Zilphia shared Myles's assessment that the union movement had abandoned democracy. She told a gathering of Montana farmers that unions had become "so reactionary and complacent that they've lost their ideals, and I don't care anything about singing for people like that."[46] As far as both Hortons were concerned, Stephens's resistance wasn't just one person's reluctance to make change; it stood for a system that lacked the will to act on its own espoused commitments and, more significantly, symbolized the union movement's decision to reject bottom-up participation. By realigning itself with the more established and conservative American Federation of Labor, the CIO had lost virtually all of its radical edge.

Similarly, as a number of historians have documented, the UPWA degenerated into an unwieldy bureaucracy that had lost touch with its membership. As that occurred, "education as a force for greater democracy was co-opted."[47]

In the meantime, Highlander, which had always prioritized civil rights, saw racial justice more clearly than ever as the most important mission of all and prepared to bring it to the center of its work. As Horton put it, "We finally came to the conclusion that we couldn't go any farther in terms of economic, political, or cultural changes until we dealt head-on with this business of racism."[48]

8 *The White Supremacist versus the Social Egalitarian*

In 1954, at the height of the McCarthy Red Scare, James O. Eastland, one of the U.S. Senate's leading white supremacists and a pivotal member of the Senate Internal Security Subcommittee (SISS), issued subpoenas to prominent civil rights activists charging them with Communist infiltration of southern education. Myles Horton was among those summoned for a hearing in New Orleans on the Southern Conference Education Fund (SCEF). Suspicion about Horton's educational purposes had hounded him for years; FBI undercover agents had conducted investigations of Horton and his school at least twice. A network of southern governors had branded him a dangerous subversive, and the state of Tennessee had repeatedly threatened to shut him down. But Eastland's subpoena would put him in the national spotlight for the first time, hardly a welcome development.[1]

Eastland's subcommittee acted as the Senate counterpart of the notorious House Un-American Activities Committee. Together, these two legislative entities devoted countless hours to holding public hearings and amassing documents that purportedly demonstrated widespread Communist penetration of U.S. institutions. Eastland exploited his role on the SISS by gaining authority to hold special hearings in local communities across the country. Ostensibly tasked to expose little-known subversives, the SISS gained wide media attention that emboldened Eastland to malign reputations, make unfounded accusations, and promote the lie that civil rights activism equaled Communist agitation.

The prospect of the hearing distressed Horton. Eastland, an unusually virulent white supremacist known for being reckless and unreliable, drew on his years of experience as a country lawyer to set traps so that witnesses would say or do the wrong thing, making them vulnerable to a contempt of Congress charge. Horton knew he had a lot to lose in any confrontation with Eastland.[2]

As preparations for the special hearing unfolded, the Supreme Court was also preparing to announce its landmark *Brown v. Board of Education* ruling, declaring school segregation inherently unequal, and, therefore, unconstitutional. Eastland, a wealthy Mississippi planter, was shaken to his core by the prospect of court-ordered racial integration. The scenario of little black boys and girls and little white boys and girls going to the same school made him sick to his stomach. During the 1954 campaign to retain his Senate seat in advance of the Supreme Court's decision, Eastland considered any action overthrowing "separate but equal" confirmation that the court itself was "Communist-infiltrated." Governors from the states of Georgia and South Carolina egged him on, urging him to use his authority on the subcommittee to collaborate with the FBI to dig up more dirt on the South's most notorious integrationists. If he could use his hearing to successfully portray Horton and others as Communists, Eastland thought, he could discredit them and thus cripple their ability to advance the cause of racial equality.[3]

SON OF MISSISSIPPI

James Eastland grew to adulthood in a world diametrically opposed to the one that nurtured Myles Horton. Born in 1904 into a wealthy

Mississippi Delta planter family, Eastland matured under the shadow of his father, who bred him to be a perfect representative of his native culture, one marked by patriarchy, white supremacy, and a strict social hierarchy. When Eastland said years later, "My father completely controlled me," he was honoring Woods Eastland, the family patriarch, who imposed on his clan his notion of the ideal community, in which mature white males ruled uncompromisingly, exercising total control over all others in their domain. Eastland accepted his role as the dutiful and obedient son, primed to take his own place someday as the incontestable patriarch, owing allegiance and deference to no one. As one of his biographers said, Eastland not only learned from his father to wield power effectively; he mastered the role his father exemplified, that of protector of "white dominance in a black-majority world."[4]

Eastland's father oversaw his son's immersion in all the practices and rituals of planter society. Some of this preparation came directly from the father himself, who would often have his son accompany him on tours of the property. A parade of well-trained, dutiful tutors supplied the other, more formal aspects of James's education. Obligatorily, he later went to the University of Mississippi, "Ole Miss," where he was steeped in its grand, genteel traditions. Although he maintained a reasonably good academic record and acquired the social graces expected of a planter's heir, he did not graduate, dropping out during his senior year after successfully passing the state bar exam, which allowed him to practice law.

Eastland's upbringing had carefully prepared him for a political career, and his father pushed him to run for office at age twenty-four. He was elected and served a single term as a state representative under an unpopular regime; facing a likely defeat if he ran for reelection, Eastland was told by his father not to run and to return home to oversee the family's plantation. By maintaining a small law practice at the same time, he could accumulate the influence that ultimately would earn him the moniker "the godfather of Mississippi politics."[5]

To many of the people who worked for him, Eastland had a reputation, like his father, for being a generous and good-natured employer. At the same time, he had a vicious temper that flared whenever anyone questioned the social hierarchy of the South. He was known to act swiftly in retaliation, whether offenders were white or black, exacting severe punishment that could result in outright banishment from the plantation.[6]

The prevailing dynamic between white owners and black sharecroppers in the Mississippi in which Eastland thrived served the interests of the planters, further consolidating their power. Planters carefully nurtured a culture of dependence by doing trivial favors for sharecroppers or loaning them small amounts of money, keeping workers beholden to their "betters." As one former sharecropper put it in John Dollard's classic study *Caste and Class in a Southern Town*, "It was to the advantage of whites not to encourage thrift or consistency of behavior, because, as long as these qualities are lacking, the Negroes are dependent on the landowners."[7] Without the limits, dependencies, and literal bonds that kept people in their place, the world of white supremacy was impossible. This "Southern way of life" that Eastland understood so deeply had treated him well; he would fight to perpetuate it. The principle was simple: "Whiteness represents full personal dignity and full participation in American life. Blackness or darkness represents limitation and inferiority."[8] Years later, when Eastland ran for reelection to the Senate in 1954, his campaign manager inquired if there were other issues besides race to highlight. Eastland's response expressed the same principle even more succinctly: "Hell, no. Stay on segregation, segregation, segregation!"[9]

BUILDING A DEFENSE STRATEGY

Eastland's March 1954 hearings targeted key associates of the Southern Conference Educational Fund, a group devoted to racial justice and the elimination of racial discrimination. Horton himself served on the board of the SCEF. Among the others subpoenaed was James Dombrowski, the executive director of the SCEF, whose role primarily entailed pressuring educational institutions in the South to desegregate. Aubrey Williams, SCEF president, who had dedicated his life to racial equality, had also been called to testify. A former head of President Roosevelt's highly touted National Youth Administration, which focused on providing work and education for young Americans, he had gained considerable attention for insisting that blacks receive the same treatment as whites in New Deal programs. Virginia Durr also had received a subpoena. Well known for her pacifism, anti-racist activism, and support of the black community in Montgomery, Alabama, she was an active member of the SCEF board. Her husband, Clifford Durr, a leading civil liberties attorney, would also join the group at the hearings to represent Horton and Williams. Later, the Durrs would be the first white people to publicly support Rosa Parks when she was arrested in December 1955 for defying the laws segregating Montgomery's buses.[10]

Not long before the hearings, the SCEF board met to develop a strategy for the upcoming encounter with Eastland, in particular, deciding how to respond to the inevitable question that had become a kind of ugly mantra of the Red Scare: "Are you now, or have you ever been, a member of the Communist Party?" Williams felt each of them had to decide for themselves how to answer. He would not invoke the self-incrimination protections of the Fifth Amendment and would deny that he had ever been a Communist. But under no circumstances would he testify against anyone else.[11]

Virginia Durr preferred silence as her approach. She would not invoke the Fifth, but would instead challenge the committee's authority to require her to respond about her political beliefs. Each question would result in one of two responses: either she would refuse to acknowledge the committee's authority to ask the question, or she would stand mute.[12]

Dombrowski also refused to invoke the Fifth Amendment, as he thought it had become, in some people's eyes, an admission of guilt. Instead, he would cite the First Amendment and his right to freedom of speech and freedom of association. A large part of the committee's strategy was to find people guilty by virtue of their associates. Dombrowski would make a point of underscoring the committee's unconstitutional approach, which abridged these most fundamental of rights.[13]

Horton was unable to make the board meeting but sent word that he, too, would not take the Fifth. He wanted to use the opportunity to expose the committee for what he thought it really was: a "segregationist witch hunt."[14] As was characteristic of many in the movement, he wasn't satisfied just protecting his rights; he would take advantage of being in the spotlight to offer a lesson about the nature of civil liberties in a democratic society.

THE HEARINGS BEGIN

On March 17, 1954, the evening before the SISS hearings were to get under way, Eastland arrived in New Orleans with his legal counsel, Richard Arens, and two compensated informants, who had been carefully primed to denounce Dombrowski, Williams, Virginia Durr, and Horton as Communists.[15] Eastland told the press that the hearing was vital to American security because it would unmask subversives posing as humanitarians and reveal their true intent to undermine and even destroy the American way of life.[16]

Eastland opened the hearings on the morning of March 18 in a high-ceilinged, dark-paneled meeting hall in the New Orleans post office building, just a few blocks from the historic French Quarter. On one wall, the iconic scale of justice had been carefully carved into an absurdly high bench from which Eastland and Arens presided. Before the bench were two small, narrow tables, one set aside for witnesses, the other barely accommodating the crowd of reporters from national newspapers.[17] Spectators packed the stuffy room and police patrolled the hall to maintain order and keep noise to a minimum. Dombrowski recalled, "It was like a movie set for a film about Nazi Germany, with big guards patrolling the aisles."[18]

The first two witnesses appeared as friends of the subcommittee, boasting lengthy service as members of the Anti-Subversive Committee of the New Orleans Young Men's Business Club. They welcomed Eastland's investigation, having long feared the dangerous agitation of many of the educators under suspicion. Going back to 1946 and 1947, they had repeatedly accused the SCEF of being a Communist front. At Eastland's hearing, they singled out Dombrowski as SCEF's "guiding light," who had "a record of continually supporting the Communist Party line." They also underscored Dombrowski's ten-year association with the Highlander Folk School, denouncing Highlander as "a center, if not the center, of spreading Communist doctrine in 13 states."[19]

DOMBROWSKI'S TESTIMONY

During the early stages of the hearing, Eastland came across as gentle thanks to his soft, restrained tone. When he spoke at length, which he often did, with his head tilted appealingly to the left, his avuncular presence inspired confidence. If he liked what he heard, he cultivated a comforting, even sympathetic presence. But once Dombrowski took the stand, Eastland's demeanor changed. He riled easily. He scowled with gruff impatience. Occasionally, his voice would suddenly spike out of frustration or anger, alarming spectators. All of this was part of Eastland's strategy to browbeat and insult witnesses in order to extract information from them about past or present Communists they may have known.

From Dombrowski, Eastland wanted information in particular about an alleged Communist named Leo Scheiner who had contributed to the SCEF. Dombrowski maintained that under the First Amendment, he was not required to answer. Eastland, in typical fashion for his SISS hearings, ordered him "to answer that question on penalty of contempt of the United States Senate."[20]

Eastland hounded Dombrowski about Scheiner for many minutes, with no success, then abruptly changed the subject to a petition Dombrowski had signed seeking exoneration for defendants found guilty under the Smith Act, which made it illegal to advocate for the overthrow of the U.S. government. Eastland and Arens seemed desperate to elicit an incriminating response from Dombrowski, who remained steadfast: "Well, I signed a petition defending the civil rights of Communists and I don't apologize for that. I defend the civil rights of any person."[21]

Goading Dombrowski, Arens then asked a question that began a particularly insulting exchange, including the following:

ARENS: Have you ever signed any petitions for murderers?

DOMBROWSKI: I am not sure what petitions I have not signed.

ARENS: You ought to recall if you have ever signed an amnesty petition for any rapists.

DOMBROWSKI: I don't recall that.

ARENS: You sign them only for Communists?

DOMBROWSKI: No, that's a very unfair question, sir.

ARENS: Can you recall anyone for whom you signed an amnesty petition who was convicted for a crime other than these 11 Communist traitors?

DOMBROWSKI: I have signed a great many petitions in my life and I am not prepared to say what I have or have not signed unless you are prepared to ask me—if you have a particular petition there I will try to remember whether or not I have signed it.

EASTLAND: You say, Doctor, that you are not a Communist. You state that you have never been a Communist. Here is a case where the United States Government in order to protect itself tried the 11 Communist leaders in this country, topflight ones. They were convicted of advocating and conspiring with a foreign power to overthrow the Government of the United States by force and violence. They were convicted by a jury in the city of New York . . . and after that you petitioned the President of the United States for amnesty. Why did you do that?

DOMBROWSKI: Mr. Chairman, the question of why or why [sic] I do certain things, of course, is a very involved thing. You have prodded me pretty deeply on my beliefs, and I have tried to cooperate and answer your questions.

EASTLAND: Yes, but what was your reason for signing that petition?[22]

Dombrowski, who was visibly fatigued and experiencing difficulty processing the flurry of questions directed at him, asked for a break. He was suffering from the early stages of a debilitating arthritis that soon would make it impossible for him to walk without assistance and caused him to tire easily.[23] Eastland agreed to pause but, sensing that he had the upper hand, continued to grill his witness about alleged Communist associates. Although the temperature outside remained mild, the high humidity created an oppressive atmosphere in the hearing room, which lacked air-conditioning. Eventually, when Dombrowski seemed barely able to continue, his shirt drenched in perspiration, Eastland called for a recess.

On resuming his testimony, Dombrowski added a strong defense of Highlander to the public record. He testified that he had heard scores of unfounded claims against Highlander over the years, but he knew its strengths and good intentions firsthand. In response,

Eastland lambasted Highlander, branding it a front, a "fraud," a program with no purpose other than "to overthrow this country." Its real program, Eastland contended, "was the destruction of America."[24] His stark and untethered characterization, so contrary to the truth, laid bare the depth of Eastland's hatred of all those who worked against southern racism.

DURR STANDS MUTE

On the second day, Virginia Durr took the stand, but her testimony didn't take long. True to her word, she greeted most of the questions posed to her with a stony silence, reflecting her conviction that the SISS was conducting an illegitimate inquiry. One typical exchange, with John P. Kohn as Durr's attorney, went as follows:

> MR. ARENS: Are you under Communist discipline?
> MR. KOHN: With that exception, you answer that question.
> MRS. DURR: No.
> MR. ARENS: Have you ever been identified with the American Committee for Democratic Greece?
> MRS. DURR: (No response.)
> MR. ARENS: Have you ever been identified with the American Committee for Spanish Freedom?
> MRS. DURR: (No response.)
> MR. ARENS: I put it to you as a fact and ask you to affirm or deny the fact that in 1948 you were in attendance as a sponsor of a session by the Committee for a Democratic Greece.
> MRS. DURR: (No response.)
> MR. ARENS: I put it to you as a fact and ask you to affirm or deny the fact that you were one of the sponsors for the American Committee for Spanish Freedom in 1946?
> MRS. DURR: (No response.)[25]

Near the conclusion of these exchanges, Virginia Durr turned her back on Eastland and Arens to powder her nose with a grand flourish, eliciting tremendous laughter from the spectators and exasperated frowns from the questioners. Durr's decision to "stand mute" especially tickled Horton and other close friends because they knew her to be incorrigibly garrulous in most situations—"a non-stop talker."[26]

WILLIAMS REFUSES TO COOPERATE

Aubrey Williams's testimony followed Durr's. When asked about the work of the SCEF, Williams answered simply that it fought "racial discriminations of all kinds."[27] As for how the fund operated, Williams explained, "Why, we operate through research. We take a problem such as the problem of refusal of hospitals to admit on the basis of color and we make a study of that. We make an inquiry based on questionnaires that are sent out to hospital administrators, hospital officials and then based upon the material which we receive we transform that into some meaningful statement and then we send that out to hospitals and to supporters of the conference, that type of thing."[28]

When Eastland and Arens instructed Williams to turn over the list of contributors to the SCEF so that they could identify possible Communists, Williams refused, knowing he risked being cited for contempt by Eastland. Williams's stubborn defense of the right of Communists to serve in the government risked even more. In a 1947 speech, reproduced during his testimony, he had said, "We take our stand and defend the right of any Communist to maintain his position as an employee of the Government of the United States. To take any less position than this is to throw overboard such primary rights as the freedom to think and to hold whatever beliefs one chooses."[29] Eastland called the speech subversive, repeatedly pressing Williams to renounce his position. Each time, Williams unhesitatingly defended his original statement.

By the time Myles Horton finally appeared, on the third day of the hearings, fatigue more than fear prevailed, as both witnesses and spectators seemed worn down by the Mississippi senator's relentless bullying. As Horton took his seat before Eastland, the similarities between the two men stood out. Both were around fifty, laughed easily, enjoyed recounting stories, and projected confidence. Both also possessed quick tempers that could erupt at any moment. Many observers, including the ten or twelve reporters in attendance, knew the two white men as sworn enemies with diametrically opposed goals.

Horton, who rarely dressed formally, tried to strike just the right pose for his once-in-a-lifetime testimony before a Senate subcommittee by appearing in a well-pressed light-colored suit. With his hair neatly combed and horn-rimmed glasses partially concealing his lively eyes, he looked a bit like a college professor responding patiently to his students' ill-informed questions.

The testimony began routinely enough. When Arens asked for his name, residence, and occupation, Horton responded matter-of-factly that he served as "a teacher at the Highlander Folk School in Monteagle, Tennessee." Horton answered Arens's follow-up question about the nature of Highlander this way: "Well, the Highlander Folk School was started back in 1932 for the purpose of educating rural and industrial leaders for democratic living and activity. The school has continued to carry out as best we can that concept of education."[30]

Arens also inquired about the school's founders. Avoiding potential problems stemming from Don West's alleged Communist affiliations, Horton responded as if West had no role in establishing the school: "I assume the full responsibility personally for having first conceived the idea of the Highlander Folk School and having gone down to the Tennessee mountains for the purpose of starting this school. There was no one with me at the time."[31] Horton had techni-cally not perjured himself, as he had been in Tennessee before hear-ing of West's similar interest in a folk school and his possibility of ac-quiring land from Lilian Johnson.

Eastland then took over, demanding to know about Mildred White, an alleged Communist. One of the paid informants at the hearings had claimed she attended Highlander, with Horton's fore-knowledge, ostensibly to "recruit people into the party." Horton an-swered that he did not remember a Mildred White but added that "if she attended she did not attend as a Communist Party member." Eastland, suspicious, wondered how Horton could be so sure. Hor-ton explained that if White had been sent by a group to attend High-lander, "she was sent by a union, not by the Communist Party. We accept no students from the Communist Party and never have."[32]

When Eastland pressed him to recall White, Horton answered that he "couldn't place her. We have had several thousand students, Senator, and it would be rather difficult—I can tell you the basis on which she came." Eastland pounded his fist on the bench in front of him, insisting that Horton couldn't possibly know her political affili-ation if he didn't remember her.[33]

Arens abruptly shifted the inquiry, asking about Dombrowski's activities at Highlander. As Horton's attorney, Clifford Durr sug-gested that Dombrowski had already spoken for himself on that topic in prior testimony. Despite an outward calm, Horton fumed, finding it infuriating to be asked to speak for someone sitting only a few feet away.[34] Horton then added impatiently: "Couldn't I give my reasons why I don't want to answer?" Eastland said, "No, I don't want your reasons. Do you decline to answer the question?"

Knowing that he risked enraging Eastland, Horton continued: "Mr. Chairman, you listened to Communists and ex-Communists talk here—" Eastland interjected, "Wait a minute," before Horton finished with: "Won't you listen to an American citizen talk?"[35]

The courtroom exploded. Eastland tried to restore order while Horton began to read a prepared statement, as Eastland had earlier, during a closed session, agreed he could.[36] As Eastland continued to rap his gavel against the high bench in an attempt to silence the witness, only a few scattered words from Horton's pleas could be heard: "American citizens," "explain reasons," "like to know why I can't." Eastland angrily motioned to two U.S. marshals standing nearby, ordering them to eject Horton from the muggy hearing room.[37]

"Take him out, take him out!" Eastland shouted, adding that Horton's attempt to insert his public statement into the proceedings would not be tolerated: "We are not going to have any self-serving declarations." The marshals applied hammerlocks, yanking an uncooperative Horton toward the exit. Those who had crowded into the hearing room hurriedly stepped aside as the marshals and a struggling Horton skidded across the floor. Many of the bystanders wore blank looks on their faces, stunned by this shocking lack of decorum. A few smiled broadly and even laughed out loud, perhaps pleased that this southern radical was finally getting his comeuppance. As the marshals dragged Horton away, the Highlander director announced to the transfixed onlookers, "They're treating me like a criminal." Then, turning his head to direct his ire squarely at Eastland, he added, "You're just putting on a show here, that's all!"[38]

When Horton protested that one of the marshals was painfully twisting his arm and that he could exit the doorway unaided, the marshal scowled, "We know about you and were warned that you would have to be thrown out. You are dangerous and we know it." Someone had convinced these marshals, who actually knew nothing of Horton, to treat him with contempt. They added a final humiliating gesture by throwing him to the floor once they were outside the hearing chamber.[39]

If Horton had been permitted to read his prepared comments aloud, he would have condemned the subcommittee for its unconstitutional practices, especially for threatening to punish him simply for expressing his opinions honestly. He would have noted that "if the First Amendment insures freedom of speech, it must likewise insure freedom to remain silent." His prepared comments noted that he did not fear an incompetent and feckless organ of government, but he did fear "the results of our timidity in advancing democratic principles." None of these words from his prepared statement ever appeared in the official report of the hearing because Senator Eastland preemptively struck them from the record.[40]

Despite the censorship of the subcommittee, much of the story was quickly circulated to the rest of the world by the *New York Times*. Splashed across the front page of the March 21, 1954, edition were separate pictures of Horton and Clifford Durr being manhandled by U.S. marshals.[41] The testimony that the *Times* quoted reflected negatively on Eastland, highlighting his badgering of Horton, Dombrowski, and other witnesses. When it was all over, the leading daily newspaper in Montgomery, Alabama, polled nine of the reporters who had covered the hearings, asking them, "On the basis of what you have seen and heard here, who of the principals represents the greatest threat to American ideals?" Four of them concluded that Senator Eastland did, two mentioned one of the informants, one singled out Dombrowski, but none saw Horton as a threat, possibly because his public appearance had been cut short so abruptly.[42] Two days later, the *Times* again filed a story about Horton, quoting his public statement at length, giving Horton more of a platform than he could ever have hoped for:

> The hysteria spread by your committee, and the McCarthy committee, has substantially contributed to the fiction that the only dynamic force in the world is communism. This I deny. Communism has never tempted me because I believe in democracy. You know, if you have made an effort to find out, that I have never been a member of the

Communist party. I suppose in the eyes of the chairman of this committee opposition to segregation in the South is subversive. But as an American, I am unwilling to assume that a legislative group bearing the authority of my Government represents a dark and dismal outlook that justifies slavery and which today equates the fight for full democratic rights for all men, including Negroes, with Communism.[43]

THE AFTERMATH

Upon returning home, Horton reported that he had fared reasonably well in his jousting with Eastland. He also emphasized that Highlander had never knowingly accepted funds or students from the Communist Party, and that Highlander continued to focus on protecting the rights of people everywhere so that Communist solutions would lose their attraction. A number of prominent citizens who had closely followed the hearings gladly made public statements praising Horton for his courage and refusal to cave in to Eastland. Former First Lady Eleanor Roosevelt, Reinhold Niebuhr, and Ralph Bunche, a Nobel Peace Prize winner, all strongly defended Horton and his educational work at Highlander.[44]

Privately, though, Horton harbored doubts about whether anything worthwhile had been accomplished in tussling with Eastland. The experience only reinforced a feeling that government can be an especially tenacious foe and what might seem like a victory at first can quickly turn into a humiliating rout.[45]

When Eastland returned to his Washington, D.C., offices, he characterized the witnesses he had examined as "particularly vicious" and contemplated charging at least some of those who had refused to answer questions with Contempt of Committee violations. But, in fact, no such charges occurred. This would be the last time that James Eastland conducted hearings on Communism in the South. The "Red roadshow" had finally come to an ignominious end, with Eastland and company vividly displaying their utter feckless-ness.[46] The tide was turning toward direct opposition to civil rights. Communist or not, subversive or not, the civil rights movement was the enemy that antagonists like Eastland most feared. It had to be stymied at any cost. For many, Myles Horton remained one of the most dangerous of the civil rights advocates, requiring every tactic to blunt his impact. Horton may have gotten the better of Eastland for a moment in New Orleans, but Eastland proved far too fierce an ad-versary to give up on the war entirely.[47]

The backlash against Horton and Highlander entered a new stage in early 1957, as Highlander's reputation for civil rights militancy soared. H. T. Swartz, director of the Tax Rulings Division of the Inter-nal Revenue Service, informed Highlander that it no longer met the requirements for the tax-exempt status it had been granted in 1937. The reasoning seemed twisted. Swartz claimed that too many of Highlander's educational projects involved pushing for specific leg-islative solutions to controversial problems. In particular, the IRS sin-gled out this statement from one of Highlander's annual reports: "Our purpose is deliberately to use education for the realization of certain social and cultural values. We do not consider other educa-tion any less propaganda, because its teachers are ignorant of the fact that they are supporting an unethical *status quo,* than our approach which consciously seeks to bring about a more just social order."[48]

The IRS finding, a Highlander newsletter reported, enjoyed the full endorsement of James Eastland himself and may even have been initiated by the senior senator from Mississippi.[49] In any case, High-lander staff regarded the tax status decision as punishment for the school's pro-integration agenda at a time when white resistance to desegregation had grown fiercer than ever. The ruling threw High-lander into crisis mode. For the rest of that year, Highlander slashed spending and salaries, bringing many of its activities to a halt until its tax-exempt status was restored in December 1957. In the school's appeal calling for the reinstatement of the exemption, Highlander's lawyers argued that while it openly sought to bring about a "more just social order," a review of its workshops and residential programs would show that the means for achieving this goal emerged from the needs of participants, not the ideological preferences of staff members.[50] The IRS declared itself satisfied with this response, but the truce felt uneasy. Highlander had never been so embattled. How much longer before the school finally succumbed to the legions of haters who despised the school's mission of seeking to usher in a new South, free of racial discrimination and proud of its multicultural heritage?

A young Myles Horton during his football days at Cumberland University, ca. 1925. All images courtesy of the Wisconsin Historical Society.

The early days of Highlander Folk School, November 1933: the main office, housed in Dr. Lilian Johnson's home in Summerfield. A later addition significantly increased this building's capacity.

CIO students doing kitchen duty at Highlander, late 1940s. Myles Horton is fifth from left. Kitchen detail was one of many responsibilities all Highlander guests were expected to assume.

Myles and Zilphia Horton square dancing, mid to late 1940s. Square dancing was one of their favorite forms of recreation at Highlander.

Attendees at a United Packinghouse Workers session at Highlander Folk School, ca. 1951. Myles Horton is in the back row, fifth from left.

Myles Horton and Rosa Parks at a gathering in 1956 to consider the progress made by the Montgomery bus boycott.

Myles Horton, former First Lady Eleanor Roosevelt, and writer Jim Stokely at a Highlander integration workshop in the late 1950s.

Highlander Reports

27th ANNUAL REPORT   October 1, 1958 - September 30, 1959

HIGHLANDER FOLK SCHOOL
MONTEAGLE, TENNESSEE

. . . Esau Jenkins and Myles Horton talk things over

Few of the school's nearly thirty years have held such problems—and such progress.

Against a background of almost continuous harassment and litigation, Highlander has continued with an expanded program of residential workshops for citizenship and integration, with more and larger citizenship schools on the Sea Islands, and with two new research and projected extension projects. Two full time and two part-time members have been added to the staff, and a director of music. Four new members have been elected to the Executive Council, which is Highlander's governing body. And during the past year there has been increased recognition of Highlander as a pioneer in adult education. Old friends have renewed their ties, new friends have rallied to the defense at home and abroad.

It is perhaps true that the spectacular nature of our recent problems has had some part in all this. While Highlander has never deliberately sought the more dangerous and difficult ways to pub-

licity, we have not on the other hand avoided them by compromise with principle. A Southern school which preaches and consistently practices residential integration, and at the same time openly trains and presses for overall integration, is asking for trouble. We have laid ourselves wide open to this kind of trouble.

We believe it is a tribute to the effectiveness of our program that the segregationist movement in the South has elected Highlander as one of its major enemies. Certainly it is because of the confidence of our friends in the job we have set out to do, that we survive and grow.

Highlander promises, in 1959-60, to continue without compromise or equivocation, to fight for integration in the South through its residential program, its extension program and its publicity. As it has always done, Highlander will practice integration in its staff arrangements, in its administration, and in its student enrollment.

2

Esau Jenkins and Myles Horton on Johns Island, South Carolina, in the store that provided a "cover" for the first citizenship schools. The front-page article from the 1958–1959 "Highlander Reports" describes ongoing efforts to expand the citizenship schools. It also reflects the pride Highlander took in gaining a reputation as one of the leading enemies of southern segregationists.

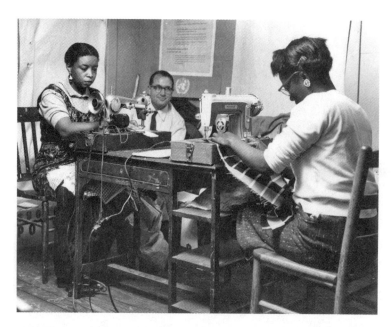

Myles Horton visiting a citizenship school sewing class for younger members taught by Bernice Robinson on Johns Island, ca. 1957–1958.

An event marking twenty-fifth annive sary of Highlande 1957. Pictured in th school's library are Parks, Myles Hort SCEF president Au Williams (on Hort left), and Martin L King, Jr.

MARTIN LUTHER KING....AT COMMUNIST TRAINING SCHOOL

The above picture was made by an employee of the State of Georgia, at the Highlander Folk School in Monteagle, Tennessee during the Labor Day week-end of 1957. The photographer was sent to the Highlander Folk School by the Georgia Commission on Education. The Highlander Folk School was abolished by an act of the Legislature of the State of Tennessee at a later date.

Those numbered in the picture are:

1. Martin Luther King, Jr., of the Montgomery boycott and the Birmingham riots. Karl Prussion, a counterspy for the FBI for **twelve years**, charges that Martin Luther King belongs to sixty Communist-front organizations — more than any Communist in the United States.

2. Abner W. Berry of the Central Committee of the Communist Party.

3. Aubrey Williams, President of the Southern Conference Education Fund, Inc., The Transmission Belt in the South for the Communist Party.

4. Myles Horton, Director of Highlander Folk School for Communist Training, Monteagle, Tennessee.

These "Four Horsemen" of racial agitation have brought tension, disturbance, strife and violence in their advancement of the Communist doctrine of "racial nationalism."

JOIN THE AUGUSTA COURIER IN THE FIGHT FOR FREEDOM
Copies available- 100 for $ 1.00 (include .30c stamps for postage)

Alert Americans Association. Box 1222, L. A., Calif. 90053
Order RIGHT WING DIRECTORY, listing all Right Wing Activities

This image, also from the twenty-fifth anniversary celebration, appeared in the *Augusta Courier* and was widely distributed to "prove" King's Communist sympathies. The handwriting around the border reads, "He's dangerous, rich, fat, sassy & powerful"; "He's not non-violent"; "Send King & all riot leaders to Russia or back to Africa."

Highlander Reports

29th ANNUAL REPORT   Oct. 1, 1960 – Sept. 30, 1961

HIGHLANDER FOLK SCHOOL
MONTEAGLE, TENNESSEE

... A meeting place for ideas

STATE GRANTS CHARTER TO HIGHLANDER CENTER

Knoxville, Tenn., Oct. 7—A charter was granted to the Highlander Research and Education Center by the state of Tennessee on August 28, 1961. This new organization (completely separate from Highlander Folk School) has been formed to carry on a Southwide adult education program including voter and citizenship education. Activities will include residential workshops and seminars, evening classes and research in related fields of adult education. Application has been made for tax exemption.

Headquarters for the Center have been established at 1625 Riverside Drive in Knoxville, Tennessee, where a building has been leased and some of the staff are living. Residential adult education facilities will later be developed on a large tract of wooded land in Jefferson County, eighteen miles away. Activities are now being carried on at the Knoxville Center and in rented facilities suitable for residential education and evening classes.

The directors who formed Highlander Research and Education Center are: Professor Scott Bates and Retired Professor Eugene Kayden of the University of the South; Myles Horton, Director of

Highlander Folk School; May Justus, author and long-time Monteagle resident; and Lewis Sinclair, an economist with the TVA in Knoxville. A twenty-three member Advisory Council will recommend policy to the Board of Directors. They also serve as the Executive Council of Highlander Folk School.

Myles Horton, the school's director, is devoting part of his time to the development of this new program. He is assisted by four staff members and a number of volunteer teachers. The staff and educational program of Highlander Folk School, in so far as it is financially possible, will be taken over if the school is forced to close down.

The new charter and the establishment of a base in Knoxville insures the continuation of the Highlander idea. We believe that our many friends whose generous financial support has made Highlander Folk School possible for the past twenty-nine years will want to play an important part in the development of Highlander Center.

A 1960–1961 issue of "Highlander Reports" announcing the granting of a charter to the Highlander Research and Education Center in Knoxville. Pictured at a Highlander meeting are Myles Horton (at left) and Ella Baker (fifth from left, with pearl earring). In the early 1970s, Highlander moved to its current location on a beautiful mountainside in New Market, Tennessee.

A civil rights meeting at Highlander, ca. 1960. At left is Thurgood Marshall; the man with the guitar is Guy Carawan. Seated in front of Carawan are Anne Braden and Septima Clark. Myles Horton is seated in front of the window at right.

334 Auburn Ave., N.E.
Atlanta, Georgia 30303
Telephone 524-1378

Southern Christian Leadership Conference

Martin Luther King Jr., *President*   Ralph Abernathy, *Treasurer*   Wyatt Tee Walker, *Executive Assistant*

November 5, 1963

Mr. Myles Horton
Highlander Center
1625 Riverside Drive
Knoxville 15, Tennessee

Dear Myles:

I am in receipt of your letter of October 24. I am deeply
concerned over the problem which you and the Highlander
Center are facing. I must confess that I was not aware of
the extreme seriousness of the situation, and the meager
financial support that you are receiving. I will be going to
Birmingham in the next few days and I will be very glad to
discuss this whole situation with Fred Shuttlesworth and
Nelson Smith. I hope we can be of some assistance.

Please extend my warm best wishes to your staff members.

Sincerely yours,

Martin Luther King, Jr.

Km

Letter to Myles Horton from Martin Luther King, Jr., dated November 5, 1963,
expressing concern about the continuing attacks on Highlander and how those
have constrained the center's fundraising efforts.

9   *Mrs. Parks Goes to Highlander*

Many people have heard how the courageous actions of Rosa Parks sparked the historic 1955–1956 Montgomery bus boycott. They have learned that on the early evening of December 1, 1955, she was ejected from a public bus and taken to jail for refusing to surrender her seat to a white man, a clear violation of the city's strict segregation statutes. They know she was subsequently booked, fingerprinted, and released on bail, and when faced with the choice of paying a small fine or appealing her case by challenging the constitutionality of Montgomery's segregation laws, she chose to appeal. They know, too, that as the appeal slowly snaked its way through the courts, Montgomery's African American community rose up in unified protest, renouncing segregation and condemning the treatment Parks had endured. Finally, they know that for 381 days, the black community as a whole shunned the buses, precipitating a bitter, drawn-out, and often dangerous conflict with whites until equality between the races on all public transportation could be guaranteed.

What far fewer people realize is that only four months before her startling act of defiance, Parks took part in an intense two-week workshop at the Highlander Folk School, an experience she described as life-changing and which clearly strengthened her resolve to become part of a historic wave of oppressed black women publicly challenging the laws of their city.

Rosa Parks was not yet famous when she first went to Highlander, but she was a seasoned activist who had served for many years as the secretary of Montgomery's branch of the National Association for the Advancement of Colored People (NAACP). A quiet and unassuming forty-two-year-old seamstress, Parks worked closely with NAACP branch president E. D. Nixon to promote anti-lynching laws, eliminate barriers to black voter registration, and protect black women from sexual violence at the hands of police and other white public officials.[1] Parks took special pride in her many years as the branch's Youth Council coordinator. She took strength from the contagious energy of Montgomery's youth, devoting hundreds of hours to mentoring them toward leadership roles in the NAACP. She often escorted the group downtown, encouraging them to drink from the whites-only water fountain, not just as an act of defiance, but also to assert their self-worth. Sometimes they went even further and, with Parks's encouragement and guidance, held demonstrations outside the municipal public library protesting its policy of barring African Americans from checking out books.[2]

In Parks's judgment, most black adults in Montgomery were so beaten down by white supremacy and the relentless terrorism of the Ku Klux Klan that they had little faith in the possibility for change. Although Parks remained an outwardly determined participant in the black community's campaign against segregation, privately, she, too, felt deeply discouraged and suffered from physical and psychological exhaustion. Her friend and confidante Virginia Durr knew that Parks needed a break, so she secured Parks a scholarship for the Highlander workshop and paid her traveling expenses.[3]

As Parks prepared for her journey to Highlander, thoughts of fifteen-year-old Claudette Colvin could not have been far from her mind. Only a few months earlier, on March 2, 1955, Colvin had refused to forfeit her own bus seat, which had led to her arrest. NAACP lawyers agreed her act of civil disobedience offered a possible test case for toppling Montgomery's entrenched segregation laws. E.D. Nixon urged Parks to get Colvin involved with the Youth Council.[4]

The two activists became close. Parks liked Colvin and enjoyed being around her, but she also worried about the pressure Colvin was under. White officials were actively portraying her as irresponsible and lawless, promoting a dubious charge that she had assaulted police officers and condemning her as defiant and profane. In fact, Colvin had an excellent academic record and enjoyed high esteem in the African American community. In terms of the actual charges resulting from her refusal to give up her seat, Colvin later recalled, "I was too smart to fight back. . . . I might have scratched one of them because I had long nails, but I sure didn't fight back."[5] And while the police officers were vulgar toward her, her only vocal indiscretion was that "I kept screaming over and over, 'It's my constitutional right!'"[6]

Parks made sure that Colvin participated actively in the Youth Council, receiving moral support from the other members. Colvin deeply appreciated Parks's concern: "She was very kind and thoughtful; she knew exactly how I liked my coffee and fixed me peanut butter and Ritz crackers, but she didn't say much at all." But once a Youth Council meeting started, Colvin noted, "I'd think, Is that the same lady? She would come across very strong about rights. She would pass out leaflets saying things like: 'We are going to break down the walls of segregation.'"[7]

NAACP leadership debated whether to press Colvin's case. Her youth and outspoken nature could create challenges in the press. As

Nixon said, "I had to be sure I had somebody I could win with."[8] They ultimately decided not to use Colvin for their test case when, shortly after her arrest, it was revealed that an older white man had impregnated her, and fears arose that whites would use this against her as proof of an unsavory character.[9] Despite this setback, the Colvin incident had heartened black Montgomery. As NAACP lawyer Fred Gray would later say about the bus boycott itself, "Claudette gave all of us the moral courage to do what we did."[10]

TWO WEEKS AT HIGHLANDER

On July 24, 1955, Rosa Parks boarded the bus for Highlander. Once seated, she grew increasingly anxious about taking a trip into this virtually all-white region. Unsure what to expect, she feared venturing into the wilds of Tennessee on a five-hour bus ride. As the bus traveled north, Parks had the sense of moving farther and farther away from familiar surroundings and into alien territory, an area populated almost entirely by white people who had no interest in protecting her. She also warily eyed the mostly white passengers on the bus, and although nothing unusual occurred, her sense of unease continued to grow. Arriving at the Chattanooga bus stop unharmed made her feel better, though she was somewhat disconcerted upon being greeted by a white woman who would drive her to Highlander.[11]

Fortunately, the hour-long car trip passed pleasantly and uneventfully. When Parks finally walked through the door of Highlander's main building, Septima Clark, the seasoned black activist and workshop facilitator, warmly greeted her. Parks began to feel safe enough to drop her guard, sensing she was among friends. It didn't hurt to learn that in this integrated residency, she was joining more than twenty other blacks, along with a roughly equal number of whites, to explore plans for desegregating schools.[12] Parks later said that spending time at Highlander "was my very first experience in my entire life, going to a place where there were people, people of another race, and where we all were treated equally and without any tension or feeling of embarrassment or whatever goes with the artificial boundaries of racial segregation."[13]

The atmosphere at the school felt surprisingly buoyant. The recent *Brown v. Board of Education* Supreme Court decision declaring school segregation inherently unequal had given workshop participants new hope. Officially titled "Racial Desegregation: Implementing the Supreme Court Decision," the workshop promised an opportunity to develop plans for desegregating participants' own communities.[14] The fact that the people gathered at Highlander "believed completely in freedom and equality for all" also meant the world to Rosa Parks.[15]

Throughout the workshop, Parks participated sparingly in the many discussions but remained an attentive and respectful listener. Her notes indicate that the breadth of anti-segregation activity throughout the South impressed her, and the optimism of both black and white activists took her by surprise. She singled out Horton for praise; his respectful attitude, uplifting ebullience, and irrepressible sense of humor raised her spirits. She later said, "Myles Horton just washed away and melted a lot of my hostility and prejudice and feeling of bitterness toward white people, because he had such a wonderful sense of humor. I often thought about many of the things he said and how he could strip the white segregationists of their hardcore attitudes, and how he could confuse them, and I found myself laughing when I hadn't been able to laugh in a long time."[16] In fact, Horton's sense of humor was legendary. As Julius Lester, a civil rights activist, noted in a journal not long after Horton's death, he "laughed continually," and not primarily because of jokes or funny stories. His laughter "was a basic attitude toward life itself," a laughter "in full appreciation of life's absurdities." Horton recognized that "it is a shameful waste of time and energy to believe in the worst of people when one can also choose to believe in the best of them, a best they might not know is even there."[17]

By the time Horton met Parks in July 1955, he was used to playing congenial host to a wide range of community leaders. Some arrived eager and hopeful. Others harbored grave doubts about the possibility of change. Horton counted Parks as one of the doubters, so he made a special effort to connect with her, seeking her out often and drawing on his considerable charm to relax her. He loved to joke about the absurdity of segregation and soon, as Parks recalled, had her "cracking up" about white sensitivity regarding race. As a leader in Montgomery's NAACP, Parks had participated in other integrated meetings but disliked them. As she put it, "Every time I went to one of those meetings, I came away blacker than I was before, because everything was discussed in terms of race."[18] At Highlander, Horton and his staff combined conviviality with seriousness to create a positive and humanizing atmosphere.

Parks found herself fully accepted at the school, not just because of her struggles as an oppressed black woman, but also owing to her rich experiences as a community leader. When she spoke, people responded to her comments with interest and respect. As she put it years later, it was one of the few times in her life up to that point when she "did not feel any hostility from white people" and could participate "honestly without any repercussions or antagonistic attitudes from other people."[19]

Septima Clark recalled how withdrawn Parks seemed when she first arrived: "She wouldn't talk at all in the workshop for two or three days—wouldn't tell at all about how hard it was in Montgomery."[20] In an effort to draw her out, Clark urged her to tell the story of escorting Montgomery's NAACP Youth Council to the Freedom Train of 1947–1948. The Freedom Train, as Parks described it to workshop participants, functioned as a special anti-segregationist traveling exhibit that displayed original versions of the Declaration of Independence, the U.S. Constitution, and the Bill of Rights. Jointly sponsored by the American Heritage Foundation and the federal government, the Freedom Train officially welcomed both blacks and whites without discrimination or racial separation. In Montgomery, as in many other southern cities, news of the Freedom Train brought menacing letters and even death threats from whites who denounced its integrationist agenda. Despite the risks, when the train came to Montgomery, Parks guided a dozen black teenagers through a display that celebrated freedoms inscribed in founding documents but regularly denied to African Americans. Behind the scenes, she and E. D. Nixon had conspired to make sure the Freedom Train stopped, as scheduled, in Montgomery, over the objections of local whites.[21] The story typified Parks's activism—quiet, unassuming, yet persistent. But doing something that daring in the Jim Crow South exacted costs, too. Hate calls poured into the Parkses' home. Both she and her husband lived for months in fear of violent reprisals.

As instrumental as Horton had been in boosting Parks's hopefulness, Septima Clark left the biggest impression. Clark, who had been a teacher and activist for forty years but had lost her job when she refused to surrender her NAACP membership, had recently joined Highlander as a staff member. She would soon become Highlander's director of workshops. Her encouragement of full participation by reticent members—like Parks—exemplified her particular style of developmental leadership. She did everything possible to support activists in recognizing that their "own experience, knowledge and skill were their most important resources in their struggle for equality."[22] Clark's perseverance and courage in the face of white resistance dazzled Parks, exceeding anything she could imagine herself accomplishing. She claimed that Clark's example made her own activities seem "very minute" in comparison.[23]

The only black female leader who compared to Clark in Parks's eyes was Ella Baker, who was emerging as one of the civil rights movement's boldest and most versatile leaders. She had taken charge of all the NAACP branches in the 1940s, would coordinate Dr. King's Southern Christian Leadership Conference in the late 1950s, and later gained renown as the founding mother and guiding spirit of the Student Nonviolent Coordinating Committee in the early 1960s. Baker inspired groups to recognize that leadership works best when shared widely and cooperatively.

Parks had met Baker when she delivered keynote addresses at two different NAACP leadership conferences in the mid-1940s. Calling Baker "beautiful in every way," Parks opened up her home to Baker whenever she visited Montgomery.[24] Baker's approach to community leadership, which closely paralleled Highlander's method, called to Parks. People didn't really need to be led, Parks recalled Baker insisting. They needed to be given the skills, information, and opportunity to lead themselves.

Now, thanks to this Highlander workshop on civil rights, Septima Clark joined Baker in Parks's exclusive club of outstanding leaders. The fact that they both led fearlessly and powerfully mattered a great deal to Parks. But just as important, they exemplified the caring, dignified, unshakable person Parks aspired to become. She wanted nothing more than to have "some of [Clark's] great courage and dignity and wisdom" rub off on her. Self-deprecatingly describing herself as "tense, nervous, and upset most of the time," Parks couldn't stop commenting on Clark's "calm determination" and unflappable self-assurance under fire as an NAACP activist, public school teacher, and Highlander facilitator.[25]

The workshop content itself also offered Parks food for thought. Focusing on potential strategies to successfully desegregate schools, participants investigated integration efforts around the country, including in places as diverse as the District of Columbia, Texas, Arkansas, and Tennessee. By the end of the workshop, one group of participants had produced a draft of a document eventually published and widely circulated with the title "A Guide to Community Action for Public School Integration." A second group had studied two communities in depth, one racially mixed and one segregated, searching for patterns in the desegregated community that might help others develop plans for ending segregation in racially divided regions.[26]

Parks stayed engaged throughout the workshop, as her copious notes affirm. At one point, she considered the pros and cons of making change gradually versus rapidly: "Gradualism would ease the shock of white minds," but it might also "give the opposition more time to build greater resistance," working against long-term reform. Later in her notes, she foreshadowed her own behavior, writing, "Desegregation proves itself by being put in action. Not changing attitudes, attitudes will change."[27] By taking bold and concerted action, the change in minds and hearts would inevitably follow.

As the workshop moved toward its conclusion, Parks, in her notes, considered the preconditions for a successful social action program. First, the people at the forefront of an action should have no record of trouble with law enforcement. Second, movement leaders should be relatively stable and economically independent—not rich, but largely debt free, and in long-term relationships. Parks had no interest in judging how people should live, but was issuing a warning that under Jim Crow, whites would use any pretext, however unreasonable, to defame African American activists. Notably, these preconditions described Parks herself. She had no criminal record and no outstanding loans, thanks to her part-time work as a seamstress and her husband Raymond's steady work as a barber. She and Raymond also had enjoyed more than twenty years of marriage.[28] One can't help wondering, based on her Highlander journals, whether she saw herself as a logical choice to take a more active role in dramatically disrupting the racial status quo in Montgomery.

Highlander workshops usually ended with participants explaining how they planned to make changes back home. Parks shared frankly that she didn't expect a lot to change in Montgomery, the fabled cradle of the Confederacy, but she did take heart from her work with youth, believing that they ultimately would engage in bold actions. Parks also underscored her admiration for Septima Clark, whose rich experience and unfaltering courage in the face of vicious racism would continue to inspire her. She really didn't want to leave Highlander, either. She hated returning to a segregated city "where you had to be smiling and polite no matter how rudely you were treated."[29] It was especially difficult to envision returning to Montgomery Fair, the local department store where she was employed as the only black seamstress. The work, carried out in a stuffy basement sweatshop for minimal pay, not only exhausted her physically, it depleted her psychologically. As she noted to Virginia Durr, who had helped pay her way to Monteagle, the discrimination she faced in Montgomery felt even worse after the sense of liberation she had experienced at Highlander.[30] Horton had sensed that dissonance. In recalling Parks at the end of the workshop, he hoped "that this tired spirit of hers would get tired of being tired."[31]

THAT FATEFUL DAY IN MONTGOMERY

Late on the afternoon of December 1, 1955, less than four months after attending the Highlander workshop, Rosa Parks absentmindedly boarded a Montgomery bus, inadvertently finding herself on a vehicle operated by a man named James Blake. She had despised him for what he had done to her back to 1943. Many Montgomery drivers subjected black passengers to the humiliating routine of having to enter the front door to pay their fare before re-entering by the back door to take a seat near the rear of the bus. That day, in 1943, Blake, a notorious racist who demeaned black women in particular, had demanded she exit the bus once she had paid her fare even though the stairwell had filled, making it impossible for her to disembark.

Enraged, he seized her coat sleeve to force her removal. She agreed to leave but first intentionally dropped her purse and then defiantly sat in the front "whites only" seat to pick it up. As Blake's rage intensified, Parks warned him not to hit her. Grasping her purse, she finally exited. From that day on, she resolved never again to board any bus driven by Blake.[32]

But on December 1, loaded down with Christmas parcels and with her mind focused on getting home to her husband, who was preparing dinner, she failed to note the driver's identity. She sat in the middle of the bus, where African Americans, by law, were permitted to sit unless the bus driver ruled otherwise. The bus was not crowded at first, but the front section reserved for whites soon filled up, causing at least one white man to remain standing because he refused to sit in the middle section occupied by four black riders. Blake barked, "Let me have those front seats." At first none of the four people of color who sat in the middle section moved. When Blake demanded even more vehemently that the four surrender their seats, three did so; Rosa refused to budge. Blake angrily stopped the bus, walking to Parks's seat. He carried a gun, like all Montgomery bus drivers. Just five years prior, a young black man had been killed in front of his wife and children for not obeying a bus driver; it was impossible to predict what Blake might do.[33] He asked, "Are you going to stand up?" Parks answered, "No, because I got on first and paid the same fare, and it isn't right for me to have to stand so someone else who got on later could sit down." Blake responded, "Well, I'm going to have you arrested," to which Parks quietly retorted, "You may do that."[34]

Later, Parks commented that everyone always said she was tired, which explained why she didn't get up. But as Myles Horton had foreseen, she didn't feel physically tired, no more than usual. "No, the only tired I was," Parks later insisted, "was tired of giving in."[35] Her refusal to give up her seat ultimately stemmed from a long history of being humiliated, of being subjected to the worst sort of treatment, of being treated like a second-class citizen, all because of her skin color.

Rosa Parks refused to give up her seat and risked arrest because she had found the will inside herself to challenge Montgomery's racial hierarchy. She could not wait any longer for others to act. As important as Myles Horton or Claudette Colvin or E. D. Nixon might have become in her life, she acted alone, for reasons that can never be fully explained. When asked where she found the courage to resist segregation that day, Parks first invoked the memory of her mother and grandfather, "for giving me the spirit of freedom."[36]

Yet, as Septima Clark observed, anyone who had seen Parks during those two weeks at Highlander "would understand just how much *guts* she got while being there."[37] Horton, too, said that judged by conventional standards, Parks would not seem to be a promising future leader. But, he was quick to add, Highlander didn't use conventional standards, "so we had high hopes for her."[38] Virginia Durr, who witnessed Highlander's impact on Parks, concluded that the contrast between life at Highlander and life in Montgomery gave her the courage to say no to Montgomery's racist systems. In a letter to Horton and his wife Zilphia in early 1956, after the bus boycott had been going on for two months, Durr wrote: "When she came back she was so happy and felt so liberated and then as time went on she said the discrimination got worse and worse to bear AFTER having, for the first time in her life, been free of it at Highlander. I am sure that had a lot to do with her daring to risk arrest as she is naturally a very quiet and retiring person although she has a fierce sense of pride and is, in my opinion, a really noble woman. But you . . . should certainly take pride in what you did for her."[39]

Rosa Parks herself later commented on how much Highlander meant to her: "I shall never forget the experience that I had there or the strength that it gave me . . . the perseverance it gave me to go on and work for freedom."[40] On her return, Parks had also confided to

Nixon that her time at Highlander had "strengthened her resolve around her Youth Council work." She now hoped to show young people by example their undeniable worthiness.[41] The dozens of activists she met during her time at Highlander also cannot be discounted. Many carried the same scars of racial hatred she bore, yet they somehow continued to exude hope. Thinking of the efforts of Horton to win her over, and more important, the many black activists who continued to inspire her, Parks commented years later that "I had a hard lesson to learn, that I could not help others free their hearts and minds of racial prejudice unless I would do all that I could within myself to straighten out my own thinking and to feel and respond to kindness, to goodwill from wherever it came."[42] Perhaps Parks was determined to emulate her role models Ella Baker and Septima Clark, absorbing their ability to stand up to the most intense pressure with composure, self-assurance, and grace. Often simmering with rage before her stay, Parks had been brought to a defiant boil during her time at Highlander Folk School; there was no turning back after that.

Just three months after taking the action that launched the Montgomery bus boycott, Parks returned to Highlander for a discussion about the status of the protest. Asked about life back home, she commented, "Montgomery today is nothing at all like it was as you knew it last year. It's just a different place altogether since we demonstrated."[43] When Horton asked Parks about the African American community's explosive reaction to her arrest, she conceded she could not entirely account for it but wondered if it had something to do with the fact that virtually everyone could identify with the humiliation she had experienced, because so many black citizens had been treated in the same dehumanizing manner. As a local reverend put it, "There was not a single colored person in Montgomery who had ever ridden a bus who had not either been abused or witnessed someone else being abused. So that everybody knew the conditions, and everybody was mad about it, and, as you say, waiting for this rallying point."[44]

In addition, the NAACP had reconsidered its litigation strategy. Since Mrs. Parks's legal case was tied up in Alabama's legal system and likely to lose because of the state's history of prejudice against African Americans, Fred Gray, the lawyer who had initially represented Claudette Colvin in her Montgomery case, worked with Clifford Durr to mount a federal case against the City of Montgomery. They found five black women who had been discriminated against and agreed to be plaintiffs, including Claudette Colvin, in a case challenging segregated seating in public transportation on the grounds that it violated the equal rights provision of the U.S. Constitution's Fourteenth Amendment. This case, *Browder v. Gale,* was eventually decided in favor of the plaintiffs in a federal circuit court and was then upheld by the Supreme Court. Thus, on December 20, 1956, 381 days after the bus boycott was first launched, officials of the city of Montgomery were notified that the public bus system must be integrated.[45]

Eleanor Roosevelt, a longtime supporter of Highlander, had written in her "My Day" newspaper column about a meeting she had enjoyed with Rosa Parks in May 1956 in New York City. The meeting apparently had been arranged by Myles Horton. Roosevelt began by commenting on Parks's quiet and gentle manner, which made her wonder how Parks could have been responsible for such "a positive and independent stand," adding that, of course, "these things do not happen all of a sudden. They grow out of feelings that have been developing over many years. Human beings reach a point when they say: 'This is as far as I can go.'"[46] Roosevelt concluded that, like other protesters who had stood up against the indignities of oppression, Rosa Parks had much to teach about the conditions that bring such change agents to a breaking point. Above all, "There is a point beyond which human beings will not continue to bear injustice."[47]

Going to Highlander probably did not serve as the breaking point for Parks. The persistent, relentless cruelty of an unjust system of segregation ultimately did that. Still, Highlander lent Parks new hope that her acts of resistance would not be in vain.

It is important to acknowledge that Highlander has never claimed that a single workshop by itself leads to transformation. Only someone like Rosa Parks, who had already accumulated many years as an activist and opponent of white supremacy, would have been able to use what she had experienced as a springboard for such decisive action. To Highlander, workshops supplied a necessary but insufficient component of the change process. Workshops had to be related to experience in the field and treated as one of many building blocks in the life of an emerging activist. But of course, Parks was no emerging activist. She was ready to act. Her history of humiliation on Montgomery buses may have provided that stimulus, or perhaps the vicious cruelty of James Blake tipped the balance. Then again, the example of leaders like Septima Clark and Ella Baker may have been the decisive influence. In any case, the impact of the two weeks she spent at Highlander, a little-known retreat center in the mountains of southeastern Tennessee, should not be underestimated.

10 *The Citizenship School on Johns Island*

The story often recounted about the emergence of the citizenship school idea places all four key protagonists at the Highlander Folk School in the summer of 1954, at a racially integrated workshop called "World Problems, the United Nations and You." Throughout the week of that workshop, the participants from Johns Island, South Carolina, and Knoxville, Tennessee, pored over an assortment of documents and contributed to spirited discussions about the possible links between the United Nations' positions and the human rights violations afflicting their communities. Much of the discussion focused on doing more to achieve a just and integrated South. As typically occurred, near the end of the workshop attendees revealed their plans for change they hoped to carry out upon returning to their local communities.[1]

Esau Jenkins, a native of Johns Island and the first of four change agents who animate the origin narrative, purportedly turned the workshop around when he called for a school to teach his people reading and writing. As remembered by Bernice Robinson, a resident of Charleston and the second of the story's main protagonists, Jenkins didn't especially care about the United Nations. But he did care about the quality of life on his beloved island off the coast of South Carolina. When his turn to speak came, he didn't hold back: "Well, I don't know about the promoting of the United Nations, but I'll tell you what I'm interested in. . . . I need to get my people registered to vote. They got to read a part of the Constitution and they don't know how to read and I'd like a school set up."[2] Robinson felt that Jenkins's visit to Monteagle had convinced him that realizing his dream of a fully enfranchised black community on Johns Island depended on Highlander's support. With seeming exasperation, he pleaded, "I need a school. I need somebody to help me. Tell me *how* I can get a school going to teach my people."[3]

In this origin story, everybody started focusing on the needs of Johns Island as if they had suddenly found a shared purpose. Even Robinson, an experienced activist familiar with the situation on the island, found that Jenkins's pleas caused her to rethink her assumptions about white supremacy's permanence. "I knew that there was a lot of illiteracy all around me, but I accepted that as a fact, that there was nothing you could do about it," she said. "But when Esau started talking, I thought, yeah, that is something to think about. People can't read." Jenkins's words "turned the whole workshop around. Everybody became interested in this, and that's all we talked about the last couple of days. What are we going to do about this situation on Johns Island?"[4]

Of all the people at the workshop, Jenkins had apparently most wanted to impress Myles Horton, the third of the four principal players in this origin story, and the one most likely to have access to resources to get a school off the ground. Horton reportedly didn't say much at first. He surveyed the group as the excitement about Jenkins's call intensified. He rubbed his cheek, as he often did when he was thinking something through. The emotion that Jenkins's speech had stirred moved him. Suddenly, he agreed the time had come to act: "Well, let me see if I can find some money for you to set up a school. You try to find a place and we'll see where we go from there."[5]

The fourth member of the quartet, longtime teacher and social activist Septima Clark, had extended invitations to both Jenkins and Robinson to attend the Highlander workshop in the first place. She knew them intimately. She had met Jenkins when he was a child and she was an eighteen-year-old teacher on Johns Island. Robinson was her niece. Both were valued collaborators on the Charleston NAACP Executive Board that Clark had been affiliated with for years. Though this was only her second Highlander workshop, Clark was reputed to already love the place, calling it refreshingly different for refusing to tolerate any form of segregation. Her positive experiences with the school, her deep knowledge of Johns Island, and her skill as an activist and organizer all spurred her to take up Jenkins's challenge to breathe life into the citizenship school idea.

This citizenship school origin legend, though accurate in many ways, ultimately does not quite hold up to the facts. For one, no record exists indicating that Bernice Robinson attended the 1954 United Nations workshop. Her first of many Highlander workshops did not occur until she accepted Septima Clark's invitation to attend the following summer, in 1955; even then, Esau Jenkins was not present. At the United Nations workshop that Jenkins attended, he probably did not ask Horton for a school. He wanted to get more Johns Island residents to register to vote, but the idea of establishing an actual citizenship school lay in the future. For the same reason, Myles Horton wasn't asked to find money to set up a school, though he enthusiastically agreed to do so once the citizenship school idea later took hold.[6]

In a way, it doesn't matter much that the origin story doesn't square perfectly with the facts. In most respects, it rings true. The problem with the story is that it reinforces the impression that magical things happened at Highlander, and that they happened very quickly when Horton personally supported them. As usual, the truth was more complicated. The kind of change that Highlander worked for took time, much more time than is usually recalled in popular narratives. Almost two and a half years would elapse between the first Highlander workshop that Jenkins attended, in the summer of 1954, and the actual opening of the first citizenship school on Johns Island in January 1957. As historian Peter Ling argues, that time was necessary to develop the latent leadership skills possessed by the protagonists and their many collaborators. In the end, Highlander's purpose was not achieving community development goals so much as it was "people development," which involved the complex work of helping people learn to articulate and reframe issues so they could acquire the self-confidence to resolve problems themselves.[7]

What the origin story does capture, though, is Esau Jenkins's steely determination and his refusal to let anything stand in his way. His commitment would cement the support of collaborators like Robinson, Clark, and Horton, allowing them to play decisive roles in helping to turn the nascent citizenship school idea into a reality. Though Robinson could not have learned of Jenkins's intentions at the 1954 Highlander workshop, his passion, which she must have experienced many times at other gatherings, such as meetings of the Charleston NAACP, would ultimately convince her that she needed to be involved.[8] In addition, her first visit to Highlander, which happened a year later than the origin story suggests, also made a deep impression on her, not least because of the example set by Horton and Clark, reinforced by Zilphia Horton's invigorating musical leadership.[9] During the year that elapsed between the summer of 1954 and the summer of 1955, Clark also had emerged as one of Highlander's most valued leaders. Without question, her painstaking work with Jenkins, Robinson, and Horton proved decisive in coaxing the first citizenship school into existence. Finally, after much deliberation and many visits to Johns Island, in which he kept his focus on "people development," Horton raised the funds to pay for the building where the school was housed. Without the money that Highlander attracted to fund the project, primarily from the Schwarzhaupt

Foundation, much of what occurred might never have gotten off the ground.[10]

In fact, Highlander's best work always resulted from rich and extensive collaborations, not because a single bold leader guided loyal followers to positive outcomes. Highlander drew from the strength of many people who knew their communities well and who positioned themselves strategically to devise locally appropriate means for bringing about meaningful change. Highlander's leaders knew that only when responsibility for a change initiative gained the strong support of a core group of activists could the community as a whole be convinced of its value and take the necessary strides to carry it forward.

Despite this understanding of how social change works, until recently, most accounts of the citizenship school movement have given too much weight to Horton's role. As Katherine Charron has claimed, Highlander "shaped the narrative of the citizenship school's origins that was sold to the outside world."[11]

Horton is himself partially responsible for this bias, as he regularly underplayed the impact of his three collaborators. Others, too, often exaggerated his impact, owing in part to white supremacy's tendency to give the only white man in the group primary credit, lavishing attention on his analysis of the school's emergence. Recently, though, there has been a tendency to emphasize the influence of the other individuals, eliminating Horton from the story altogether.[12] Such revisionism is understandable, particularly given the decades of adulation that Horton has enjoyed as the "founding father" of Highlander, and the desire to award Clark, Jenkins, and Robinson long overdue recognition. Still, history will likely show that the first citizenship school grew out of a years-long, complex, sometimes planful, sometimes chaotic collaborative process that built up community leadership—and in which all four protagonists played decisive roles. To put it another way, there is reason to believe that without the full participation of any one of the four key players, something critical would have been lost, preventing the citizenship school movement from taking off as it did.

If history needed an indication that Horton wasn't the single inevitable architect responsible for the leadership that developed the citizenship schools, his own track record working in other communities during the same period offers supporting evidence. In towns like Whitwell, Tennessee, and Altoona, Alabama, as well as Monteagle itself, efforts to strengthen local leadership did not develop into self-sustaining projects. In Kodak, Tennessee, for example, Highlander had high hopes. Community development work began in 1953 and seemed promising because the effort did not begin as a Highlander suggestion but came from a concerned member of the Kodak community who wanted to reform the local schools and improve delivery of public services. In addition, survey data gathered at the beginning of the project uncovered a number of potential leaders who expressed interest in working on some of the town's pressing concerns. Highlander also successfully lobbied Kodak residents to participate in a series of workshops to spawn new leadership and deepen ongoing engagement. Somehow, though, the Kodak work never quite took off, perhaps because, as Horton put it, the townsfolk "lacked the incentive to solve their community problems themselves."[13] In short, Highlander's efforts did not lead to further organizing because the fruits of such efforts just didn't matter that much to the people in the community. The Schwarzhaupt Foundation, which provided support for these earlier projects as well as for Johns Island, learned that community development projects can't be "cooked up" but have to grow organically from a locality's needs. Leadership emerges when a crisis or pressing problem poses a challenge that motivates people to think and respond with a sense of urgency.[14]

Change came to Johns Island because of the urgency felt by Jenkins, Clark, Robinson, and others. Whatever happened in Whitwell or Altoona or Kodak didn't really touch the people living in those communities. On Johns Island, the changes that were put in place would dramatically alter the quality of people's lives. In her ground-breaking study of Highlander, Aimee Isgrig Horton, who married Myles years after he was widowed, pointed out that sites where social change was not sustained lacked "the kinds of crisis situations, the social ferment, which, beginning with the Bugwood Strike, had provided the school with a basis for initiating a program" and which drove the push for transformation.[15] In addition, John Glen's observation seems right: citizenship schools "took hold . . . primarily because residents of the Island were not so much concerned with something called community development," which was too abstract and amorphous a concept to promote lasting change. Change on Johns Island was driven by "one single, essential problem: illiteracy as a barrier to voter registration."[16]

CONNECTING JOHNS ISLAND WITH HIGHLANDER

One of Highlander's many strengths stemmed from its network of previous visitors, which became a powerful tool for spreading the word about its programs. Aimee Horton noted that "the majority of participants were . . . recruited by former participants who, because they were enthusiastic about what they had gained from the workshop experience, encouraged others" to get involved.[17] The citizenship schools fit that pattern in that a less well-known fifth activist, Anna D. Kelly, a prominent black YWCA leader in Charleston, attended a Highlander workshop in the summer of 1953 that impressed her deeply. She found it to be a welcoming, relaxing, and informative place, completely free of racial self-consciousness. Kelly said she encountered no stereotyping, no racial barriers, no favoring of one group over another. It was also a wonderful place to network with other community leaders. Most remarkably of all, she enthused, Highlander fed people well and kept them stimulated the whole time.[18]

Kelly's conviction that Highlander created a true community of equals finally convinced her good friend and YWCA colleague Septima Clark to pay a visit during the early summer of 1954, just weeks after the *Brown* decision had been handed down. Clark was bowled over. She came away from this first workshop appreciating the comforts of Highlander and its incredibly relaxed interracial atmosphere, but she was most impressed with the school's emphasis on discussion and its use of the experiences of participants to frame problems and devise possible solutions. As an experienced teacher, she could see more clearly than most how Highlander's dialogic methods followed from its democratic goals. Used to meetings where long, drawn-out speeches predominated, Clark delighted in Highlander's far more interactive and open-ended approach. She delved more deeply into the school's pedagogy when she worked on a brochure for Highlander called "What Is a Workshop," which advised clear definition of a topic while staying flexible enough to adapt "to the interests of the group / or the resources of the people available." Because of Highlander's commitment to racial equality, Clark also grew "more vociferous on the integration angle."[19]

Just a few days after that first Highlander workshop, Clark wrote to Horton, "Every chance I get I'll sell Highlander and you shall hear from me when I have something to offer or need help. I have faith to believe that you . . . are going to see your convictions blaze forth over the whole world."[20] A little later in the summer, Highlander invited Clark to attend a second workshop on the United Nations and to bring a guest with her whom she thought might benefit from the Highlander experience.[21] She chose Esau Jenkins.

When eighteen-year-old Septima Clark first encountered six-year-old Esau Jenkins in 1916 on Johns Island, harsh poverty, widespread disease, and abysmal sanitary conditions were major challenges there. In addition, the two-thirds of the population that were black, many of whom spoke an English-based Creole dialect known as Gullah, suffered from vicious racism. Though only about ten miles from Charleston, Johns Island remained isolated until the 1930s, when the Works Progress Administration finally constructed a bridge connecting the island to the mainland and opening up new possibilities for many of its people. Still, poverty, disease, racial bigotry, and limited educational opportunity continued to prey on its residents, hobbling growth. Clark returned to Charleston in the late 1940s after a long career teaching in Columbia, South Carolina. She reconnected with Jenkins, and they collaborated as members of the Executive Committee of the Charleston NAACP. Clark also began working again on Johns Island, first assisting Jenkins with a vacation Bible school he had organized and later helping to finance and publicize an urgently needed immunization campaign that was launched to combat a terrible outbreak of diphtheria that killed 68 children in 1953, a tragedy that struck a huge proportion of the roughly 2,700 black residents.[22]

As for Esau Jenkins, he had dropped out of school in the fourth grade to work with his father as a carpenter and truck farmer, growing into a respected leader of the Johns Island black community and a successful businessman. But as an adult he still bitterly recalled his hatred of the schools he attended as a youngster, not because he hadn't wanted to learn; he was an avid learner even back then. What he hated were the overcrowded classes and absence of books. He also despised the stigma that black segregated education suffered from on Johns Island, symbolized for him by the fact that their schoolhouse was painted a particularly ugly shade of black. It was not a disinclination to learn that caused Esau Jenkins to despise formal schooling; it was the insistent malice of Jim Crow that he could not get out of his mind.[23]

His abhorrence of racial discrimination and the ways in which it kept his neighbors down never diminished. In 1945, he scraped together enough money to buy a bus, which he used to transport students to the all-black high school in Charleston because there was no high school for African Americans on the island—until Jenkins himself successfully campaigned for one a number of years later. Before long he was also providing transportation for black adults who needed to get to jobs on the mainland. His passengers included many local women who served the wealthy households of Charleston or held positions in the city's profitable tobacco plants. The men he transported usually owned land on Johns Island but couldn't grow enough produce to make ends meet, so they had to take jobs as longshoremen or as laborers in Charleston's fertilizer factory.[24] At a time when it was unheard of, Jenkins also often organized trips to New York City so his neighbors could experience a place where black people held a range of jobs not confined solely to menial lines of work.[25]

One day Alice Wine, one of his regular passengers who always sat near the front of the bus, spoke to Jenkins about wanting to become a fully recognized citizen, someone who could vote. She knew that as a black person under Jim Crow, she would have to pass a literacy test to get registered. She wondered if Jenkins would help her. As Jenkins recalled, Wine said, "Mr. Jenkins, I would very much like to become a registered citizen, but I cannot read this constitution because I did not get but just so far in school and I cannot pronounce these words. But if you are willing to help me, I will show you that I would be one who would be willing to vote in every election."[26]

What began with Alice Wine soon extended to the entire busload. Each morning Jenkins tutored his passengers on the South Carolina constitution, guiding them through difficult vocabulary words and sounding out technical terms. Despite many hours of instruction, Jenkins realized his school on wheels was not enough to teach large numbers of disenfranchised blacks the rudiments of reading and writing. Once he visited Highlander, he wondered if the unassuming school for adults in rural Tennessee might be able to provide just what he needed.

Despite the United Nations angle of the 1954 workshop, Jenkins's primary concern was finding a way to bring change to his Johns Island community, possibly by getting more people like him elected to office. But this, too, was impossible without more black people gaining eligibility to vote. At the workshop's final gathering, when participants shared what they planned to do once they returned home, Jenkins vowed to run for trustee of the local school board, even though he knew he could not win in the absence of a substantial block of black voters. But he wanted to show, as he put it, "that a Negro can run for office and not get killed."[27] He knew that running for school board trustee, even without winning, would inspire his neighbors, providing a new incentive for them to register to vote. The records of the meeting do not indicate any mention at that point of setting up a special school on Johns Island to overcome adult illiteracy.[28]

People who knew Jenkins regarded him as unstoppable, someone with the persistence and sense of mission to fuel a movement. Septima Clark said his greatest gift "was his love of people and his determination to do all he could to help them."[29] Jenkins recalled having asked himself early in his life, "Am I my brother's keeper? The answer that I got was, You are. So then I decide to myself, since I'm no better than anybody, I don't feel that I'm worse than anybody. I decided to do anything I can to help people in order to help myself."[30] He understood something that Myles Horton also swore by: He couldn't want something just for himself. If it were worthwhile, it had to be available to everyone.

Highlander staff called Jenkins "relentless": "Every night of the week he would be going out to a different church or community center, even in his own church, or going to all these surrounding communities in the low country of Charleston, speaking to people, passing on the things they needed to know about everything from health to schools to voting."[31] Still, though, he knew he needed the help of a place like Highlander to bring more people into the movement.

In a letter Jenkins wrote to Horton in mid-September 1954, two months after his first visit to Highlander, he seemed to sense the school could be a loyal ally, and he wanted to demonstrate how much he had already accomplished. Jenkins wrote that he had gotten the support of the local PTA to show and discuss a number of film strips and films at the high school, films that had been shown at Highlander focusing on the need for social justice and racial equality. He also organized a series of twice-a-week interracial fellowship meetings involving black youth from Johns Island and white youth from Charleston. And he made sure that Highlander knew about his decision to run for the Johns Island school board, refusing to be intimidated by concerns that doing so would rile the white community or endanger him and his family.[32]

Finally, he invited Myles and Zilphia Horton to come to Charleston in November to pay homage to J. Waties Waring, a United States district judge based in Charleston who had done much to advance the rights of black people in South Carolina. Waring had stood up for civil rights by supporting pay equalization for teachers and eliminating the so-called white primary, but he paid an incredibly high price for daring to do so. He and his wife Elizabeth were abused and threatened until they finally concluded they could no longer live in South Carolina. In 1952, they escaped to New York City, where they would live for the remainder of their lives. They returned briefly to Charleston in November 1954 so that the community could honor Waring.[33]

Although Myles could not attend the dinner for Waring, Zilphia was there and filed a glowing report, highlighting the remarkable energy of Esau Jenkins. She called him a tireless man who, despite his limited education, had found a way to become "president of the Johns Island PTA, Superintendent of the Baptist Sunday School, assistant pastor of the church, President of the Citizen's Club of 200 members, Chairman of the Progressive Club, and member of the Executive Board of the NAACP of Charleston."[34] She was fascinated and charmed by life on the island, thoroughly enjoying the opportunity to be immersed in local culture and delighted to be invited to sing twice for the community. She felt confident that the trip would yield worthwhile results in terms of identifying and building up community leadership. Her report on Jenkins's organizing efforts also played a pivotal role in moving Highlander toward much deeper involvement.[35]

SEPTIMA CLARK LEADS THE CITIZENSHIP SCHOOL

Highlander quickly came to regard Johns Island as an ideal site to test out its community development approaches and to advance integration and black rights. Between November 1954 and the summer of 1955, Highlander staff visited the island dozens of times, led largely by Clark, who was brought on as a part-time staff member in February 1955 and whose educational experience and knowledge of Johns Island made her an ideal coordinator. In December and then later in the spring, Horton had visited the island for extended periods to become acquainted with its culture and to get to know the people better. His report from December 1954 indicated that Jenkins's leadership potential was considerable and that he had already developed the habit of thinking ahead. Still, Horton was frustrated by Jenkins's tendency to schedule meetings dominated by endless speeches, instead of using his growing influence to engage more participants and build deeper leadership capacity. This conflict between the two men partially arose from different assumptions about public meetings. Horton saw them as opportunities to hear from many people and to give a widening circle of community members a chance to lead. Jenkins saw them as a time for an established leader to make pronouncements or to lay out next steps without a lot of consultation with others. Horton lamented that Jenkins did not understand Highlander's approach to leadership development, even as he admired Jenkins's drive and optimism. For the time being, he decided not to push Jenkins too hard and to keep their interactions informal and low key.[36]

Horton also understood that as a white man he had limited ability to effect change on Johns Island, a place populated largely by black people. Whatever came out of their collaboration had to be led by African Americans. As historian Katherine Charron has said, "Horton harbored no illusions about how his white skin limited his effectiveness."[37] During his December 1954 visit, Horton had repeatedly failed in his attempts to engage the local populace in Highlander-style discussions, probably because they had been inculcated with the expectation that whenever a white man held the floor, their primary task was to listen, not to offer opinions. Their tepid responses almost certainly reflected uncertainty and lack of trust. Perhaps, too, their silence was a reaction to an unconscious sense of superiority that the strong-willed Horton projected. In any case, he eventually recognized the need to defer to Clark, who was not only black but had a deeper understanding of the culture of the islanders. From the start they responded more positively to her, owing to the fact that she had "learned their ways, turned her ears to [their] language" and "didn't put herself above them."[38] Clark was still teaching in Charleston, so she had to juggle work and her island responsibilities. Although this was unfair since other Highlander staff were full time, as a leader in the civil rights movement, Clark had grown accustomed to managing multiple roles simultaneously.

In March 1955, Myles Horton, Jenkins, Clark, and Zilphia Horton met to talk about how to get more people involved in the projects on Johns Island. Clark led the meeting, moving cautiously because of fears that Jenkins was not yet comfortable sharing leadership with her. He saw his work as a one-man operation and "had not yet grasped the importance of having more people doing different things to a common end."[39] She framed most of her interactions in the form of questions, as was the style at Highlander, both to draw him out and to pave the way for broader participation in the project. For example, when Jenkins said he would get his daughter to conduct a house-to-house survey of the number of school-aged children on the island, Clark wondered whether others outside his family circle might also be able to help with the survey. Because of such interactions, Jenkins became increasingly aware that he could not make the progress he wanted by exclusively corralling his relatives to perform key tasks. Horton watched closely as Clark coaxed Jenkins into a more collaborative mindset.[40]

To Horton, it was essential to bridge the divide between Jenkins, whose instincts continued to favor self-reliant leadership, and Highlander's democratic commitments. As he saw it, that divide undermined their shared purpose. For Jenkins, the chief purpose entailed increasing the number of black voters so that people of color could assume more positions of leadership. For Horton and Clark, something more was at stake. "A . . . fundamental change was needed which depended not only on making good on the right to vote but also on raising the level of sophistication with which the suffrage was exercised."[41]

Not long after that meeting, in late April 1955, Jenkins wrote a letter to Horton indicating that he was beginning to understand the importance of developing more leadership from all around the island. He critiqued himself, saying, "I have found that giving others something to do in helping make better citizens in the community is very important. My old way of doing was slow."[42]

Still, the connection between getting more people registered to vote and broad-based leadership development remained elusive. It was only sometime after the summer of 1955, when Jenkins, Clark, and Horton all began to envision an actual school for adult learners where unregistered islanders could acquire the skills they needed to pass the literacy test, and, in the process, gain the confidence to become more active members of the local community, that they all saw more clearly how both of these goals could be achieved.

Earlier, Horton had discovered that state funds for adult education were going unspent on Johns Island. At least one school administrator claimed that adults on the island didn't want to learn, but, as Horton noted, "Esau had gotten them to want to learn. So how can we get more people to want to? Why did Esau's people want to read? So they could vote. The reason was immediate and specific."[43] Once the decision was made to focus on the creation of a citizenship school, Clark gained full authority over the project and assumed primary responsibility for moving it forward, even though her position was still part time. Horton may have been the undisputed expert on leadership development, but it was just as clear that Clark's forty years of teaching experience made her the expert needed to plan and establish a literacy school for adults.

Both Clark and Horton realized that part of the problem of getting more adults involved was the tendency for seasoned teachers to fall back on methods and materials that worked relatively well with children but left adults feeling disrespected and discounted. Previous efforts to work with adults "didn't treat them with respect . . . didn't treat them with dignity. They treated them like little kids, they were contemptuous of them. They actually put them in seats for children; they called them daddy-long-legs, these big old lanky people sitting in a chair for first graders. They just treated them like dirt. So that becomes obvious that you have to treat people with respect."[44]

Additionally, the exacting discipline and formality that were standard operating procedure with children did not translate well to adults, who wanted a more open, conversational kind of experience. Textbooks that focused on the lives of children, designed to pique their interests, also had an off-putting effect on adults. The new school would need to treat adult learners as adults with minds of their own, as people who had accumulated a variety of rich experiences that set them apart from children. For both Horton and Clark, the most important thing was to recruit a teacher for this first school who did not carry the baggage of a career teacher. Clark said she wanted someone with a fresh approach whose lack of familiarity with standard teaching procedures would allow her to be more open to a Highlander-like program and who "would be willing to follow suggestions from the school."[45]

Horton and Clark didn't always agree; as Clark later put it, sometimes we "had to just shout it out."[46] They clashed in particular over the focus for the citizenship school. Horton felt a relatively short training period was enough to get blacks prepared to pass the literacy tests and gain eligibility to vote. Clark knew Horton hadn't read the election laws, or he would have known how much instruction people actually needed to pass the literacy tests. He assumed incorrectly that a large group of potential voters could be successfully registered without the deep literacy training Clark favored.[47]

Horton also questioned some of Clark's teaching methods, often calling them "new-fangled."[48] But newfangled or not, her ideas worked. They made a decisive difference in eventually helping thousands of people become literate. Like Horton's, Clark's vision didn't stop with literacy; she also wanted people to hone their political awareness, to become more politically active and politically wise enough to reach sound, defensible judgments. But she was adamant that her ambitions for her fellow citizens be built on a foundation of basic literacy.[49] Only then, in her view, could black people become what she called "first-class citizens." Clark prevailed, insisting that the school follow a fairly intense schedule: two hours a night, two nights a week, for at least two or three months, and sometimes considerably longer.

When Clark first came to Highlander in 1954, she was already an experienced activist and committed freedom fighter who had played a significant role in advancing the case for salary parity for South Carolina's black teachers and expanding the influence of teachers who chose to join the NAACP. Although her NAACP activism would result in the termination of her Charleston teaching contract in 1956, Highlander would then make her a full-time director of education and co-leader of the citizenship school project, giving her "free space" that enabled her to blossom into a genuinely transformational leader. As Horton looked back on those days, he came to regard Clark and, later, Bernice Robinson as the ones who made things happen. While giving himself credit for making sure activities on Johns Island followed a nontraditional and nonacademic path, Horton let Clark decide how the school would be organized and run.[50]

BERNICE ROBINSON, THE IDEAL TEACHER

It was Clark's idea, which Horton enthusiastically supported, to select her cousin Bernice Robinson as the teacher for the first citizenship school. Robinson had attended Highlander workshops, was an experienced NAACP activist, and knew the Sea Islands well.[51] She had a high school education and had worked as a successful beautician and seamstress for most of her life. Robinson resisted the idea at first. She had wanted to help since attending that first Highlander workshop in the summer of 1955 and was especially committed to doing whatever she could to increase black voter registration, but she just couldn't see herself as a teacher. Clark and Horton persuaded her to think otherwise. They regarded the lack of teaching experience as a strength, as a kind of prerequisite for working well with adults. They didn't want teachers "accustomed to working by a strait-laced curriculum. They wouldn't be able to bend, to give." Adults needed someone who was known in the community, who cared about the community and knew how to communicate with people in a natural way, but also someone who understood the Highlander philosophy and could teach using Highlander methods.[52] Because of her work experience, not in spite of it, she became a seasoned, outspoken, and highly adaptive leader who showed remarkable courage during periods of great stress. And her high school diploma made her comparatively well-educated for the time and place. In short, she was a very talented woman, whose gifts Septima Clark, in particular, recognized from the beginning and helped develop even further.[53]

Robinson had at least one other quality that made her especially fitting to be the first citizenship school teacher: she knew how to listen. Even Horton, who prized his own listening ability, fell short of her standard. Horton could be impatient, unwilling to hear out a long-winded story or stay focused on a speaker who had difficulty coming to a point.[54] Robinson, on the other hand, had acquired "a good ear" as a result of her many years as a beautician whose clients expected her to "listen to their problems" and let them "tell you all of their life stories."[55]

Right from the start, Robinson used her skill as a listener to let her students guide her toward a focus on "what they wanted to know."[56] On January 7, 1957, she launched the first citizenship school, not by telling the original fourteen students what would be covered, but by asking them what they wanted to learn.[57] Her own sharing about the class revealed her commitment to treating them as equals: "I'm not going to be the teacher, we're gonna learn together. You're gonna teach me some things, and maybe there are a few things I might be able to teach you, but I don't consider myself a teacher. I just feel that I'm here to learn with you, you know, learn things together."[58]

Robinson's speech was genuine. She knew that many of her students had been discouraged before by adult learning classes, and she wanted this time to be different. She wanted to convey the feeling that they were part of a community of learners, with everyone encouraged to contribute something that would create the best possible learning environment for all. Horton had understood that dignity and respect must accompany all efforts to teach adults; Robinson knew how to both model and embody those all-important attitudes.

When her students started sharing what they wanted to learn, their initial answers were not about voting registration or the South Carolina constitution, but about things that mattered in their everyday lives—reading the Bible, making sense of the newspaper, filling out a mail order, deciphering letters from their relatives. As she put it, "I just had to reach them on their level" and as long as she did, "we got along well."[59] In addition, Robinson must have understood that literacy was not only a road to voting; it was a path that would allow oppressed people to do many things beyond politics that illiteracy had made impossible.[60]

Robinson's effectiveness stemmed partly from her realization that by beginning with things that were familiar, just as Brazilian educator Paulo Freire recommended, students could participate more naturally and comfortably. As they gradually opened up about themselves, she copied out stories they recounted, which became primary texts for initial lessons in reading. She summed up her method by saying "I used all that trying to meet them where they were."[61] At the same time, she also challenged her students, urging them to study the United Nations' Universal Declaration of Human Rights, which she pinned on the classroom wall. Whether she knew it or not, she was following Myles Horton's philosophy: see learners as they are with one eye, and with the other eye, see them as the learners they are in the process of becoming.[62]

One big focus during those first classes involved learning to write their names in cursive, which gave students a sense of independence because "printing didn't count for signing checks." Mastering cursive was no easy task, but Clark's "new-fangled" suggestion helped: Robinson wrote their names out beforehand, and students traced the examples. Many students told Clark that learning how to sign their names made them feel different. "Perhaps the greatest single thing it accomplishes," Clark said, "is the enabling of a man to raise his head a little higher." Suddenly they had become a part of the community: "They were on their way toward first-class citizenship."[63]

Together, Robinson and Clark pioneered a variety of instructional strategies in this first citizenship school that were soon tried out in the chain of islands nearby, and then in other parts of the South as well. What united the strategies was their emphasis on respecting students' voices and experiences and focusing on topics that truly mattered to them and helped them in their everyday lives. Clark found "that you don't tell people what to do. You let them tell you what they want done. Then you have to have in your own mind certain things that you feel they need to do. And so you get their thoughts and wind your thoughts around them . . . but if you have a cut-and-dry program for them, you'll lose out every time."[64]

These pioneering activists embraced Highlander's belief in the dignity of adult learners and their capacity for growth, regardless of the limits of their prior education. None of the earlier, unsuccessful efforts to educate Johns Island adults had stood so firmly behind these unassailable principles.[65] Their instructional philosophy also directly aligned with Highlander's: "The direction and substance of a program must emerge from the people and not [be] brought to the people however well intentioned. . . . If a program is going to work, the people must have the power of making decisions about what they want to do."[66] This method, which resembled how Clark taught when she began her career on Johns Island, might have grown out of talks the two women regularly enjoyed, or it might have emerged from Robinson's uncanny ability to listen closely and to capture respectfully exactly what her students were expressing.[67] Robinson often gave credit to Highlander for the impact of its instructional methods on her teaching. Indeed, Highlander may have inspired her to be interactive, respectful, and open to her students' experiences; but most of what she did resulted from her collaborations with Septima Clark and her own responsiveness to the feedback her students supplied.

By all accounts, despite her lack of formal training, Robinson was "an exceptionally good teacher . . . who improvised a curriculum based on her students' needs and aspirations."[68]

Upon visiting Johns Island to observe Robinson for the first time, Horton recognized that something extraordinary was going on.[69] Bernice Robinson had found a way to address the educational priorities of all three of the citizenship school's founders. Septima Clark wanted many things, but she especially lobbied for developing the students' reading and writing skills. She argued that literacy itself should be the foundation for the school. Robinson's methods emphasized reading and writing. Jenkins's goal was to develop reading and writing skills as a means to an end: dramatically increasing the black vote. The results greatly exceeded expectations: fourteen students were enrolled when the first class started; thirty-seven were enrolled when it ended. All of the initial fourteen successfully registered to vote on the first try, as did the others not long afterward.[70] Finally, Horton sought to develop the community's leadership skills and promote civic empowerment. By using discussion strategically in the context of literacy education, Robinson offered opportunities for the students to confront community problems and explore possible solutions.[71]

The campaign against illiteracy, then, was no minor skirmish; it was a fight for freedom in all the senses of that word from which none of these champions of racial justice would retreat. Historian David Levine is particularly insightful about the "double oppression" that state-imposed illiteracy had foisted on black people. It not only prevented them from enjoying the advantages of reading and writing— "better job opportunities, civic power, access to culture, written communication with others"—it also "diminished their sense of self-worth and validated a social system which often equated lack of book learning with inferior intellect."[72] That double oppression denied black people their humanity and, in so doing, imposed on them what was universally understood as "a badge of inferiority." The citizenship schools strove to do their part to eradicate that badge once and for all.

AN EXPANDING SOCIAL MOVEMENT

Within a year, the citizenship school on Johns Island had spawned three additional adult education programs, one in North Charleston and one each on the nearby islands of Edisto and Wadmalaw. Robinson also taught in the North Charleston school and soon assumed responsibility for all of the schools in the Low Country of South Carolina. In the meantime, Clark traveled widely, seeking to spread the word about citizenship school education to other southern communities. Perhaps the most astounding early success occurred on Johns Island, where in 1958 alone, over 600 black people successfully registered to vote, and the voting rate of those registered reached nearly 100 percent.[73] By the spring of 1960, there were five times as many eligible voters on Edisto Island as there had been in 1958, and during the two-month winter session of 1960–1961, 105 out of 111 black learners in four of the established schools had qualified to vote.[74] Between 1954 and 1961, Highlander helped establish thirty-seven literacy programs in South Carolina "involving nearly thirteen hundred participants."[75] With few exceptions, all of these learners eventually gained access to the franchise.

Led by Septima Clark, Highlander organized eight new schools in Huntsville, Alabama, and Savannah, Georgia, during the winter of 1960–1961. After a brief period of adjustment in which Clark and Robinson revised their methods to meet the specific needs of these communities, the results were almost as impressive as they had been on the Sea Islands of South Carolina. Eighty-six of the 115 enrolled learners in the Huntsville program were registered to vote by March

1961, and in Savannah, seventy-four of the ninety-two learners who took literacy classes officially registered to vote by the middle of 1961.[76] By 1960, there were also emerging citizenship programs in west Tennessee, southeastern Georgia, and Montgomery, Alabama, all supported by Highlander trainings and workshops.[77]

As the citizenship schools spread, Horton began to make plans to hand off the program to an organization better able to manage the complexity of this ever-growing movement. He attempted to interest Dr. Martin Luther King, Jr., in having the Southern Christian Leadership Conference (SCLC) adopt it as an important part of the SCLC's commitment to civil rights. King was reluctant at first, primarily because the citizenship schools did not seem to advance the direct action side of the movement, which he especially valued. Unlike the demonstrations and boycotts and marches that defined direct action, citizenship schools were a quiet, less obtrusive, more drawn-out way to further racial justice. They didn't attract much attention and so didn't offer the public relations advantage of a bus boycott or a march for jobs and freedom.[78]

Eventually, Septima Clark was able to convince King of the value of these schools by arguing that demonstrations and other forms of direct action rarely brought about tangible results. Citizenship schools, on the other hand, boosted voter registration that directly fueled black empowerment. Her argument sealed the transfer, which Horton hastily executed.[79] Horton assigned Clark to the SCLC program in mid-1961, keeping Robinson on the staff at Highlander.

Clark and Robinson responded with anger to this sudden change. They felt the transition to SCLC happened much too quickly and, far worse, that it had occurred without their input. Horton had not bothered to consult with them, making the move independently and unilaterally, as if their opinions didn't matter. They liked nothing about the arrangement, especially the plan to separate the two of them, as they had worked so effectively together over the years. Both women were embittered and outraged by the lack of discussion about this major change in the work they had led. They regarded it as part of a pattern in which both Highlander and SCLC consistently failed to fully value and recognize the contributions of women.[80]

By July 1961, Septima Clark and Bernice Robinson had grudgingly accepted their new roles in helping to implement what was now known as the Citizenship Education Project under the auspices of the SCLC. Funding, which came primarily from the Field Foundation, was also transferred from Highlander to SCLC. Andrew Young, an SCLC staff member, became the director of the project and was joined by others, including Dorothy Cotton and Annell Ponder. A training facility located in McIntosh, Georgia (now Midway, Georgia) was identified, and most of the teacher training occurred there. The facility, which became known as the Dorchester Center, had originally been an academy for freed black Americans and later became a lively community center.[81] From 1961 to 1965, "some 1600 young and older volunteer teachers" participated in SCLC workshops. "They, in turn, taught Citizenship School classes for more than 25,000 adult students and, together, as Mrs. Clark was able to report in 1965, these movement teacher-leaders and their students 'were responsible for the enrollment of more than 50,000 registered voters!'"[82] During the first nine years of the Citizenship Education Project's existence, something like 3,500 citizenship school teachers would participate in workshops at the Dorchester Center, which made it possible for an estimated 125,000 citizens to gain access to the ballot box.[83] Years later, Dorothy Cotton, who helped lead the project for the SCLC through most of the 1960s, would say that "Citizenship Education Project training was the base upon which so much of the civil rights movement was built. Thousands of people came through our sessions, and their hometowns were never the same again."[84]

Even in the best of times, Highlander lacked the capacity to continue to support an ever-expanding citizenship school movement, but the increasing number of threats to its existence made the transfer to the SCLC absolutely necessary. For years, Highlander had been investigated and attacked for its liberal policies, especially for its refusal to compromise on integration. To much of the white South, Highlander's total commitment to equal rights could only be explained by the unfounded claim that it was consciously aligned with communism. As a result, hundreds of politicians and law enforcement officials insisted, despite a complete lack of evidence, that Highlander was an official training school for the Communist Party. In addition, people who saw Highlander as an instigator of the civil rights movement thought that shutting down the school in Monteagle would permanently cripple the movement as a whole.

Although there had been many attacks on Highlander over the years, perhaps the most effective and extreme involved a four-page pamphlet published by the Georgia Commission on Education in October 1957 called *Highlander Folk School: Communist Training School, Monteagle, Tennessee.* Prompted by Highlander's twenty-fifth anniversary celebration, at which Dr. Martin Luther King, Jr., appeared as the keynote speaker, the publication recirculated the old canards that Highlander staff and guests were "unAmerican, immoral, Communist conspirators responsible for every major civil rights controversy since the *Brown* decision."[85] Most of the pamphlet's text was based on discredited testimony from the 1954 Eastland hearings, and the picture accompanying the pamphlet, which had been snapped by an anti-Communist investigator posing as a journalist, showed Horton, King, and Aubrey Williams listening calmly to an uncontroversial Highlander speaker. Blown up to poster size, this picture, with the caption "Martin Luther King at Communist Training School" would be recycled repeatedly, over a period of many years, to "prove" that Highlander was communistic, subversive, and dangerous. FBI files indicate that FBI Director J. Edgar Hoover himself received numerous copies of these materials, accompanied by dozens of notes from public officials and ordinary citizens urging him to suspend the charter of the school.[86]

In February 1959, as the pressure on Highlander continued to build, the Tennessee legislature passed a resolution to investigate the school for its supposedly subversive activities. With the help of ardent segregationist Bruce Bennett, attorney general of Arkansas, who had done much to stir up the opposition to Highlander throughout the South, a series of hearings was held to reveal the school's ostensible transgressions. Almost nothing substantive was uncovered. Some documents indicated that Highlander's original charter had never been filed in Grundy County and that a transfer of property to Myles Horton had occurred under somewhat questionable circumstances, but that was all. As one reporter put it, all the investigation really did was reaffirm and draw attention to what everyone already knew: "beyond a doubt . . . the school is interracial." Despite the lack of damning evidence, both houses of the Tennessee legislature agreed that a suit should be brought to revoke Highlander's charter.[87]

On the evening of July 31, 1959, county and state officials raided the school while Myles Horton was abroad, attending an adult education conference. In John Glen's recounting of the raid's details, it was obvious that the officials were looking for anything that would incriminate Highlander. They found liquor in Myles Horton's private home, along with a half-empty wooden keg, which they took as evidence that the school was producing moonshine or perhaps selling beer without a license. It was on the dubious strength of these revelations that Clark, a lifelong teetotaler, and a number of other staff members were arrested. In September, Highlander was found to be in violation of the statute which prohibited the sale of liquor without a license. The judge approved the revocation of Highlander's charter and ordered that its main building be padlocked. It was then, on September 26, 1959, that Horton famously remarked, "You don't need buildings to run a school." Highlander was an idea, and no public official could "padlock an idea."[88]

The case continued to be battled in the courts for another eighteen months, but on April 5, 1961, the Tennessee Supreme Court upheld the original ruling that Highlander should lose its charter. The state had been dead set on destroying the school, and it finally prevailed. It had halted what it thought was the center of operations in the march for black rights. But as Myles Horton said years later in an interview with Bill Moyers,

> only a racist white person could make [that] assumption, that some white people had to be doing that kind of thing. So they assumed because a lot of the black[s] had been at Highlander long before the civil rights movement and during the civil rights movement, blacks couldn't do anything themselves, so it had to be some white people. So they got four or five governors together and closed Highlander. And it was only after they closed it they found out that they, you know, didn't have anything [to do] with the civil rights movement, the black [people] were [running] the civil rights movement.[89]

A NEW CHARTER FOR HIGHLANDER AND A NEW PARTNER FOR HORTON

Although it was a great hardship to witness the destruction of the original Highlander Folk School, Horton and his colleagues were not so easily deterred. Without missing a beat, they chartered a new organization in Knoxville to continue Highlander's work, officially renaming it the Highlander Research and Education Center.

Though the loss of the original Highlander was crushing for Horton, this period in his life also became a time of rejuvenation and new possibilities, in part because of the move to Knoxville under a new charter, but also because of his marriage to Aimee Isgrig. Horton and Isgrig met at an educational conference in Colorado, returned to Highlander together for a weekend visit, and were married soon thereafter, almost exactly at the same time that the state of Tennessee was ordering the school's closure.

Born in 1922, Aimee Isgrig had grown up in Wisconsin and from an early age showed an unusual interest in social justice. Educated in a Milwaukee lab school run by teachers with strong progressive backgrounds, Isgrig applied what she was learning to an analysis of pressing social issues and became a believer in the power of group deliberations. She attended Rockford College, the alma mater of Jane Addams, and gained an appreciation for Addams's action-oriented example. She went on to earn a master's degree from the University of Wisconsin at Madison in adult education and completed all coursework for a Ph.D. at the University of Chicago before accepting a position as the director of the Illinois Commission on Human Relations. In this role, which officially lent her very little authority to make change, she provided much-needed support to a number of communities grappling with racial discrimination.[90]

After marrying Horton in April 1961 and getting to know Highlander's culture, she became an enthusiastic supporter of the school. She was struck by the motivation of the students and taken aback by the composure and commitment of teachers with few credentials and only limited formal education. She attributed all of this to the freedom the Highlander community enjoyed and its unalterably positive outlook about the future.

Almost immediately, Isgrig began research on Highlander, eventually producing the first complete historical study of the school from 1932 to 1961. She presented this work as her dissertation at the

University of Chicago in 1971, and in 1989 it was published as a book, with a glowing introduction by Pulitzer Prize winner David Garrow.[91]

Ever humble and self-effacing, Aimee Isgrig Horton described herself primarily as a learner whose dissertation "represents the culmination of what I learned about" Highlander.[92] But during the first years of her association with the school, she wrote widely about its programs and its history and helped it transition quite successfully from Monteagle to Knoxville, linking civil rights to the rights of disadvantaged Appalachians. She also played a major role in cataloging Highlander's archival materials, which had been "hastily deposited" in a "dark, third-floor attic" of the rented house on Riverside Drive in Knoxville that had become Highlander's new home.[93] All future researchers of Highlander's history are indebted to Isgrig for her careful documentation of Highlander's first thirty years and for ensuring that Highlander's official papers were preserved and properly organized.

11 *Highlander and SNCC*

LEARNING TO PREACH WHAT MATTERS

John Lewis, the future congressman from Georgia, was just eighteen in the fall of 1958 when he started his second year as a divinity student at American Baptist Theological Seminary (ABT) in Nashville, Tennessee. Lewis loved ABT and was thrilled to reunite with the many good friends he had made there the year before. Coming from a very poor family, he also loved ABT's simple comforts—the fact that he had a whole bed to himself struck him as luxurious, as he had always shared his sleeping space with two or three of his brothers.

At ABT, Lewis also found he had a knack for preaching, a skill every ABT student needed to master. Those who could preach thrived; those who could not often dropped out. Among the most passionate preachers at ABT was his friend and colleague James Bevel. Bevel was a force of nature whom Lewis admired inordinately. No one could match his passion, drive, and sheer volume. In their close-knit peer group, Bevel "set the tone." As Lewis recalled, "He could make you think. . . . He loved nothing better than a good argument, and it didn't really matter what it was about. It was like push-ups for the brain to him, a workout that made the mind sharper and stronger."[1] Lewis wanted to translate that kind of thinking into preaching that could make a difference in the world.

During that fall of 1958, Lewis met thirty-year-old James Lawson, whose passion for social justice gave Lewis a new sense of purpose. Having recently settled in Nashville to pursue a graduate degree in divinity at Vanderbilt University, Lawson carried himself with the wisdom of an older man whose desire to do something noteworthy with his life drove his actions. He declared himself a conscientious objector during the Korean War and served fourteen months in jail for draft evasion. He then gained extensive experience as an activist for both the Fellowship of Reconciliation and the Congress of Racial Equality, two of the nation's leading advocacy groups for nonviolent direct action. When Lewis saw Lawson for the first time, he was set to deliver a public lecture about justice as a unifying theme of all organized religions. Even before Lawson began speaking, Lewis couldn't help noticing there was something remarkable about him. Despite his ordinary appearance—tall, soft spoken, bespectacled— he had a way about him that evidenced an extraordinary "aura of inner peace and wisdom."[2] At the age of eleven, Lawson had undergone a kind of conversion experience when, after announcing proudly to his mother that he had slapped a white boy for using a crude and derogatory racial epithet, she "proceeded to give him the first lecture he had ever heard about the concept of Christian love."[3] From that time on, he became a practitioner of what he called "New Testament pacifism."[4]

The lecture Lawson delivered launched a series of weekly workshops about justice and the power of nonviolence that Lawson wanted to open up to the entire Nashville community. Lewis felt compelled to participate. The workshops included an extraordinary set of techniques and strategies to actively but nonviolently resist unjust laws. Behind it all, Lawson preached a way of being in the world, a combination of love, peace, and compassion, that animated how to respond to almost any conflict situation. The workshops transformed Lewis; they became the focus of his life.[5]

Lewis invited Bevel to join the workshops, wanting his friend to experience the euphoria that came over him at every gathering. Bevel was skeptical. He only joined the workshops after Lewis and other Lawson protégés, close friends such as Bernard Lafayette and the fearless Diane Nash, began to participate in sit-ins at segregated restaurants and department stores all over Nashville, using Lawson's techniques. The viciousness with which whites lashed out in response to the respectful and nonviolent protests that Lawson's students staged alarmed Bevel. He decided to join the workshops in part to look out for his dear friends, and in part to connect with a movement that he realized might change his life. Once he joined, he devoted himself to the student movement as faithfully as Lewis and all the others.[6]

In late 1959, Lawson broached the idea for the Nashville group to attend a Highlander workshop. Almost everyone knew something about the school and what it had stood for over the years. They knew that Horton's fierce, uncompromising commitment to integration was a violation of Tennessee segregation laws and that every workshop he held invited the censure of white supremacists whose threats to shut down the school never abated. As Lewis later put it, "What Jim Lawson was doing that fall . . . Myles Horton and his staff had been doing for decades up in those wooded mountains."[7] But Bevel again doubted and balked. He imagined Highlander as a place with a lot of glittering generalities but not much substance. For him, as for most blacks, "The idea of an integrated school up on a mountain, surrounded by blue lakes, sounded like a fairy tale."[8]

By the time the group would make it to Highlander, a lot would have changed. On February 1, 1960, four African American students from North Carolina Agricultural and Technical State University in Greensboro had staged a quiet sit-in at a whites-only Woolworth's lunch counter and asked to be served. They went ignored until the store finally closed rather than serve them. The next day many more students of color showed up and again were refused service until closing. Day after day, more students sat in at the lunch counter; each day they were ignored and went unserved. Within a week, hundreds of mostly black, nonviolent demonstrators and an ever-growing group of white antagonists who heaped abuse on the protesters were crowding into the Greensboro store, and the protests were spreading to nearby Durham and Winston-Salem. The disruptions created a chain reaction of protests across the South. During the second week of February, the students in Nashville, under Lawson's leadership, readied themselves to apply what they had learned. They hoped to show the whole country what a highly disciplined, nonviolent army could accomplish.[9]

Their first sit-in happened on February 13 with 124 orderly students, almost all of them black, taking their places at lunch counters throughout downtown Nashville. These serious, proud students knew what was at stake for them and how much their white opponents were likely to condemn or even harm them for their actions. They sat at the historically segregated spaces with remarkable commitment and composure, understanding the risks they faced because they were breaking the law, but also knowing at some deep, abiding level that it was the right thing to do.[10] As in Greensboro, these initial sit-ins occurred without incident.

Then, on February 27, even before their daily sit-in began, students got word of officials' plans to arrest them after allowing white bigots to taunt and threaten them. Despite the dangers, they took their usual places at lunch counters in the downtown area. As Candie Carawan (then Candie Anderson), who would gain fame as Guy Carawan's partner and one of the guiding forces of Highlander's cultural program during the civil rights era, recalled, "Right away the toughs started throwing things over us and pouring catsup in our hair; putting out cigarette butts on our backs."[11] All that wasn't a surprise, but the passivity of the police really shook her. They just watched as the rioters heaped abuse on the nonviolent demonstrators. Finally, the police intervened by arresting the sit-in students, completely ignoring their white aggressors. This pattern repeated itself day after day.

When the Nashville group arrived at Highlander on April 1, many of them had already participated in countless nonviolent demonstrations and endured jail numerous times. More than any other group that attended that special workshop, the Nashville students saw themselves as battle-hardened activists. Julian Bond, one of the leaders of another sizable group from Atlanta, especially admired the Nashville contingent for its distinctive "group personality." Its members had "panache and confidence in each other," Bond noted. But more than that, they had already accomplished so much. "Unlike us they had really taken over the leadership of the sit-ins in Nashville."[12]

About ten days before the workshop, Myles Horton had singled out the students and the sit-in movement for praise. He said the sit-ins marked "a new phase of democratic action in America . . . which will lead to fuller participation by Negroes in all phases of economic and political life." He insisted that the black students must lead the fight for racial equality, but that white students had an important role to play as well by supporting their brethren in whatever ways the black student leaders needed. Horton encouraged the students to remain independent to avoid being co-opted by mainstream civil rights organizations such as the Southern Christian Leadership Conference (SCLC) or the long-standing National Association for the Advancement of Colored People (NAACP).[13]

ENCOUNTERING HIGHLANDER AND MYLES HORTON

On April 1, 1960, eighty-two students, forty-seven of them black and thirty-five of them white, representing twenty different colleges, showed up for Highlander's Seventh College Weekend workshop, which had been retitled "The New Generation Fights for Equality."[14] John Lewis, James Bevel, and Bernard Lafayette all attended and became actively involved in the many discussions. A sense of urgency prevailed at this meeting because it was the first large gathering of sit-in participants since the beginning of the protests and the participants' first opportunity to discuss their situation and explore possible next steps. A lot of the students who wanted to talk about their experience of going to jail found themselves challenged by Horton to defend the rationale for their actions. As Candie Carawan remembered it, Horton asked questions to push students to clarify their thinking, prodding them to make the case for going to jail: "By the end of the discussion we came to the conclusion that if we wanted to make jail part of our tactic, we'd have to be willing to stay in."[15]

Despite his initial resistance, Bevel was won over by Highlander. In part, he liked the isolation, the sense of being part of a completely self-enclosed community. But most of all he liked the staff, how they helped students take hold of an issue and analyze it thoroughly. Horton became an intellectual hero to Bevel for his ability to clarify people's thinking about almost any issue. Bevel regarded him as a kind of Socrates whose penetrating questioning allowed everyone to zero in on the truth. And, as Lewis said, Horton's extensive experience interacting with a wide range of people prepared him well for the brashness and edginess of those like Bevel. Bevel later said that Horton asked questions that pushed people to examine their assumptions or "challenge you on your inferior feelings. He sort of decrudded Negroes from being Negroes and . . . [made] them think of themselves as men and women. . . . He . . . destroyed all the false assumptions of the oppressor and made us deal with the fact that we were cowards and that we were lying, and were not serious about being who we said we were."[16]

At first, Bevel didn't know what to make of Horton. Horton seemed to revel in getting students to question themselves and their cause. His voice didn't help matters. Horton spoke in a "moderately high-pitched voice, not especially pleasant. It tended toward nasality and was as southern white in accent as it could be."[17] Candie Carawan also noted that Horton's voice and manner added to the tension; it was "almost like you're arguing with the white power structure."[18] Given what that voice seemed to represent, could it be trusted to support the cause of racial justice? Horton left Bevel feeling dizzy and doubtful. He was not inclined to listen to a white man talk about the problems of poverty and race, but Horton was hardly a typical white male, and Highlander was hardly a typical retreat center. It had a solidity and spirit that invited discussion and exploration. It didn't discourage disagreement and conflict; it saw value in making the most of conflict and using it to bring about positive results. Highlander generated an energy that "even Bevel couldn't resist," John Lewis recalled.[19] Still, in the middle of at least one session, Bevel reached his boiling point, leaving abruptly and slamming the door behind him. As Taylor Branch put it, it was "Myles Horton who first cracked Bevel's sense of mastery."[20]

John Lewis's best friend, fellow activist Bernard Lafayette, was also touched by Horton's approach. Quieter and more modest than Bevel, Lafayette followed Lewis, from the beginning, in opening himself up to Lawson's mentorship and learning how to use nonviolence to advance racial justice. For him, Highlander was a place where he and his fellow activists "could get away, think, plan our strategy, and also connect with ourselves." It became a "retreat from the battle in Nashville." In that first workshop, though, Horton's temerity and his questioning of the basic assumptions behind the civil rights movement rattled Lafayette. At one point, Horton asked, "Well, why shouldn't white folks have the right to eat with whomever they like?" Lafayette got mad. "I stood up and we had a good old fuss. I didn't then understand the concept of being a devil's advocate. What Myles was doing was causing me to think critically about why I was doing what I was doing. This was one of the things he consistently did."[21] Lafayette recognized that Horton provoked students to think more deeply, relentlessly challenging a particular point of view no matter how much it stung. Some of Horton's actions made Lafayette furious, even though he understood that Horton pressured students so they could be as clear as possible about what they believed. He "was always pushing you further," Lafayette recalled. "You think you have come to some conclusion about something, and there he is, pushing out the walls and you have to reach out and grab something. That's what a good teacher does—keeps making you rearrange the blankets to make room for broader ideas."[22]

In his autobiography *The Long Haul,* Horton reflected on the idea that he infuriated people with his unremitting challenges and that, in a way, it was cruel of him to be the cause of so many people's discontent. He believed in changing society by first preparing individuals to be effective in the face of extended struggles. "There's a lot of pain in it, and a lot of violence, and conflict, and that is just part of the price you pay. I realized that was part of growth—and growth is painful. A plant comes through the hard ground, and it breaks the seed apart. And then it dies to live again."[23] For Horton, pain and discontent were inescapable when educating for radical social change.

As Horton facilitated discussions about the student protests and how adults might be reacting to the activists, he often posed as a "liberal white man" or an "average Negro businessman," prodding students to defend their actions from a consistent philosophical ground, whether legal or moral. Septima Clark's summary of the workshop said, "Nearly every one of the students stated that he was eager to act according to the law, but most of them acknowledged that they had not thought clearly through the implications of their own undertaking." In the end, the Nashville contingent, including Lewis, Bevel, and Lafayette, argued for nonviolence as a way of life, with obedience "to a higher than civil law" a moral requirement.[24] Lafayette held that when a law "perpetrates discrimination . . . you have a question whether or not that law is morally right, and so you can't respect this immoral law, and the fact that you don't have any involvement in this law to begin with that makes this law entirely a moral question."[25]

Bevel's focus was on the impact of the students themselves and their communities. Students needed to dramatize the hatred they faced, just as Christ had done, to offer a principled lesson to the community about the protesters' true and just intent. When over a hundred students were jailed in Nashville for their participation in the sit-ins and then were immediately freed on bail, Bevel wished the situation had developed differently, without the intervention of lawyers: "If the students had stayed in jail, the public officials would have started to rethink the situation. It wasn't that we overlooked the lawyers, but we wanted to appeal to the community" to achieve a moral victory in community members' hearts. Remaining in jail could have changed "the heart of the Mayor" and changed "the heart of the Chief of Police . . . This is the idea of teaching them by subjecting ourselves to [their] evil."[26]

Like Bevel and Lafayette, Lewis was impressed with Horton and eager to learn from him. He admired him especially for his obvious commitment to racial justice and his ability to provoke students to think more deeply. But during that first Highlander weekend, he was actually most taken with a different member of the staff: Septima Clark, the school's education director and creator of the citizenship school. Her background as a teacher and her grassroots success working with people on the margins who had little or no education captured his imagination. He loved her "down-to-earth, no-nonsense approach and the fact that the people she aimed at were the same ones Gandhi went after," people at the bottom who rarely had champions.[27] Lewis's experiences with Clark taught him that organic intellectuals like Clark, with all of their commitments to supporting the quiet, behind-the-scenes person, ultimately made the biggest difference. He concluded she was the sort of person the movement most needed, someone who understood what it was like to have so little and yet knew how to support, encourage, and love people into meaningful action. Lewis saw what Taylor Branch called Septima Clark's ability to strike "a miraculous balance between leathery zeal and infinite patience." Clark predicted Lewis's profound and long-term impact on the civil rights movement. When a distinguished scholar visiting Highlander said Lewis was an unlikely leader because of his country ways—he stuttered, split infinitives, and wasn't a smooth reader—Clark exploded, "What difference does that make?" She recognized even then that he possessed the heart of a leader and predicted great things for him.[28]

The probing discussions and provocative questions weren't the only experiences participants recalled from this first Highlander workshop. The singing also stood out. They sang a lot. Led by Guy Carawan, a versatile musician and engaging singer who years earlier had worked briefly with Zilphia, was just beginning to reconnect to Highlander. In the interim, Carawan had learned "We Shall Overcome" from Pete Seeger. Through workshops such as the one Lewis and the other college students attended, Guy became the first person most students heard sing what would become the anthem of 1960s protests. Lewis remembered how much everyone was drawn to the song and how perfectly it "fit the movement we were becoming a part of."[29] But there were other songs, too, that Guy Carawan introduced to the movement and that become an important part of the student protests. There was "Amen, Amen" and "I'm Going to Sit at the Welcome Table," and especially "Keep Your Eyes on the Prize." All the students at the Highlander workshop not only heard and sang these songs; they took them back to their campuses so that they could be reexperienced with friends who had been unable to make it to Highlander.[30]

The power of song to unite people and strengthen their collective purpose became more evident than ever during that pre-SNCC experience. As Stephen Schneider has eloquently stated: "For civil rights activists, singing became an important means of keeping together in time, whether it be in meetings, in prison, or on the march. Freedom songs provided a fabric by which individuals became a collective body capable of enduring humiliation and violence; the repetition of movement anthems, and the feedback created by hundreds of people singing in unison, provided individuals under attack with a larger body of strength on which to draw."[31]

As the workshop was nearing its end, Horton grew more explicit about Highlander's role in supporting the students' work. Highlander existed to help people, not to push them in any particular direction or make them affiliate with one organization or another. Highlander's strength grew out of its success in bringing people together to think, strategize and take collective action according to their own initiatives. He spurred students to "avail themselves of the opportunity of each other's presence to talk about some of the problems" they faced, noting that the meeting had marked the first time since the sit-in protests began that a group of people "representing a variety of points of view and a number of different colleges" had gotten together. The students were presented with a unique opportunity to share perspectives, deepen thinking, and, perhaps "further the things you believe in." Whatever conclusions are reached, Horton declared, Highlander had "no interest in engineering" a particular outcome. Highlander merely wanted "to help you do what you decide to do."[32]

At the conclusion of the 1960 workshop, Horton cautioned students to preserve their independence from adult organizations by following their own paths and maintaining a creative and hopeful spirit. Lewis was inspired. As he put it, he "left Highlander on fire." He had come to understand that "to light fires and refuel those whose fires were already lit" stood as Highlander's most important purpose.[33]

Sociologist Charles Payne expressed roughly the same idea when he said that "the development of efficacy in those most affected by a problem" mattered more than anything to Highlander. Individual goals and objectives counted much less than the people in a community coming "to see themselves as having the right and the capacity to have some say-so in their own lives."[34] These were the things Highlander believed in and tried to instill in its many disciples. John Lewis counted himself among them.

ELLA BAKER AND THE FOUNDING OF SNCC

On Easter weekend 1960, just two weeks after the sit-in protesters met at Highlander, Ella Baker convened a meeting that she called the Southwide Student Leadership Conference on Nonviolent Resistance to Segregation. Many of the same students, joined by scores of others, converged on Shaw University in Raleigh, North Carolina, the historically black university where Baker herself had been valedictorian. The avowed purpose was to conceptualize a new, independent, student-focused civil rights organization. Widely regarded as one of the African American community's most effective organizers, Baker, like Horton, recognized the untapped potential of young people. She lamented the lack of racial progress made since the Montgomery bus boycott and saw in student leadership an opportunity to electrify the civil rights movement by bringing youth and adults together into a stronger, more unified movement.[35] At the same time, she rejected efforts by Dr. King and other members of the SCLC "to capture the youth movement."[36] She believed that students' strength would come from their independence, which would also empower them to become more constructive partners of groups like the SCLC and the NAACP. Inspired by her confidence and vision, students emerged from the Raleigh conference as members of a new organization—the Student Nonviolent Coordinating Committee

(SNCC), with Ella Baker serving as the group's primary adult advisor and, unofficially, its biggest booster.

Baker was not only a great organizer but also renowned for her first-rate skills as an educator and developer of grassroots leaders. She often argued, at least as insistently as Horton, that strong, charismatic leadership in a movement for participatory democracy was self-defeating. A different kind of leadership worked better, she contended—more humble, caring, and behind the scenes. For Baker, leadership had little to do with filling a position and almost everything to do with collaborating with others to support a group's collective development. Her response in 1970 to historian Gerda Lerner's question about community leadership directly aligned her with Horton when she said, "I have always thought what is needed is the development of people who are interested not in being leaders as much as in developing leadership in others."[37]

Like Horton, Baker believed that one principal way activists exerted leadership was through carefully crafted questions. Prathia Hall, a SNCC member and Baker admirer, praised her for her nondirective and question-centered teaching style: "Raising a question and then raising another question and then helping us to see what was being revealed through the answer was her mode of leadership."[38] Another activist, Lenora Taitt-Magubane, commented that Baker's inclination to rely on "key questions" frequently wasn't recognized or appreciated as leadership. She delayed intervening, Taitt-Magubane pointed out, "because she wanted the decision to come out of the group and not be hers." Still another SNCC activist, Mary King, observed that Baker maintained a "Socratic presence" by asking questions that brought the focus of discussions back to purpose and intent. "Now let me ask this again, what is our purpose here? What are we trying to accomplish? Again and again she would force us to articulate our assumptions."[39] As biographer Barbara Ransby notes, Baker acted on the belief that "people had many of the answers within themselves; teachers and leaders simply had to facilitate the process of tapping and framing that knowledge, of drawing it out." As at Highlander, "debate and the open exchange of ideas became critically important."[40]

Horton's own love of questioning grew out of his belief that this was a nonintrusive way to get people to think differently. The right questions at the right time could help a group "examine the underlying reasons for a problem, or why the problem was so persistent, without the facilitator or leader ever having to supply any of the answers."[41] The questions one asked didn't tell the group what to do or what decisions to make, but they did provide a direction or open up a new line of thought. As Horton put it, "You can get all your ideas across just by asking questions and at the same time you can help people to grow and not form a dependency on you."[42] Part of the skill of questioning entailed using close listening to build on what had already been said, so that the question functioned as a natural outgrowth of the discussion's give and take. The question needed to be organic, not artificially "injected" by a facilitator.

Horton actually thought answers were overrated. In one of his last interviews, he reaffirmed the lessons he had learned at Ozone and practiced throughout his life: "I don't much care for answers. . . . You are letting [people] down if you give them answers." He added that "giving answers is not as good a way of education as asking questions and making people face up and think through things for themselves. When you can get people to think about the process they are going through, this is the beginning of their education."[43]

Ella Baker's most important contribution as a teacher and a leader was probably her notion of group-centered leadership. One of the educational assumptions that united Baker and Horton, as well as the world-renowned educator Paulo Freire, was this notion that learning is "a collective and creative enterprise requiring collaboration and exchange at every stage." For Baker, this especially meant creating space for everyone to speak and contribute. Learning to be silent had real value, as did learning to interrupt "to make sure that others were allowed to speak and that the more confident speakers were made to listen."[44] In order for group-centered leadership to work, no single person could be designated as the leader or the official spokesperson all the time. Rather, as many participants as possible had to assume multiple leadership roles so that the contributions of individuals more accurately reflected the broad range of viewpoints and feelings represented in the group.

Ella Baker, like Septima Clark, "functioned as an organic intellectual for groups" because "she validated and relied on the collective wisdom that resided in poor and oppressed communities."[45] She had enormous respect for the everyday experience of marginalized populations and believed they possessed the thoughtfulness and social intelligence to generate discerning critiques and take informed actions. Although she personally received a rigorous formal education, she reserved her greatest admiration for people with street smarts, for the learning that took place "in the meeting places and unions hall of New York City, as well as at rural and urban churches, barber shops and kitchen tables throughout the South."[46] She recognized that retreat centers like Highlander provided a central location where the everyday wisdom of ordinary people could be brought to bear on the most difficult problems, while also diminishing the barriers of race, class, sexism, and elitism that so often derailed productive dialogue.

In May 1960, with SNCC still not yet a month old, Highlander held a smaller follow-up workshop for students and older activists called "The Place of the White Southerner in the Current Struggle for Justice." To kick off the gathering, Horton urged everyone to forget their particular role in society, whether as student, parent, or community leader, and to affirm that "we are here, all of us . . . to try to learn from each other."[47] What interested Horton most, which he tried to formulate as a question for the group, was the role whites might play in supporting their black colleagues who had rightly become the undisputed leaders of this urgent fight for equality. The answer given by many of the black leaders who participated, including Ella Baker, Septima Clark, Rosa Parks, and Fred Shuttlesworth, Birmingham's most visible black leader, reminded whites that they had an important role to play in lobbying against segregation laws, expanding black voting rights, and, in general, fostering "constructive relations between the races." At the same time, black leaders cautioned whites not to fall into the trap, common to even the most progressive groups, of following old patterns of interaction in which well-meaning whites ended up dominating discussion and decision making, thereby marginalizing black voices.[48]

Another Highlander gathering in November 1960 continued exploring the theme of whites' role in the freedom struggle. Entitled "The Place of the White College Student in the Changing South," the workshop focused on white participants who found themselves still searching for a "place" in the new student movement for integration. For one thing, blacks and whites lived in separate communities, and the stakes of activism differed for the two groups. White participants saw black participants as facing more immediate and dire consequences than they did; they also made greater sacrifices—going to jail, risking their jobs, walking instead of riding—"because it is *their* struggle and they are the ones being pushed around." But at least one passionate African American activist from Nashville "emphatically rejected this view, repeatedly insisting that this is everyone's struggle."[49] Many agreed, though an uneasiness with the idea lingered, as if in practical terms it didn't seem to fit the facts. Embracing the notion that the freedom struggle was everyone's struggle had the potential to change everything; "Direct action with all its risks and the possibility of sacrifice is no more or less difficult for a white person than a Negro."[50]

In the end, participants agreed that any union between blacks and whites should focus on racial justice and also strive to transcend the necessity of that union by working together to create a better and more humane society overall. True integration "must come through common efforts to improve aspects of society that have little or nothing to do with race. If the organization and dedication growing out of the sit-ins can be applied by the students to the solution of all shared problems at the same time as they work to get rid of discrimination, a radical and creative movement can be born in the South."[51] The summary conclusions from the workshop sounded utopian, perhaps even beside the point, but they grew out of the hopeful spirit that surrounded the meeting. With the help of groups like SNCC and yeasty environments like Highlander, ushering in a new era of radical equality for all seemed like a distinct possibility.

SNCC AND THE GREAT COMPROMISE

It is probably fitting that an institution as important to the civil rights movement as Highlander—with its unique status as "movement halfway house"—became the place where SNCC chose to hold one of its most decisive meetings, in August 1961.[52] It couldn't have been lost on the students as they gathered in Highlander's new quarters in Knoxville that the state had closed down Highlander's Monteagle site, primarily for its commitment to integration and advancing the cause of racial justice—the very things the students were fighting for. SNCC students had already met repeatedly with Highlander staff during SNCC's first eighteen months of existence, and now they were coming together one more time to hash out an especially contentious organizational issue. Should SNCC remain a group exclusively devoted to making change through direct actions such as sit-ins, freedom rides, and marches? Or should it also create a space for the more indirect goal of expanding the black electorate by challenging restrictions on the registration of African American voters?

The advocates of direct action, primarily the group from Nashville, were convinced of its primacy. It had proved highly effective in grabbing people's attention and putting pressure on white leaders to introduce real changes in southern communities. SNCC's very existence, after all, had grown out of the students' commitment to collective direct action. At the same time, a strong contingent had emerged contending that the historic disenfranchisement of southern blacks deserved equal consideration. The Kennedy administration had recently introduced a foundation-funded program called the Voter Education Project, which would provide financial support for efforts to register more black voters. Many saw this as a golden opportunity to pursue a highly worthy objective and to receive financial support for doing so. Partisans of direct action feared that the voting rights issue was risky and would dilute the impact of the in-your-face street activism that had proved so effective and given SNCC so much visibility. They wanted to continue to be free to focus on provoking and confronting the powers that be. Diane Nash, one of SNCC's most powerful and vociferous leaders, saw the Kennedy-engineered voting rights initiative as an attempt to buy out students; similarly, John Lewis thought it was a "trick to take the steam out of the movement, to slow it down."[53] As the discussion dragged on and the passions on both sides grew ever more intense, some concluded that the only way to move forward was by creating two organizations—one oriented toward direct action and the other toward voting rights. Baker strongly opposed the idea; "it was her aggressive intervention that calmed the situation, abated the rancor and preserved unity." She knew from her experiences with the NAACP and the SCLC that "organizing for voting rights did not preclude direct action. . . . Any attempt to register black voters would precipitate confrontations with white registrars and public officials in small towns and big cities."[54] In reality, then, the two strategies were not nearly as far apart as they seemed. In fact, Bob Moses, who would soon play a large role in furthering the goals of the voting rights wing but did not participate in this particular debate, had already been won over by the claim of Mississippi freedom fighter Amzie Moore that "in hard core areas of the Deep South, voter registration was 'direct action.'"[55]

Baker also knew that a split would weaken SNCC just as it was coming into its own. She felt that "SNCC had too much important work to do to consider a division." Speaking with uncharacteristic urgency, she warned that breaking up SNCC at such a crucial juncture would play right into the hands of the enemy. Acknowledging the passion with which Baker expressed her thought, the students knew she must be right: "No one rose to challenge her."[56]

What emerged from this historic meeting was a compromise, not entirely satisfactory to either side, in which SNCC encompassed two strong, singular factions—one committed to direct action and one committed to voting rights. Although Baker did not publicly favor one group over the other, she must have been pleased to help birth the new wing devoted to voting rights. For one thing, direct action and expanding black voting rolls required two completely different kinds of leadership and sensibilities. Direct action was more periodic, requiring short bursts of energy and connection. What it did best was to dramatize a situation and get people to pay attention in the moment and sympathize with a specific oppressed group. But voting registration drives were painstakingly slow, requiring months and even years of building trust and forming relationships in remote rural environments where challenging the status quo was always resisted and often dangerous. As Barbara Ransby has said, this second approach to making change "was Baker's model, and in 1961 it became SNCC's model" as well.[57] Of course, Baker's model was also Highlander's. The long-term impact of the meeting at the transitional Highlander site can hardly be overstated.

Both Horton and Baker understood at a deep level what the SNCC students were experiencing as they became more and more caught up in the excitement and fervor of the freedom movement. Everything in their lives seemed secondary compared to the all-consuming nature of the work. Education, jobs, connections with family and non-movement friends all took a back seat to achieving their movement goals. It was hard and painful but also exhilarating, because, in a very real sense, they had never felt so free. Horton understood this exhilaration and talked about it tellingly in his autobiography:

> I think that people aren't fully free until they're in a struggle for justice. And that means for everyone. It's a struggle of such importance that they are willing, if necessary, to die for it. I think that's what you have to do before you're really free. Then you've got something to live for. You don't want to die, because you've got so much you want to do. This struggle is so important it gives a meaning to life. Now that sounds like a contradiction, but I encourage people to push limits, to try to take that step, because that's when they are really free.[58]

TWO GREAT MOVEMENT TEACHERS

Myles Horton and Ella Baker embodied the best of democratic education during their work with the young college students who formed the Student Nonviolent Coordinating Committee, helping it develop into one of the black freedom movement's most powerful forces for social change. As Francesca Polletta has shown, their success with the SNCC organizers stemmed from a number of commitments. One was their intention to be deliberately educational, "to give people the tools to articulate their grievances and goals and to organize to realize them." Horton and Baker were absolutely adamant, regardless of the discomfort they might cause and the impatience they might engender, about preparing students "to weigh options and articulate positions," even if it meant undermining consensus or delaying movement toward a final decision. They saw great virtue in getting the SNCC activists to bring their differences out into the open and to keep the conversation going until it was clear which position should prevail. They were just as committed to the role of relationship building, both in helping a fledgling organization like SNCC recognize its strengths and in relating to people in grassroots organizations who demonstrated leadership potential. Their brilliance in managing dialogue in which they guided a kind of "endless meeting" brought multiple viewpoints and unheard voices to the forefront of the group's often contentious deliberations.[59]

As collaborators and as the leaders of their respective organizations, Horton and Baker consistently committed to what Polletta calls "developmental democracy," which meant that the rationale behind most of their interactions with the students was pedagogical.[60] The success of any one action or engagement mattered less than the ongoing growth of the students as activists, leaders, and change agents. As Horton often said when comparing organizing to education, it was more important to take the time and effort to promote learning than to secure an organizational advantage. Baker, too, underscored the habits and attitudes that were most likely to sustain students' long-term leadership development. As movement teachers, they were creative, resourceful agitators, responding on the spot to local conditions, making the most of unexpected developments, turning defeats into formative lessons, and knowing "when to exploit teachable moments."[61] They did all of this in service of the group as a whole, working to make it more collaborative and unified. Under their guidance, individual betterment invariably took a back seat to the advancement and solidarity of the collective, because building up a group's collective strength served as the only reliable path to the kind of radical social change Baker and Horton believed in so passionately.

12 *From Civil Rights to Appalachia*

By the spring of 1964, Highlander had begun to shift its focus away from direct involvement in the civil rights movement and toward the problems of poverty in Appalachia. The values of the movement remained central for Highlander, and they endured as an underlying theme of every one of its new initiatives. But the yearning to do more locally, in a region where chronic unemployment and economic suffering continued to increase, called the school to return to its roots, to refocus on the region that had birthed the school in 1932, and "perhaps to achieve a true balance between its original goals of developing a new social order and preserving the . . . cultural values of the mountains."[1]

As always, the school would commit to helping people learn from one another, thereby gaining greater control over the decisions that shaped the quality of their lives. Its educational assumptions remained the same: "The best experts on a particular problem are the people who must live daily with the problem. The best teachers are people who have grappled with a particular problem and who can then share their experiences with other people like themselves. " And the best solutions to a problem are the ones that emerge out of a community's attempt to identify and analyze a problem and to enact a course of action that reflects the needs of the community as a whole. In the case of Appalachia, the focus would not only be on better solutions to chronic problems, but also on the development of a growing cadre of local leaders tasked with moving their communities to greater self-reliance.[2]

Part of the challenge facing the school in turning to Appalachia had to do with the complexity of the problems. Appalachia couldn't be defined as a single issue. It entailed an extensive network of interlocking problems that called on Highlander "to develop a new integrative vision and educational strategy" in order to reverse a century of exploitation.[3] Pervasive strip mining had degraded the land, toxic waste disposal threatened water supplies, absentee landowners resulted in a reduced tax base, failing public schools limited children's futures, occupational hazards from coal mining and industrial farming resulted in the twin plagues of black lung and brown lung, and the union movement was pathetically weak. This overlapping complexity, exacerbated by Appalachia's entrenched poverty, made progress difficult. Highlander knew better than to exaggerate or oversell its potential. A single residential workshop, or even a series of them, wouldn't make much of a dent in such a complex set of problems. What a Highlander workshop could do, though, was "provide a vehicle through which a community group, or its representatives" could temporarily escape the pressures of daily living and gain some insight into the strengths and opportunities available to that community.[4]

Highlander's decision to focus on Appalachia by exploring ways "of helping the poor to organize themselves," primarily through leadership development, coincided with federal efforts to reduce poverty, increase employment, and expand educational opportunities by funneling billions of dollars to ailing cities and impoverished rural areas.[5] Expressions of concern about the challenges facing Appalachia occurred during a Highlander residential workshop for white student activists organized by SNCC in March 1964, just a little over two months after Lyndon Johnson's inauguration and the decision of his administration to wage a so-called war on poverty. The gathering, which attracted thirteen students, explored some of the growing hardships facing coal miners in eastern Tennessee, including low wages, failing mines, and the decline of labor unions, all of which made the problem of getting by in Appalachia even more challenging than in the past. In 1962, the United Mine Workers had attempted to strike for higher wages but was stymied by a lack of funds. When money for medical and hospital coverage for strikers ran out, small bands of individual workers engaged in wildcat strikes, making the union seem unstable and untrustworthy.[6]

What must have been especially galling about these challenges was the fact that while working people suffered, many coal companies flourished. The Virginia Coal and Iron Company, for instance, enjoyed a 65 percent profit margin in 1965, larger than any other American corporation for that year.[7] As Frank Adams put it: "As capitalism thrived in Appalachia, so did welfare." In spite of, or perhaps more accurately, because of various efforts to control, channel, and manage the people of Appalachia, their dependency, their poverty, and their sense of hopelessness continued to grow.[8]

The picture that the workshop painted of the economic difficulties besetting miners struck everyone as both honest and grim. Participants were daunted by the poor long-term prospects for Appalachian residents but remained determined nonetheless. As Sam Shirah, chair of the SNCC White Student Project, told the group, "The people of the community expect us to become part of their community, not to come as college students, concerned about theory and ideas only. We are dealing with people's lives. We must attempt to make the transition from thought to responsible action."[9]

The Appalachian initiative that Highlander eventually settled on emerged from a question that Myles Horton had raised about what it might take to breathe life into a small community that had fallen on hard times. What would happen if a group of activists rented a house and just started meeting people, with the object of learning about their shared concerns? Could such a simple set-up bring about meaningful community development? Horton was eager to experiment with the idea. He knew that Appalachia had already been analyzed to death: "Appalachia has probably been studied, surveyed and researched as much as any area in America. Many people have come to help us, but look at the mess we're in today." Maybe by refraining from direct intervention and focusing on promoting people's self-education and self-development, whatever approach Highlander devised would be empowering, not draining or disabling, for the residents of the community.[10]

Just as important, Horton knew Appalachia suffered from "top-downism," in which outside "experts" who believed that mountain people lacked the intelligence to make decisions for themselves had concluded, without consultation, what should happen in Appalachian communities. Poor people, as a result, never learned how to organize themselves and act on their own behalf. On those rare occasions when ordinary people gained a say in how things might work, the issues were trivial. Horton recalled one large industry that trained all its foremen in group dynamics, but confined their discussions to things like eating arrangements or using the suggestion box. Off limits were the nitty-gritty issues of wages and working conditions.[11]

Better to assume from the beginning that poor people as a whole are creative and eager to explore ideas when given an opportunity, Horton believed: "Even though the poor are often short on education, they are long on folk wisdom." In any event, "Unless we plan to continue to run things for them, sooner or later they must take the responsibility and it is easier to learn from the beginning than after a plan has been well formulated by someone else."[12]

Excited to move ahead, Horton selected four young men to carry out this community experiment in the summer of 1965. Two of them, John Chater and Horton's son Thorsten, had taken community organizing classes together as students at Goddard College, an experimental institution that Horton knew well from his association with its highly progressive longtime president, Tim Pitkin. A third, Sam Clark, was a student at Amherst College who had spent some time at Goddard and Highlander, where he had gotten to know both Thorsten and John. Finally, Robert Flint, a graduate of the University of Hawaii who had volunteered with the Peace Corps in Ecuador and interned in Mexico with the Community Development Foundation, also agreed to join.[13]

By the beginning of May, the four men had rented a house in the center of Habersham, a small Tennessee town near the Kentucky border suffering from joblessness, primarily because much of the work in the coal mines was now being done by machines. The men planted a garden and encouraged townspeople to drop by. They visited with the principal at the local school, met with the coordinator of the town's new Head Start program, checked on welfare allotments and food assistance programs, dropped by the courthouse to find out what sort of cases were preoccupying local judges and attorneys, lingered in the town's taverns, and attended houses of worship. They got to know Habersham but avoided intervening directly with any of the problems the town faced.

Three months went by in a hurry, and the Habersham experiment came to an end without any apparent impact. In a series of meetings with Horton, the four men expressed disappointment that so little had happened. Not wanting to make excuses, they nevertheless felt that three months wasn't enough time to get a change initiative going, and that their anxiety about not intervening in the town's affairs made them feel passive and ineffectual. They also had found it difficult to transition from simple pleasantries to more substantive conversation about the community's needs. Horton, though, saw the project as a positive step forward. "You cannot place too high a value on what you did," he wrote. He urged them not to be discouraged. "Nobody knows what to do in Appalachia." He wasn't nearly as interested in the results as he was in simply making a pioneering effort to engage with a small Appalachian community.[14] Soon thereafter, Horton proposed a more proactive project to Highlander's executive council, the Appalachian Self-Education Program (ASEP).[15]

ASEP introduced strategies such as discussion circles, open-ended questioning, and analysis of personal experience so that leaders-in-training would be better prepared to facilitate community conversations. The program gave people practice in community decision-making built on democratic deliberative processes. As future Highlander director Mike Clark (no relation to Septima) put it, "Too many Appalachians are done for, done to, done with, and done in." The point of the self-education program was to combat all of these factors and to provide the "encouragement and education which will enable people whose traditional pride is now too often twisted into hostile bitterness and hopelessness 'to do' for themselves."[16]

Mike Clark, who became Highlander's director in the early 1970s, not long after Horton stepped down, played a central role in the development of the self-education program before becoming Highlander's head. A native of western North Carolina, a graduate of Kentucky's Berea College, and a fierce opponent of strip mining in eastern Kentucky, Clark was an ideal choice to get the program moving. Like Horton, he recognized the perils of top-downism that had long plagued the region, but he also had a deep understanding of what inhibited mountain people. For one thing, Clark noted, they had little experience working in groups because they had been discouraged from doing so by existing institutions and prevailing custom. He also knew that mountain people tended to say little in public meetings even when discussion leaders actively welcomed their ideas. "Meetings to them mean a church where a preacher decides what is right or a school meeting where the principal tells them what to do about the school or a civic gathering where the county judge tells them how to vote," Clark lamented. "Meetings are just one more way they are kept down; either through parliamentary procedure or technical jargon which they don't understand."[17]

Another factor limiting Appalachian progress stemmed from the lack of a structure for holding discussions in which people could come together as equals to voice opinions and contribute ideas. Unions provided that structure during the labor movement, and many black churches valued members' voices during the civil rights movement. But mountain people had "no such common structures where people feel free to talk."[18] In essence, ASEP was designed to establish structures to encourage the habit of meeting together, valuing one another's experiences, and learning how to plan cooperatively for the future. Ultimately, Clark noted, the point was "to get poor people thinking for themselves and acting on their own decisions."[19] In addition to exposing leaders-in-training to the elements of discussion circles, Highlander workshops would also introduce them to cultural aspects of community development, including how to use singing, instrumental music, art, and local folklore to strengthen emotional bonds, enhance regional pride, and deepen ongoing social change initiatives. Of course, the cultural program had been an important part of Highlander's tradition from the beginning. By the late 1960s and early 1970s, Guy and Candie Carawan were lending their considerable talents to a further strengthening of the cultural side of fostering democratic activism. Through intensive study of local traditions and culture, their focus on Appalachian arts brought people together around a common history and shared experiences. Clark also recognized that culture helped people develop a positive image of themselves and their communities, giving them strength to continue to engage in political struggle. By building pride in heritage and exposing people to a wide variety of cultural traditions, Highlander built participants' unity around a set of values and activities that underscored their sense of shared purpose.[20]

EARLY PADGETT AND THE MINERAL SPRINGS ASEP

One of the first successes attributable to ASEP involved Early Padgett, a jack-of-all-trades with a third-grade education from the tiny town of Mineral Springs, Tennessee, not far from the state's southeastern border. After participating in a number of ASEP workshops, he returned to Mineral Springs to start a group for poor people to discuss some of their problems. He brought together a diverse set of people that included ex-miners, loggers, farmers, and housewives, some as young as eighteen and a few pushing seventy. As diverse as they otherwise were, he confined his invitations to poor people because of concern that no one would speak out if the group included middle-class people like teachers, social workers, or missionaries.[21]

They met in an old schoolhouse. Padgett told them that he wanted these gatherings to be a chance for people to talk about their ideas and problems, but also encouraged them to share their hopes and dreams for their community. He asked them not to bring up money, because nobody had any. Instead, he emphasized, "Let's talk about what we could do if we have as much money as we needed."[22]

Drawing on Highlander's framework, Padgett organized the group to serve the people who showed up. There were no rules of engagement, no parliamentary procedure, no chairperson to please. They just talked, one by one. At first, Padgett would ask someone to share ideas for the community, then others would react. Each person got a chance to say something about how to help the community, with others commenting on what they had heard. Gradually, the group became more comfortable just talking, without the assistance or intervention of a facilitator. The discussion kept getting deeper, and Padgett contributed less and less. He took notes, though, and at the beginning of the next meeting, he would report on what had been discussed and ask people if they had any new thoughts about what had previously come up. In this way, the group "began to see that they did have good ideas and could learn from each other."[23]

During those first meetings, the group brought up the need for new roads and the importance of training out-of-work people for new jobs. They expressed opinions about the quality of the public schools and talked about creating a school for children with intellectual disabilities. They invited the county superintendent to their meeting to answer questions about the school they had in mind. This meeting was as informal as all the others. The superintendent was not invited to make a speech or to share his vision for the schools, but to focus on this one pressing issue by listening to what the townspeople had to say and by responding to their concerns. "He talked on an equal basis with the group. He had to deal with their questions."[24] The participants' success grew out of the sense of community solidarity they had built up through their meetings: "*They* had talked it over, had made a decision, and the superintendent was at *their* meeting as a result."[25]

These simple encounters with authority figures like the superintendent and, later, the road commissioner, taught the group members that their ideas had as much value as those of so-called experts. They also learned more about how the schools were run and how money for roads was allocated. At the same time, the superintendent and the road commissioner started to pay attention to this engaged group of people in Mineral Springs, and they began to think twice before making decisions without broader community input.[26]

Over a period of many months, the group met weekly, with roughly ten people attending each meeting. Most of the time Padgett took notes, but if he missed a meeting, someone always volunteered to keep the minutes and take attendance. Early Padgett had started the group, but now they had progressed far enough to keep it going on their own. As time went on, they didn't always have a weekly meeting, but they continued to convene on a regular basis. It was empowering to be better informed and to be treated by public servants with the respect they had always felt was lacking. Now, when that respect wasn't shown, they were much more likely to demand it.[27]

What Padgett did bore striking resemblance to what Horton himself had tried to do some forty years before in the tiny village of Ozone. Like Padgett, Horton had dispensed with rules for discussion and simply provided an open forum for people to talk about their problems and ideas. Emerging from these informal exchanges was a new shared confidence, a recognition that the town's residents had plenty of good ideas, and that ways to make positive local changes were within the community's collective grasp. Mike Clark, who admired what Padgett had accomplished but recognized that it was hard to point to concrete results, later implied that contributions like Padgett's should not be underestimated. "It can be frustrating for people to put in years fighting for something and to see that conditions don't improve much," he said. "But we almost always improve the people's ability to deal with that problem. And in the long run that creates a ripple effect, which improves the country's ability to create a true democracy."[28] For Clark and Horton, that was the long-term point of ASEP: to move Appalachia, however slowly, toward more participation, more shared decision-making, and the building up of a more authentic democracy.

As Horton would say a few years later, "I believe our only hope lies in democratizing the decision-making process."[29] For him, this meant tying learning and decision-making together, because decision-making contributes to learning and learning makes people better decision-makers. As he put it, "The motivation for decision-

making, like the motivation for learning, comes through genuine involvement in an undertaking considered worthy of the effort and
possible to achieve."[30] With the support of ASEP, poor Appalachian
communities gained experience deliberating about issues that really
mattered, giving them new reason to go on learning to produce even
sounder decisions for navigating the future.

A MORE INCLUSIVE POOR PEOPLE'S CAMPAIGN

Working for a more authentic democracy also meant reframing the
struggle for civil rights to include brown people and indigenous cultures and other groups that had traditionally been marginalized.
While helping to conceptualize the Washington, D.C.–based Poor
People's Campaign for the Southern Christian Leadership Conference (SCLC) in late 1967 and early 1968, Martin Luther King announced that he planned to make that campaign far more inclusive
than it had ever been before by organizing an enormous "bottom-up
coalition of poor people" composed of Mexican Americans, Puerto
Ricans, Native Americans, African Americans, and whites. Myles
Horton was called on to recruit Appalachian whites and, with the
help of singer and cultural program director Guy Carawan, proved
quite effective in doing so.[31]

During a March 1968 Minority Group Conference in Atlanta that
Horton attended, Dr. King brought together some eighty non-black
poverty activists to plan the Poor People's Campaign. At the conference, he roundly condemned the American economic system for
its inequity and chronic unemployment, while also highlighting the
theme of lack of access to land as a major cause of poverty. This
theme recalled especially the lost opportunities of the post-slavery
era, while also providing Native Americans and Latinos with a historical example they could relate to. Of course, so could Appalachian
whites, who believed even then that their poverty was linked to the

hegemony of absentee landowners, many of whom controlled great swaths of Appalachia while paying virtually no taxes on them.[32]

What contributed to the success of this gathering was the openness of King and other SCLC leaders to the ideas of this diverse group of representatives. Native Americans spoke at length about the consequences of losing fishing rights to their ancestral waters. Puerto Ricans pleaded for support in their quest for independence. Mexican Americans underscored their concerns about police brutality and lack of educational equality. And "white Appalachians talked of the ongoing fight against coal companies' degradation of the land and water supply" and the powerful corporate interests that perennially blocked change.[33]

Horton wrote a hopeful follow-up letter to SCLC leadership calling King's vision of "a bottom-up coalition" a "glimpse of the future" that "could lay the groundwork for something tremendously exciting and significant." Horton urged the SCLC to take the lead in building a "bona fide coalition," because no other organization was in as strong a position or had as much responsibility to make such an alliance a reality.[34]

Sadly, Dr. King's tragic assassination on April 4, 1968, dashed all hopes for a new and more expansive SCLC. Without King's leadership, the SCLC returned to its more conservative and less inclusive roots and lost sight of the diverse coalition of poor people Horton was so enthusiastic about. Although Highlander sparked dialogues among a wide variety of groups during the Poor People's Campaign and then held regular workshops in Tennessee so these groups could explore their common problems, these efforts were short-lived and largely disconnected from other movement activities.

Unfortunately, what Horton had called "a glimpse of the future" did not materialize, not only because of King's assassination but also due to the federal government's increasing disillusionment with the so-called war on poverty. But this notion that poor people of all colors and backgrounds must find a way to unite behind a set of shared principles continued to drive Horton for years afterward.[35]

THE APPALACHIAN LAND OWNERSHIP STUDY

One of the most successful efforts to bring thousands of diverse Appalachians together around a single powerful issue proved to be the Appalachian Land Ownership Study, which was carried out in the late 1970s by a massive coalition of scholars and ordinary citizens who wanted to document something they had suspected for many years—that Appalachia was dominated by a cadre of wealthy absentee landowners paying little or no tax on the valuable land they controlled. Although this was not a Highlander initiative, it was co-directed by Highlander staff member and Oxford Ph.D. John Gaventa and grew out of Highlander's commitment to giving people the resources and strategies they need to solve their own problems.

Gaventa, who would win a MacArthur "genius grant" and who served as director of Highlander in the early 1990s, saw the school as a place to "help people who have a problem . . . gather the facts. Our philosophy is not that we can teach them how to fight these battles, but that we can put them in touch with other people who have similar problems and let them find the solution together."[36] Gaventa, who was one of the early leaders of the community-based participatory research movement, believed that by joining others in learning how to conduct rigorous, large-scale inquiry on topics of pressing concern, people could begin to find solutions to problems that had long plagued their localities.

One of the reasons that Gaventa prized participatory research had to do with its role in moving people from opinion to knowledge. "Opinion is when people play back what they've heard," Gaventa said, "and knowledge is when people have had an opportunity to reflect back on their own reality and their own position and to investigate their reality, and that's when knowledge is developed." For Gaventa, this was a crucial distinction and one that made places like Highlander necessary for supporting people in making that critical transition from "popular opinion into popular knowledge."[37]

With Appalachian Alliance researcher Billy Horton (no relation to Myles Horton), Gaventa co-directed the Appalachian Land Ownership Study Task Force, which investigated landownership in some eighty counties in the six states that comprise central Appalachia—Virginia, West Virginia, Kentucky, Tennessee, Alabama, and North Carolina. The task force evaluated how much land was owned by absentee landlords and, most importantly, assessed the extent of the tax burden shouldered by the largest landholders. It was an ambitious, astonishingly comprehensive study, involving 55,000 parcels of property and "20 million acres of land and mineral rights." In each of the eighty counties investigated, "over one hundred socioeconomic indicators were gathered . . . in order to examine the association between ownership characteristics and community well-being."[38] Though it was a complex, highly sophisticated survey of landownership across the massive central Appalachian region, most of the data were collected by engaged local citizens who regarded the issue as enormously important and urgent: "From the beginning, the landownership study was regarded as a project that would integrate research, education and action. People affected by the ownership patterns and active in response to them were to be an integral part of a research process culminating in the collection of data to be used in their local struggles around land issues."[39]

The study was not only exacting and comprehensive; it took perseverance and grit to pull it off. In addition to the immense logistical challenges, there was a "fear factor" arising from the consequences likely to be suffered by people directly challenging the status quo. As with the voter registration drives and sit-in demonstrations of the 1960s, there was real risk and sacrifice in pursuing such a potentially revealing and critical investigation. It took great courage to conduct "public interest research which threatens an established power base."[40]

The study found that Appalachia's enduring poverty stemmed in large part from a long string of policy choices that had repeatedly favored the rich and powerful. Despite the enormous wealth in coal, timber, and minerals to be found in Appalachia, little of the wealth stayed there. In addition, the land that offered up this generous bounty was subject to a startlingly low rate of taxation. In spite of Appalachia's riches, "The region's local governments remain poor. Funds are lacking for even minimal services found in other parts of the country. The reason for the disparity lies in the failure of the tax system to tax adequately and equitably the region's property wealth."[41] At least one reporter drawing a direct connection between the findings of the study and the problems that have plagued Appalachia for decades wrote: "The major owners of the region's surface and subterranean wealth . . . pay such a piddling tax sum on their holdings that local governments and the Appalachian people are chronically impoverished." Evincing the perverse satisfaction that must have been shared by many others, the reporter concluded that this study "is more comprehensive, more authoritative, more pertinent, more powerful" than those of the past. It "documents in specific and overwhelming detail . . . what the people of the region have always known in a general way": they are "not poor by accident."[42]

No one who has spent time in Appalachia could be surprised by the findings, but as Gaventa pointed out at the time, "The documentation of land ownership and taxation in county after county establishes for the first time the pervasive pattern of inequity, and this factual information should provide the basis for long-needed changes."[43]

After the multi-volume report of the task force was released in April 1981, and then again after a book-form synthesis of the study was issued in 1983, activism around land and taxation reform accelerated. In all of the states investigated, there was a great deal of initial activity to curb the power of the largest landholders and to reconsider tax systems that gave them an unfair advantage. Most of these attempted reforms did not have any long-term impact, though, and few, if any, of the Appalachian Land Ownership Study's recommendations were actually implemented. According to at least one relatively recent retrospective account of the study, it did not "result in significant structural changes in Appalachia."[44]

Nevertheless, the study continues to be widely regarded as a landmark investigation, not only because it pioneered important participatory research methods and demonstrated that such research could be rigorous, but also because it launched work in community development and democratization that continues to have an ongoing impact in Appalachia. Many of the individuals who participated in the study had life-changing experiences that continue to inform their research and activism, as was the case for Susan Williams, who went from working on the land study to becoming education director and lead archivist at Highlander Research and Education Center.[45]

John Gaventa's position at Highlander meant that the school was linked to the study in many ways. Logistically, Highlander served as the site for many of the workshops that taught citizens how to collect and analyze data. Philosophically, the Land Ownership Task Force built on many of the school's principles and traditions. In keeping with Highlander's democratic nature, the study became a true collaborative endeavor involving dozens of scholars, activists, and ordinary citizens, all working together to present a more accurate picture of the region and to use what was found to push for needed changes. According to Billy Horton, "This was first and foremost a citizen-based survey. It is a result of local people seeing a need for information and devising a plan to get it." What emerged was a rigorous and scholarly study that will be "used because the same people who needed the information and went looking for it are now ready to apply the findings in their home communities."[46]

Of course, to claim that the land study grew out of Highlander's new Appalachian focus might appear to give undue credit to Myles Horton. Actually, he played little or no role in carrying it out and, in any case, lacked the skills to coordinate such a large-scale research project. Even Highlander as an institution was itself reluctant to take explicit credit. When people claimed the study would not have been successful without Highlander's involvement, Mike Clark, who served as Highlander's director at the time, downplayed its role and praised the citizens who volunteered: "People who see problems first-hand know best how to deal with them. This is one more example of people in the region seeing a need and doing something about it. They were the ones who recognized that every problem Appalachia has . . . can ultimately be traced back to the question of who owns the land."[47]

At the same time, it is hard to imagine that the study would have been conducted in quite the same way if not for the researchers' deep and abiding understanding of Highlander's history of educating and activating ordinary people, many with little formal education. As Horton noted in his autobiography regarding the citizen volunteers in the study, "Anybody interested was welcome to help out." It didn't matter what level of education they had. They were trained in research methods and interviewing techniques at Highlander and then traveled to different localities in the six-state region to study courthouse records and to talk to local residents. People attending Highlander were encouraged to do their own research, however rudimentary, just as Highlander had always "tried to get them to learn from their own experience." For Horton, teaching people to work together to address and solve chronic problems continued to be Highlander's central mission. Certainly, in the case of the landownership study, many people were inspired to take action by what the study so convincingly documented about the roots of inequality in Appalachia.[48]

Additionally, by utilizing participatory research, the land study functioned as a program of research "consistent with Highlander's educational ideas," in which ordinary people acquired the skills to study a problem that was directly affecting them. For Horton, the parallels to self-education were clear: "Research, like education, must grow from the problems of the people, not from problems in the researcher's head."[49] Participatory research also intrigued Horton because of the emotional effect it often had on people. It gave them a "sense of their own power to do something," motivating them to use the method "to research any kind of problem."[50]

Horton was especially impressed with the broad range of people who participated in the land study and who became "so incensed by what they were finding—and so empowered by knowing how to get information—that they started organizing" even before the research had been completed.[51] For Horton, few examples better captured the claim that knowledge—in this case, rigorous, research-based knowledge—is power. He couldn't claim that he had much to do with making participatory research a Highlander tradition, but he was delighted to be a part of the process and to learn from it.

13 *Leadership and Research in Ivanhoe*

Women played prominent roles in many of the collaborations be-tween Highlander and Appalachian communities in the 1980s. One of the most successful of these collaborations featured Maxine Waller, a charismatic leader from the small mountain village of Ivan-hoe, Virginia, and Helen Lewis, a Highlander staff member and in-defatigable participatory researcher who initially visited Ivanhoe to facilitate workshops on local economic development. While there, Lewis encountered an underlying optimism and vitality among the town's women, spurring her to deepen her involvement. For two years, she maintained a regular, almost daily presence in Ivanhoe, helping to support many of the community renewal efforts that emerged. The partnership exemplified Highlander's democratic spirit, and though Myles Horton had little to do with the initiative di-rectly, it embodied everything he had ever preached in supporting adult learners to become agents of social change.

Lewis's work as a community-based participatory researcher also interested feminist theologian Mary Ann Hinsdale, who was associ-ated with the Glenmary Research Center, a missionary group seeking strategies for better meeting the needs of struggling rural communities. Over the next few years, Hinsdale would adopt many of the participatory research methods that she had learned from Lewis to better understand Ivanhoe's special challenges firsthand. Natural collaborations developed and evolved, enriching each woman's perspective on the complexities of community development. The result was a book that the three women agreed to co-author, *It Comes from the People*.[1]

Significantly, the book is dedicated to the memory of Myles Horton. Although Horton died before this book was completed, he is described in the acknowledgments as an "activist, radical hillbilly, educator and local theologian in his own right." The last sentence of the acknowledgments affirms, "Myles would have liked this book." Presumably, he would have liked it because of the conviction he so deeply shared with the three authors, that authentic and lasting social change must ultimately "come from the people."[2]

At the same time, Hinsdale, Lewis, and Waller highlight a leadership dynamic in Ivanhoe that Horton too often discounted during his most active years: the critical role played by female leaders in nurturing the quality of community life. Lewis recognized that in Ivanhoe and other similar Appalachian communities, women's patterns of leadership allowed people to respond more creatively and strategically to economic and social challenges. In particular, women functioned as leaders who put less emphasis on economic growth and more on developing people through education, heightened cultural awareness, and strong relationships.[3] Women also stood out as resourceful and resilient leaders who were often better equipped than men to adapt to problems plaguing crisis-ridden communities. Lewis thus gained recognition for work that expanded on the ideas of Freire and Horton "by incorporating feminist pedagogy and philosophy."[4]

Although Highlander under Horton's directorship had recognized female leaders such as Rosa Parks, Septima Clark, and Bernice

Robinson, it was slow to single out women as important agents of change who led in a distinctive way. According to Sue Thrasher, Horton didn't recognize the importance of the women's movement until many years after he had retired.[5] It took the active and persistent intervention of female staff, including Helen Lewis, Sue Thrasher, Juliet Merrifield, and Candie Carawan, as well as many others, to turn Highlander into a place where women leaders routinely enjoyed the same respect as men. Candie Carawan has praised Helen Lewis, in particular, for acting on the idea that "women were at the heart of many community struggles and had the stamina and skill to make a huge contribution to social change." Lewis made long-term commitments to community life, particularly in the support she gave to "women just emerging to speak out and take on issues—in a deep and engaging way."[6]

In the decade prior to the work in Ivanhoe, Lewis had become a leader in the participatory research movement, building on the work of scholars around the world and, specifically, on the collaborations that mobilized the Appalachian Land Ownership Study. In Ivanhoe, she worked closely with the community, primarily as a "familiar outsider," someone who strives "to guide, lead, teach, and facilitate in a collective way." The goal throughout "was to involve others in 'doing it,'" to emphasize "the democratic nature of the relationship, equal responsibility, horizontal communication patterns." She was careful to keep her own engagement to a minimum, while still feeling free to "express . . . opinions and argue some points." Hardly neutral or value-free, she "pushed people, especially Maxine concerning her leadership and management style."[7] Not only was this Lewis's way, it was Highlander's way as well, and it made all the difference in the quality of relationships she developed and the thoroughness of the collaborative research she was able to complete with her two colleagues and Ivanhoe's team of local activists.

At its economic peak in the 1940s, the town of Ivanhoe, Virginia, had a population of some 4,500 people supported by two large employers—National Carbide and the New Jersey Zinc Company. Significant deposits of zinc, lead, and iron greatly contributed to the town's fiscal stability during the postwar period. However, when National Carbide closed in the mid-1960s, close to 500 jobs went with it. Some fifteen years later, New Jersey Zinc also shut down, causing the loss of another 350 positions that the community had come to depend on. When an assortment of other small businesses folded because of low demand, Ivanhoe fell on very hard times.

In 1986, just as Ivanhoe seemed to be hitting bottom, a plan quietly developed by county commissioners to sell off the old industrial park previously occupied by National Carbide came to the attention of the town's residents. The people rallied, rising up to physically block the selling of the park. Driven by community leader Maxine Waller, who had become the head of a new organization called the Ivanhoe Civic League, a publicity campaign called "Hands across Ivanhoe" was set in motion. Thousands of current and former residents joined hands to dramatize their support for their town. They raised $13,000, and the industrial park survived. Even more important, the campaign brought people together and gave them new hope for the future. Waller remembered that "for the first time in years, the streets of Ivanhoe were filled with people, hugging and seeing each other again and crying together about the old memories." By putting aside previous differences and working more cooperatively than they had in years, it seemed that the people of Ivanhoe were ready to usher in a new era.[8]

Energized by the "Hands across Ivanhoe" event, the townspeople proceeded to engage in a huge clean-up of the entire community, including the industrial park, in hopes of attracting new industry.

Waller, in particular, pinned her hopes on finding a factory that could take over the cleaned-up space and save the town. As she recalled, "We wanted this wonderful factory and it had to have smoke coming out of it and it would employ the people. I just knew that was the answer for us, so I went out to get this factory. . . . I wanted this white knight waving an American flag to come down the street and have all these wonderful jobs. I wanted GM and I wanted GE and I wanted IBM to come in here and save us, but this didn't happen."[9]

WALLER COMES TO HIGHLANDER

Early on, the reborn Highlander Research and Education Center, located on a breathtaking site in New Market, Tennessee, about twenty miles east of Knoxville, was instrumental in Waller's organizing. Waller first visited Highlander in early 1987 through a Southern Appalachian Training Program fellowship. When asked what she hoped to accomplish through her Highlander experience, she said matter-of-factly that her goal was to bring a factory to Ivanhoe "because the people were tired and cold and hungry and they wanted a job. And I wanted a factory and that was it." Her fellow participants, many from towns suffering like Ivanhoe, shared their experiences, noting that sometimes a town can end up with the wrong kind of factory, including one that kills people. Waller was aghast, inquiring "Are there factories that kill people?"[10]

With Highlander's help, Waller began to read widely, learning for the first time in her life about Third World economies and how Appalachia had been colonized and exploited in ways that matched the colonization and exploitation experienced by developing nations around the world. She watched the film *Global Assembly Line* and was shocked to find out that women laborers on assembly lines in the Philippines were regularly subjected to horrific and dehumanizing working conditions, sometimes even at risk to their lives.[11]

Though new to her, the colonization theme came up often in her reading. John Tiller, a local miner whose voice informed federal testimony about the destructive effects of strip mining, said, "Appalachia was a colony in the truest sense of the word. It has all the earmarks—the absentee landlords; nothing built of permanence. You can look at the whole area—the poor roads, the poor schools, the lack of facilities—and realize that there's no solutions, and no planning for any solutions for the poor colony of Appalachia."[12] Highlander co-founder Don West called Appalachia an "exploited colonial area" whose relationship to "the mother country" was complicated but ultimately dehumanizing. Those in control "may make generous gestures now and then, send missionaries with up-lift programs . . . [and] 'superior' religion, build churches and sometimes schools. They'll do about everything—except get off the backs of the people, [and] end the exploitative domination."[13] Helen Lewis had spent years closely studying the theory that likened Appalachia to a Third-World colony. She co-edited a volume with Linda Johnson and Dan Askins, *Colonialism in Modern America: The Appalachian Case,* which greatly strengthened the claim that life in Appalachia matched the exploitation experienced by many colonized regions.[14]

Waller also learned a great deal from the people of Ivanhoe. Longtime residents who had worked for National Carbide or New Jersey Zinc began to open up to her about how hard it had been to work for these companies. They had shown little concern for workers and had no loyalty to the community. Workers remembered the environmental and physical harm caused by the mines, including a dangerously tainted water supply. They spoke out strongly against getting stuck with such employers again. Everyone seemed to agree: "We want to get the kind of industry we want, one that is good for us, and one that we can live with."[15] As Waller continued to visit other Appalachian communities, she also realized what a mistake it was to let a single industry take over a town. For residents to stay in control, they needed to diversify and not rely on an exclusive source of revenue or jobs. As she put it, "The people of Ivanhoe—if it is good or if it is bad, if it is a failure or if it is a big success—the people of Ivanhoe have to be in charge. We will do it together."[16]

In May 1987, Waller visited Highlander again, along with two other community members. Highlander staff asked, "Who's in charge in Ivanhoe? Who makes the decisions?" The Ivanhoe residents slowly realized that virtually all of the decision-making power resided in the hands of the banks, the leading businesses, and members of the professional classes, like lawyers and doctors. Those same people also controlled all the town's resources. As Waller put it, "That was an eye-opener for all of us—to find out that someone [the elite] who had played a big political part in our lives was the landlord here."[17] She suddenly wanted to learn more about the economics of towns like Ivanhoe. One of her realizations was "that none of our money stays here, so why . . . [wouldn't] we be poor?" She was coming to understand that the rent and mortgages that Ivanhoe paid almost always went to outsiders who "never bring it [back] into our town. That's the reason we are economically depressed."[18]

GETTING EDUCATED

As she became more aware and better informed, Waller recognized the practical value of gaining new skills. She didn't have a degree, but she was learning to read more deeply and analyze situations more critically. She had little formal education, but she began to say with confidence, "I've got an education all right." She noted that the so-called well educated, to whom she initially felt inferior, still made the mistake of seeing factories as the saviors of their communities. It seemed to her that many of these people were disadvantaged by a kind of "educated ignorance," which set her to wondering even more: who were the truly well educated? Such questions led her to pose even more questions, especially of those in power: "Who made these decisions and why? Did you make these decisions because it was good for us, the taxpayers, or did you make these decisions because it was good for you? And how much [in] taxes do you pay? And who buys lunch at the club?"[19]

This habit of asking questions, which Highlander practiced religiously and Myles Horton regarded as central to his own practice, became a necessary part of Waller's efforts to resist exploitation. Tom Gish, another lifelong Appalachian connected with Highlander, said,

> Had we asked the right questions and insisted on the right answers at the right time, we might have been saved from a TVA [Tennessee Valley Authority] that devastates an entire area for its strip coal; from a Corps of Engineers that builds dams simply to build dams; from a Forest Service that serves only the lumber industry; from an Appalachian Regional Commission that seeks not to assist, but to eliminate an entire culture rich in its heritage. . . . We just need help in seeing and understanding all the alternatives. Give us all the facts—and I mean all of them—and we will make the right decisions.[20]

Asking questions can, of course, also make a person unpopular. Those in power tend to spurn people who raise a lot of questions, labeling them as troublemakers or, as so often occurred in rural areas, accusing them of being Communists. Waller didn't mind. When a county administrator accused Waller of not learning to work within the system, she shot back: "If the system, the so-called system, is set up to make people cold and make people hungry and uneducated and . . . die in poverty, then God help the damn system. Because the system is wrong. There needs to be a new system because this one is not working."[21] A community household survey that emerged from Helen Lewis's participatory research revealed that many people felt the system was not working for them either. They wanted greater educational opportunity at the high school and community college level in particular, but numerous concerns also arose that the town's longtime administrators had been ignoring the best interests of the people. Citizens called for improved roads, more local stores, greater self-sufficiency, and doing more to create "a place where our kids will want to stay."[22]

The survey clearly revealed what the townspeople saw as priorities. In addition to greater educational opportunity, they wanted to address the needs of the elderly living alone, support the unemployed, and pay more attention to the needs of single mothers and their children. An analysis of the survey helped the town gain a clearer view of its strengths and led to a series of citizen-based activities designed to further fuel the social momentum that had already been created.[23]

Lewis proposed that the town create an education center to provide graduate equivalency degree (GED) classes and literacy instruction. It was an opportunity to help the town develop further despite the absence of new industry. Not surprisingly, one of the first people to take advantage of this new opportunity and to earn her GED was Maxine Waller herself. Another early attendee, Linda Copeland, found the classes difficult and quit. But a feeling inside her wouldn't let go and pushed her to return. Gradually, she realized that "the more you learn, the more you want to learn." She admitted that math had always been her hardest subject, but here, too, "the more I learned about math, the more I want[ed] to learn about math. It is just the greatest thing . . . that I have ever done for myself. . . . You just want to run out and tell the world, 'Hey, I finished school!'"[24]

Ivanhoe Tech, which is what everyone called the education center, became a hub for the community. In addition to the GED program and literacy classes, community college courses were offered that ranged from accounting to clogging, and a library appeared, thanks to the increasingly generous donations of appreciative townspeople.

The vast majority of the students enrolling in classes were women, and soon Ivanhoe Tech became a popular site for support groups and gatherings of peer tutors. Lewis noted that this "coming out" of women "growing in self-confidence and skills is a most exciting process."[25] As discussions about the economics of Ivanhoe continued and educational opportunities increased, Lewis noted that there was "less of a sense of helplessness and more of a growing sense of power about the future and possibility of" determining next steps.[26]

Ivanhoe Tech also began a Maternal and Infant Health Outreach Workers program, which created a popular course on community health. To fulfill the course requirements, enrolled students wrote and performed skits on Ivanhoe's health needs by portraying how women had historically dealt with poverty, job loss, and the like. One woman recounted a reliance on alcohol to cope; another framed a narrative about being victimized by age discrimination; still another dramatized how educational opportunities had brought new hope. A fourth woman told a story of debilitating stress, and a fifth acted out a tale of how she suffered abuse at the hands of her husband. Through the dramatizations, the students were able to identify common health problems and the resources needed to address them.[27] They were also an echo of the powerful dramatizations Zilphia Horton had helped to improvise in collaboration with struggling union organizers who resided for weeks at Highlander in the 1930s and 1940s.

THE IVANHOE HISTORY PROJECT

Perhaps Ivanhoe Tech's most ambitious and far-reaching activity was the Ivanhoe History Project, supervised by Helen Lewis. Originally conceived as a way "to reclaim" Ivanhoe's forgotten past, a worthy goal in its own right, it became much more. It became a way "to understand the changes of which Ivanhoe had been part and to use this understanding to help the community rebuild itself."[28]

Although the twelve community members who joined the project drew on a variety of materials, the core sources were the fifty-three oral histories that they collected, transcribed, and edited. By the time the project was completed, it had resulted in two 300-page volumes, *Remembering Our Past, Rebuilding Our Future* and *Telling Our Stories, Sharing Our Lives,* whose theme was the exploitation of Ivanhoe by powerful northern industrialists. For Waller, these documents were more than history; they provided clues for how to conceptualize and plan for a future in which locally owned and operated businesses would offer a more sustainable basis for promoting both economic growth and community well-being.[29]

Kay Early, an original member of the history group who was initially drawn to the project because it would be a "fun" way to study Ivanhoe's past through lectures and textbooks, was startled to learn that there would be no lectures and textbooks, and no outside experts. Instead, the group was tasked with taking full responsibility for researching and writing the history. Whatever ended up in the final product would be the result of the group's labor, commitment, and persistence. The work was sometimes monotonous and tiring, but the challenge to write the truth about the town by separating fact from fiction kept women like Early going. In the process, she discovered she could be an effective researcher, a capable writer, and a meaningful contributor to a more honest narrative about the town. In the end, one of the deep satisfactions of writing this history was the reaction of Ivanhoe's residents. They "were surprised that a book as good as ours could be compiled . . . by ordinary people."[30]

As the history was being completed, the individual members of the group responded to a crucial question: "What have you learned from the study of Ivanhoe's history that can be applied to the future development of the community?" Not surprisingly, Maxine Waller's comments set the tone for many of the responses: "In years past," Waller said, "we've relied on the land to take care of us, and it did. And

I think it's high time that we started taking care of the land." Early also expressed frustration about unchecked pollution that factories had created. Too often in the past, people had welcomed industry even if it "belched out sulfur dioxide and run the creek yellow." Her emphasis was on seeing "people grow and get closer together and have a better quality of life." What kind of factory, if any, she wondered, could support these good things? Linda Dunford, another member of the history project, suggested that a factory was not necessary to promote economic development, especially in a place like rural Virginia where recreation and hiking trails and appreciation of nature could draw people to the community and bring in new revenue. One of the few males in the group, George Lyons, agreed that a lot of important things could take precedence over industry, including better water and sewage systems, stronger schools, affordable housing, and safer, more reliable roads. Finally, one of Maxine Waller's most important lessons consisted of learning to put the value of employment into proper perspective. Of course jobs were needed, but their importance could be exaggerated. They weren't that important to school-aged youth and retired persons, for instance. Finding ways to stimulate and support these age groups also proved essential. In the case of seniors, establishing the right priorities could sometimes spell the difference between life and premature death. In short, Waller had badly underestimated the importance of accounting for the "complete age span" in assessing the community's needs.[31]

BALANCING CHARISMA AND COLLABORATION

Highlander also worked with Waller in exploring her leadership practices. People often called her a charismatic or natural leader. She once shared with a group, which included Myles Horton, that she had come to Highlander to learn to be a leader. Horton laughed, saying, "No, she came out here to teach us how to be leaders. She was a leader before she came out here. All we did was give her the space to grow with her leadership."[32] In the years before his death in January 1990, Waller had a number of occasions to converse with Horton about community leadership. He rarely gave direct answers to her questions, usually responding with further questions, such as "What does that mean to you?" or "What do you think the answer would be?" or "What do you *want* the answer to be?"[33]

Horton did, though, share his cautions about the seductions of charismatic leadership, something he understood firsthand from his days as a union organizer. He advised her to be careful about being "out front" all the time. When Horton's oral history *The Long Haul* was still in manuscript form, not long before his death, he shared it with Waller; it became her bedside reading. She took special note of his reflections on domineering leadership and his realization that he was in danger of succumbing to the temptations of being the all-powerful charismatic leader. One thing he learned from those days was that his work needed to focus on developing local leaders. As long as he dominated, he was part of an oppressive situation, preventing untested local people from emerging as leaders in their own right.[34]

Waller herself was aware of how powerful her leadership was; over time she developed a nuanced understanding of the intersections between leadership and change:

> Whatever I did wrong, with all the mistakes that I made, my leadership was necessary. I *am* a charismatic leader. But before you can have dreams become reality, you have to have a dream. And I went out on a limb and had a dream. It would've been wonderful if fifteen people could [have] come together in Ivanhoe and said, "OK, we got a dream and we are all going to step out here on a limb, and we're gonna do it," but it didn't happen that way. And it doesn't happen like that. . . . There is a time for a charismatic leader and there's a time to move on. I am all for that![35]

Waller never wanted to be the only one making things happen in Ivanhoe, but drawing others into leadership roles took time. At first, she expected people to lead as she did, in an intense, demanding, and self-motivated way. But it wasn't long before she saw the value of getting everyone to discover their own leadership styles. She wasn't sure how to encourage multiple approaches to leadership, but by creating space for others to lead, by pulling back a little, as Horton had suggested, she began to see the possibilities more clearly. One of her colleagues, Lucille Washington, was a leader who, as Waller observed, "really leads in her own calm way. She don't get up and make speeches. . . . She's not the Martin Luther King leader," but she could get up in front of a workshop group and spend half an hour "telling them how to make puppets."[36]

Waller's developing leadership style emphasized nurturance and support as much as it did serving as the chief spokesperson and most visible manager. She increasingly played the role of buffer, using her authority as a well-known and established leader to get people who had been reluctant to talk with one another to lower their guard and work as partners. She began to refer to herself as a "backseat leader" more than a "frontseat leader," someone who frequently refused to take charge in order to create a space for others to do so.[37]

For many of the people working in Ivanhoe, it was hard to imagine the community's initiatives being sustained without Waller's strong, inspiring presence. For years, she proved the one willing to put forth the effort when everyone else had given up. And she willingly absorbed criticism when the residents of Ivanhoe charged the Civic League with making mistakes: "My charismatic leadership gave me so much feelings toward it that the pain and persecution didn't affect me because I was still dreaming. . . . [A] lot of things I could tell you about now, like the threats my family lived through and things like that. If I hadn't been a dreamer, if I had been a more structured realist, I would have stopped right there. But I didn't."[38]

It is intriguing to compare Maxine Waller to Myles Horton in this respect. Horton too had to struggle with the temptation to be the outspoken, dominant leader, and in many ways his long-term success as Highlander's director has to be attributed, at least in part, to his inclination to give in to that temptation. As much as he strived to be a democratic leader, he remained the dominant figure at Highlander for decades, the one who often made the final decisions about how Highlander would be run. At a number of points in the 1970s, many of the female leaders at Highlander who were of childbearing age asked for childcare facilities and better medical coverage for families. Because Horton and then-director Mike Clark underestimated these family needs, such benefits were not provided until much later, and only then because strong women used nonviolent resistance to oppose the old policies and to demand something far more equitable and progressive. At Highlander's fiftieth anniversary celebration in 1982, Mike Clark apologized for his slowness to act on behalf of women and families, but there is no record of a similar apology from Horton.[39] Horton did eventually come to see the value of meeting these family needs, but for a long time, despite his commitment to democratic deliberations and belief in grassroots change, he blocked those changes and insisted on having the last word about Highlander's priorities.

Waller seems to have had an easier time practicing collective leadership, which she said she learned from Horton, who taught her "to accept people—to know that everybody, every person in this whole world is intelligent. Everybody has knowledge about something. It might be that somebody can't read or write, but they know how to carve, or they know how to make a quilt. Learning to accept people for themselves has been one of the most valuable lessons I have learned."[40] When Lewis brought a group from Highlander to visit Ivanhoe in May 1992, over five years after the Civic League emerged, the visitors validated the collective nature of the group's leadership. They acknowledged Waller's impact but were even more impressed that Ivanhoe was guided by "*so* many leaders." Lewis said the commitment to sharing leadership and power grew out of a sophisticated understanding of collaborative leadership in which people, especially women, didn't have to be spokespeople but could still find invaluable ways to "lead in their own way."[41]

At the very end of *It Comes From the People,* an interviewer asks Maxine Waller to explain the meaning of the word "it" in the book's title. Leading, as always, in her own way, here is how Waller responds: "The magic. It's *magic!* It's development, it's justice, it's *social* justice, it's education, it's power, it's the word, it is love. . . . The word 'it'—is everybody here in Ivanhoe. It's the golden robe of people, it is powerful, it's youth, it's faith and hope. It ain't charity. What it *ain't* is charity. What it *ain't* is apathy. What it *ain't* is oppression. What it *ain't* is sexism, racism, classism. All the 'ism's' it ain't. But it *is,* it is the people in control of their lives."[42]

14 *Myles Horton, Internationalist*

In the early 1970s, Myles Horton retired as head of the Highlander Center. As his obligations to the school gradually lessened, he developed a passion for international travel and for bringing Highlander-like programs from all over the world closer together. In *The Long Haul,* he referred specifically to this opportunity: "If there are places anywhere in the world where educational centers or research programs have been started by people who have been at Highlander and they want to have a relationship not only with Highlander but with other people who are doing similar things around the world, then I'd like to be of help in connecting them."[1]

BUILDING NEW RELATIONSHIPS IN NICARAGUA

In August 1977, Horton wrote a simple note to an American expatriate living and working in Nicaragua named Geraldine O'Leary. He wondered how he might become involved with people doing popular education in Latin America. A mutual friend had recommended O'Leary, but Horton knew nothing about her, and she knew nothing of him. To introduce himself, he wrote the briefest of notes:

Dear Geraldine O'Leary,

Since 1932, when Highlander was started in the Southern mountains, I have worked with adults struggling against poverty and repression and would like to get in touch with people in South and Central America carrying on similar activities.

Elizabeth Chase gave me your name. I would greatly appreciate hearing from you.

Sincerely yours,
Myles Horton[2]

Along with this note, he sent background materials on Highlander.

Horton was hardly new to the work of popular educators in Latin America. Just three months after the success of the Cuban revolution in 1959, Horton had contacted Cuban officials and conferred with their department of education about a possible pilot project modeled on the principles behind the Johns Island schools. He contended that immersing Cubans in an intense adult residential experience combined with deep literacy training "would contribute towards the democratization of Cuba."[3] He had also been instrumental in helping to bring thirty-five adult education specialists together at a conference in Cuautla, Mexico, in December 1962 to form the first Inter-American Adult Education Seminar. The object of the gathering was to promote greater communication among educators working throughout the Americas and to collaborate on addressing some of their common problems. The conference presented an opportunity to extend the work of the citizenship schools to countries grappling with depressed literacy rates and low levels of political participation. At the time, Mexico was having some success experimenting with literacy centers that, like the citizenship schools, did more than just teach reading and writing. They also focused on fostering civic awareness and political activism.[4]

Later, in the mid-1970s, Horton visited Peru and Brazil in hopes of creating a new inter-American adult education partnership that would be centered in the southern hemisphere. He had his heart set on supporting the partnership, but only if Latin American educators took the lead and issued invitations from a host country located outside of the United States or Canada. As he put it, he "was determined not to be a part of another North American–led gathering."[5]

Although none of these initiatives ended up having much of a long-term impact, they were illustrative of Horton's long-standing commitment to linking the struggle for freedom and social justice in the South to ongoing campaigns for liberation throughout the Americas and the world.

About a month and a half after Horton sent his letter to Geraldine O'Leary, he received a warm response. Her lengthy letter began a four-and-a-half-year correspondence between the two activists, offering a rare real-time look at how Horton developed relationships and created new projects from scratch.

Now married to a man named Edgard de Macías and going by the name Geraldine O. de Macías, she expressed delight with Horton's message and spent a good part of an evening translating the Highlander materials into Spanish for Edgard, a Nicaraguan native. She also shared the materials with a close friend who had a decades-long tie to the labor movement in Nicaragua and who responded enthusiastically. Speaking for herself and the two men, she told Horton, "We felt a certain oneness with your ideals and activities."[6]

O'Leary, a graduate of the Maryknoll Seminary in Ossining, New York, had arrived in Latin America in 1969 as a twenty-four-year-old Catholic mission sister. She moved to Nicaragua to help with relief efforts after a devastating earthquake nearly destroyed the capital city of Managua in December 1972. Within a year or two, she had fallen in love with and married de Macías, who was a carpenter by trade but also the first in his family to receive a university degree. De

Macías, a strong critic of the Somoza family dictatorship, found that his opposition to the regime made it difficult for him to hold on to a job.[7] Relying on contributions from international agencies, he helped establish and then direct an organization called INPRHU, or the Institute for Human Development, which, among other things, promoted emancipatory adult education. Like Paulo Freire, O'Leary told Horton, they used drawings, photos, and slides "to stimulate small groups to discuss a series of themes [leading] to self-awareness, self-respect and motivation to change their lives." While working with de Macías, O'Leary recognized the power of these methods and how threatening they could prove "to any oppressive regime." Working alongside her husband, she had the satisfaction of teaching adults and experiencing "the thrill of watching illiterate urban and rural people wake-up before my eyes." O'Leary and de Macías had tried to spread the Freirean methods, though they experienced only limited success because the fear of exile, torture, and death at the hands of the Somozas prevented both teachers and participants from engaging fully with the underlying liberation focus of the work.[8]

O'Leary concluded her first letter by entreating Horton and people like him to continue to call attention to the "oppressive regime that exists in Nicaragua, supported directly and indirectly by North American military aid." The human rights violations were widespread, and "U.S. government officials here are, in general, the worst examples of naïve, ignorant, uncaring and amoral officials that I have ever encountered."[9]

Soon, Horton responded. He recognized the terrible odds that O'Leary and her husband were up against but added you are "maximizing your efforts to do something about the situation, and what you are doing is very encouraging."[10] He also commented on a number of parallels between himself and de Macías, including the fact that they were both the first members of their families to graduate from college, and that their methods for working with poor rural people utilized the same problem-centered approach.

Horton commiserated with O'Leary, saying that Appalachians for too long had also been conditioned by "top-downism," in which they were fed facts and "told what to think and what to do." Taking control over their situation was not only difficult, however; it was dangerous, because doing so upset the power relations that benefited multinational corporations and absentee landlords. Horton shared his conclusion about the kinds of situations in which they both found themselves: The only solution is for people to "learn together and struggle together against repression." Otherwise, "there is no hope for democracy."[11]

To illustrate Highlander's literacy approaches, Horton told O'Leary about the citizenship schools. He attributed the success of the program to ordinary but highly motivated people, with relatively little education, making the most of their two or three months of training to steer their neighbors toward literacy and an awakened civic consciousness. He said that the program "was based on our knowledge that there can . . . never be enough full-time professionals to release the energies and stimulate the ideas and actions necessary to make democracy reality."[12] Simply put, education, like democracy, had to be everyone's business.

Three months later, on March 16, O'Leary wrote back with tragic news. On January 10, Pedro Joaquin Chamorro, the editor of *La Prensa* and a leader of the resistance movement against the Somoza regime, had been assassinated, triggering a general strike and widespread violence in the capital city of Managua and beyond. In 1974, Chamorro had become head of the Democratic Union of Liberation, which united many of the middle-class critics of Somoza into a single opposition group. De Macías had served as secretary general of the organization, so he and O'Leary had known Chamorro well, making his loss all the more poignant for them. They had erroneously seen Chamorro as "untouchable" because of his influence, popularity, and international alliances, underestimating how much of a threat he had been to the Somoza dictatorship.

In the middle of all the upheaval, O'Leary had somehow gotten hold of *Unearthing Seeds of Fire,* the 1975 book about Highlander that Frank Adams and Horton had collaborated on. She read it closely and told Horton that "it made me feel like I really knew you." She added that it reminded her of movements she had been a part of in Nicaragua, in which people of real dedication and accomplishment "allow themselves to be taught by those they are trying to help."[13]

O'Leary waited until the third page of her letter to divulge that she had given birth to a daughter—Alana Libertad Macías O'Leary—on February 10. Alana, she said, "is Irish for beautiful, Libertad for liberty because she was born during the strike and hopefully during the year of Nicaragua's liberation."[14] O'Leary would prove to be mistaken about the timing of Nicaragua's liberation, but only by a year.

On May 27, 1978, O'Leary again wrote about the protests and unrest that continued to grip Nicaragua, especially in rural areas. Her feelings were mixed: "It means living with constant uncertainty, but it is such a relief that *something* is happening." She further noted that "the eternal fence-sitters" had been shaken out of their lethargy and were finally starting to stake out positions. Included among these were parents who began "to take the side of their children" in supporting a series of school strikes. Even Protestant leaders, usually more conservative and cautious than those in the Catholic Church, officially took a position in favor of human rights and general reform. O'Leary especially lamented the poor health of young children, most of whom were suffering from hunger and inadequate nutrition.

She closed by noting that her daughter Alana was continuing to grow and that "she's so much bigger than the typical Nicaraguan that no one believes her age—and it's only because she's fed well."[15]

Then a long silence set in. For many months Horton heard nothing from O'Leary. He wrote a series of short letters, ultimately begging for a response, but none came.

In August 1979, Horton wrote to O'Leary yet again, more alarmed than ever and fearing for her safety after having not heard from her for well over a year. Horton knew that a bloody civil war had been raging in Nicaragua. The Sandinista guerillas were reported to be advancing on the capital, and Father Ernesto Cardenal, the Catholic theologian and poet, publicly defended the Sandinistas' use of violence and armed struggle as the only available alternative to Somoza's murderous death squads. In essence, he said that fighting Somoza was like fighting Hitler, which left no alternative but to employ force.[16]

Finally, after eighteen months, a short letter from O'Leary dated October 23, 1979 arrived at Highlander, interrupting the silence. The news was all about the new regime. On July 17, 1979, Anastasio Somoza Debayle resigned, and within a couple of days a new Sandinista-controlled government was installed. O'Leary's tone conveyed a combination of exhaustion and exhilaration: "We came through the war unscathed though very tired of rice and beans and very grateful when the fighting finally came to an end." O'Leary and de Macías's neighborhood witnessed very little of the actual fighting, though much of the rest of the city became a dangerous battleground for weeks. One eighteen-year-old girl from their part of town was killed and brought home to her family to be buried in the backyard. "It still seems impossible that it is all over and a new day has come for Nicaragua," O'Leary enthused. She also reported that de Macías had received an appointment as vice-minister of social welfare in the new government. It felt odd, she noted, "to have him now part of the system of government." She felt energized by the zeal and enthusiasm of the people but also recognized there "were many practical problems to be faced." She continued: "The work to do is enormous and sometimes it seems things are progressing so slowly, but at least, it is now without the fear of before." She signed off, "In the Year of Liberation 1979."[17]

Horton's follow-up letter in December began with an expression of profound relief that O'Leary, de Macías, and Alana were safe. Barely able to contain his curiosity, he then pelted O'Leary with questions about de Macías's new position, her ongoing work with INPRHU, and Paulo Freire's role in supporting the new regime's plan to raise the country's literacy level. He imagined that Freire "must be very hopeful about the possibility of liberating educational programs now that the country is rid of Somoza and the heavy hand of the United States."[18] Horton also shared with O'Leary the possibility of holding an organizational meeting at Highlander to establish a Latin America–based conference of liberal adult educators, a dream he had harbored for some time. He wanted to make sure to include INPRHU. He added that he hoped to involve Deborah Barndt, a leader with the Participatory Research Group, based in Canada, who was conducting collaborative research applying Freire's ideas. Horton and Barndt had met each other for the first time in Peru, agreeing then to find a way "to bring people together from Latin America and North America."[19]

On January 14, 1980, O'Leary wrote to share the latest news. De Macías was now vice-minister of labor in the new government, which she regarded as an especially good fit for him, though, as the work mounted, it also felt like "the ministry of constant conflicts." She, too, had been appointed to a new position in the adult education section of INPRHU, collaborating with the Ministry of Health on efforts to aid women and children. Much of this work involved preparing and delivering national radio programs to disseminate up-to-date information to new mothers about breast feeding, nutrition, and child rearing.[20]

She also told Horton that she found his idea about an interAmerican adult education conference "very interesting" and referred him to Father Fernando Cardenal (brother of Ernesto, the leader condoning violence in the liberation movement), who was in charge of the national crusade to eliminate illiteracy.

Despite improvements in government efficiency, O'Leary shared that conditions were bad. Food scarcity, inadequate medical care, and rampant unemployment continued to trouble Nicaragua, exacerbated by a spike in the number of robberies. She recounted a close call involving three masked armed men who broke into her home office, stole a number of items, then got away in a colleague's car. The police were called but never responded. O'Leary was away taping a radio program and later learned from Alana's caregiver that the child had slept through it all. Fortunately, no one was hurt, but O'Leary felt increasingly vulnerable. Characteristically, she left the most important and personal news for last. She was expecting another child and so felt "really busy."[21]

In the months that followed, Horton's hopes of traveling to Nicaragua rapidly came to fruition, thanks to O'Leary. She had put him in contact with Georgia and John McFadden, who regularly led trips to Nicaragua, and helped him reserve a coveted space on a tour scheduled from August 21 to August 30, 1980.

VISITING NICARAGUA AND THE LITERACY CAMPAIGN

As it turned out, Horton's visit to Nicaragua could not have been better timed. He had been in Nicaragua for two days when, on August 23, Nicaragua's five-month literacy campaign, one of the world's most ambitious attempts to bring literacy to hundreds of thousands of poor, unlettered people, came to an end. As a result of this first stage of the campaign, over 400,000 Nicaraguans had gained a significant foothold on literacy.[22] And some 100,000 brigadistas, or literacy workers, many of whom were middle-class urban teenagers, had acquired a completely new outlook on the challenges facing their country. As one historian put it, the literacy crusade was a monumental effort in which just about every person who could read and write was encouraged to play a role.[23]

The brigadistas had undergone extensive training to help bring their "students" to literacy. Although they were assigned to both urban and rural areas, the ones who spent time in the countryside were exposed to an especially positive and inspiring culture of possibility in which mastering country living, with the help of their new comrades, became just as important as teaching the rudiments of literacy. By providing young people from the city with the opportunity "to work and live side by side with the rural poor, the crusade made it possible for program participants to develop new friendships, commitments, and appreciation of one another."[24] For everyone involved, the sense of unity and solidarity fostered by the literacy crusade counted as a once-in-a-lifetime experience.

Not long after Horton arrived in Nicaragua, he met Valerie Miller, who was writing her doctoral dissertation about the crusade.[25] She agreed to translate for Horton as he attempted to converse with a few of the 1,500 brigadistas as they returned to the capital on the morning of August 23 in a convoy of trucks, exhilarated by their experiences as literacy workers. One of the things that struck Horton as he talked with these young people was the depth of their learning, which meant at least as much to them as the satisfactions of teaching.[26] The returning brigadistas, inspired by what they had accomplished, then joined thousands of other people converging on Managua's largest plaza to celebrate the campaign's completion. "An afternoon of parades, speeches, and songs" filled the day and "the festivities, and laughter, went on throughout the evening, and people danced until dawn."[27] It was the first great success of the revolution, a five-month journey from ignorance to knowledge, that proved what people working in unison could accomplish together. Maria Ulloa de Alaniz, who was among the thousands of new literates, recited a poem that caught

the spirit of the day. It began by bidding goodbye to useless ignorance, while affirming the profound satisfactions of the crusade:

> So I turn to all those brigadistas
>> who, with honor and glory,
>> helped us fulfill this great mission,
> We salute you.
> We toast you with congratulations,
>> because you know how to overcome this stagnation.
> You used your minds and your hearts,
>> and even risked your lives for our liberation.
> So from my grateful soul,
>> I want to bid you good-bye,
>> because now in Nicaragua,
>> ignorance has been overcome.
> Forever we have won.[28]

In the middle of this vast celebration, Horton somehow ran into
Deborah Barndt, who was on a Canadian fact-finding tour. She too
had gleefully joined the celebration in Managua's central plaza. Recalling their earlier meeting in Peru, they looked at each other and
declared: "This is where the gathering should be," meaning the convening of committed adult educators from across the Americas that
they both had envisioned.[29]

The other highlight of Horton's trip proved to be his tour group's
meeting with Father Fernando Cardenal, the director of the literacy
crusade. Cardenal called the campaign an "essential part of the revolution and designed not only to make people literate but to show the
rural people that the revolution had significance."[30] Regarding
methods, Cardenal said that "they were the best we could come up
with, but even if they had not been so good the crusade would have
succeeded since the whole country was involved."[31] Horton heartily

agreed. He knew that methods and materials helped, but they weren't the decisive thing. What mattered more was fostering a spirit of collaboration and engendering a deeply held sense that the quest for justice and equality was worth any sacrifice. A few days into his trip and after talking to many of the people who made the literacy crusade possible, Horton wrote in a note: "Method and organization is important, but even if incorrect, the crusade would have succeeded. What they were learning to read and write about and why they thought it was important was more important than any material or method." Nicaragua's literacy crusade proved unique because so many people acted on a felt responsibility to promote literacy and to commit to a campaign that went beyond educating people, as it served just as significantly "as a nation-building project."[32]

Before the meeting with Father Cardenal ended, someone asked him why so many priests held government posts. According to Horton, Cardenal replied that "the revolution was a great act of love, that he was obligated to live out his vocation of love and the revolution gave him this opportunity." Cardenal added that "the crusade was part of the revolution that hadn't killed anyone, but has killed the past."[33]

Father Cardenal's idealism and commitment were palpable, but so were the challenges facing the country. As Valerie Miller put it, Nicaraguans were charged with nothing less than giving life to the idea that "the new Nicaragua was to be egalitarian in nature, founded on citizen participation and the redistribution of power and wealth."[34] But Nicaragua also had a huge advantage in carrying out this daunting task. The exhilaration of the revolution and the sense of mutual responsibility that people felt toward one another pushed them "to work to their maximum potential." The difficulties and problems they faced were generally accepted as inevitable, and while sometimes quite disheartening, as Miller observed, they were "always providing new grist and material for their work mill and always expanding people's knowledge and understanding."[35]

For Miller, two accomplishments of the Nicaraguan National Literacy Crusade stood out. First, "by providing the poorest and most abandoned members of society with concrete literacy skills and a special awareness of their own potential and ability to express themselves, the campaign prepared people to be active, thoughtful participants in the new economic and political structures that were being formed." Second, Miller noted the importance of the experience to the brigadista literacy workers: "Their new understanding of poverty and commitment to the poor and programs of social change increased the likelihood of their future involvement in the revolutionary process as public servants and committed professionals and workers."[36]

For Horton, the opportunity to be in Nicaragua at the conclusion of the crusade fulfilled a dream of wanting "to see a country during the beginning stages of a revolution."[37] In a thank-you note to the Mc-Faddens, who led the tour, he called the trip "one of my most exciting experiences."[38] Not long after returning to the States, he also wrote O'Leary (whom he now called Gerrie) and de Macías, thanking them profusely for everything they had done to make him feel at home: "I miss you and Genevieve Paz [their second daughter] and especially Alana. I suppose it is unusual to have such a feeling of affection for an entire family, but I guess it was love at first sight for all of you. Please give a special hug to Alana for me and tell her that I am hoping to see her in my house here on the mountain."[39]

A little less than a month later, O'Leary wrote back to tell Horton how wonderful it had been to be with him, and how exhausting, too! "Frankly, Myles," she wrote, "you are a unique experience!" She added that his remarkable energy and enthusiasm had made his visit an especially rich experience for everyone involved.[40]

The August tour of Nicaragua also led to an array of new contacts. In December 1980, Edgard de Macías visited Highlander—O'Leary couldn't get away—and was delighted by the reception he received.

He enjoyed exploring ways to enhance communication between "grassroots community groups in Nicaragua and Appalachia."[41] Learning about Highlander's history, its current activities, and its participation in a struggle that resembled Nicaragua's also left a deep impression.[42] Those gathered envisioned a plan to have Highlander staff visit Nicaragua and for Nicaraguan activists to meet at Highlander sometime in 1982. Soon thereafter, Deborah Barndt invited Horton to be part of her group's 1981 conference and to take part in a session on popular education and research centers. She also asked Francisco (Chico) Lacayo, Nicaragua's new vice-minister of adult education and assistant to Father Cardenal during the literacy crusade, to co-present with Horton. Barndt praised them both for "their wealth of experience in the use of community-based education and research for social change" and urged them to take advantage of a full planning day that she had blocked out so that they could "coordinate their input for the conference." It is likely that Horton asked her to do this, as he was eager to meet Lacayo and develop a closer relationship with him.[43]

The subsequent conference in Toronto delivered on everything Horton had hoped for. While there, Horton and Lacayo spent a good deal of time together trading stories, making plans, and enjoying each other's company, though Horton was careful throughout always to let the charismatic Lacayo play the starring role. Horton wanted to work with a Latin American leader who would take the lead in building an adult education network. With Lacayo, he had found his man. He assured Horton that Highlander could be involved in helping the revolution move forward by bringing like-minded activists and researchers together, both in Appalachia and in Nicaragua. Before parting, Lacayo delighted Horton by asking for a copy of *People of the Cumberland,* an old Elia Kazan film about Highlander's efforts in the 1930s to support downtrodden workers and adult learners that Lacayo wanted to show to people back home to help them understand Highlander's history and mission.[44]

In the meantime, O'Leary worried about the direction of the revolution. Not long after the initial excitement of the literacy crusade had died down, the tone of her letters changed. They lacked her earlier hopefulness as O'Leary recounted the failure of the Sandinistas to deal respectfully and nonviolently with the dissent being expressed by many people living on Nicaragua's east coast, near the small city of Bluefields. Some North Americans tried to use these failures as a pretext for condemning the revolution, but O'Leary was completely unsympathetic to such critiques and continued to condemn U.S. foreign policy. Horton tried to help her understand that the reemergence of repression was entirely to be expected, partly due to the growing pains of a new regime and partly due to a failure to sustain an ongoing program of radical popular education. Paulo Freire, who also happened to be consulting with Nicaragua, had a similar analysis. He acknowledged that the path toward transformative change rarely proved to be smooth, affirming that when a new regime "hardens into a dominating bureaucracy," as it so often does, then "the humanist dimension is lost and it is no longer possible to speak of liberation."[45]

Horton insisted that the difficulties, missteps, and failures weren't reasons to reject the revolution but to further embrace its positive aspects, such as the literacy crusade. Similarly, dysfunction should not be met with resignation but with an even greater commitment to collaboration and community-based solutions, which for him included forming global partnerships with like-minded freedom fighters. Just as the crusade had demonstrated to much of the country that positive change could occur if people remained open to the general populace's abilities, so could successes be wrested out of setbacks as long as there was no compromise on democracy.

Still, O'Leary's concerns were understandable. In the months that followed, the repression that plagued Nicaragua's east coast seemed to spread, and much of the egalitarian spirit associated with the first year of the revolution waned. In a letter to Horton, O'Leary commented on the deteriorating relationship between the west and the east, stressing that "the lack of communication and suspicions is creating a real bottleneck." These ongoing tensions suddenly spilled over into her family's personal life when in January 1982 de Macías was removed from the position of vice minister of labor. Never given a satisfactory reason for the change, O'Leary suspected that de Macías's criticism of the way in which relations with the east coast had been handled caused some to doubt his loyalty. Attempts by the United States to destabilize the new Nicaraguan regime also contributed to rising suspicions among the country's leadership. Exasperated, she added, "The foreign policy of the U.S. is just so incredibly stupid."[46]

Less than a month later, Horton responded sympathetically, shocked by the regime's decision to dismiss de Macías. Echoing O'Leary's analysis, he commented, "I'm afraid the fear of an invasion by the United States has made some of the leadership there act unwisely, and perhaps irrationally at times. I think that's part of our efforts to destabilize the Nicaraguan government."[47]

Then in June 1982, disaster struck. As victims of a "classic smear campaign" in which they were labeled enemies of the revolution and threatened with violence, de Macías was forced to seek asylum in Venezuela and Costa Rica, while O'Leary resettled in the United States. She traveled to Washington, D.C., to confer with solidarity groups, church people, and the Nicaraguan embassy in an attempt to uncover the Reagan administration's role in what appeared to be a conspiracy against de Macías and herself. She concluded sadly that "fear of expressing an opinion is once again a Nicaraguan reality." After all she had been through, however, she recognized that a new beginning was always possible and pledged to continue the fight for "a truly free Nicaragua." She signed off, proud of what she had been a part of and reaffirming that "freedom is not an empty word, it is a real, day-to-day struggle, and I feel privileged for the last thirteen years that I have lived in Central America and shared in this struggle."[48]

A few weeks later, de Macías and O'Leary reunited in Washington, D.C., and formed a nonprofit called El Nuevo Éxodo, or the New Exodus, which focused on addressing the challenges faced by political refugees and supporting worldwide efforts to protect the rights of all exiled persons.[49]

TOWARD AN INTERNATIONAL NETWORK OF ADULT EDUCATORS

In the meantime, Horton continued to proceed with plans to form an international network of adult educators to gather at a major conference in Nicaragua sometime in 1983. He was hardly alone in pursuing this objective. John Gaventa, Juliet Merrifield, Helen Lewis, Sue Thrasher, and other Highlander staff members contributed significantly to making this meeting a reality. In a fundraising letter, Gaventa cited a 1980 meeting in Yugoslavia of the International Council of Adult Education that predated Horton's visit to Nicaragua and at which Gaventa and Lewis first broached the idea of a gathering with Latin American educators. The goal, as Gaventa put it, was to "form new networks of people whose work is rooted in local struggles but whose contacts and information span across regional and national borders."[50]

In July 1982, Horton and Gaventa both accepted invitations from Budd Hall on behalf of the International Council on Adult Education to attend its October conference and general assembly in Paris.[51] There, Horton joined the Policy Working Group on Literacy and "served on the subcommittee that formulated the policy statement on literacy in the industrial countries." He also attended some unscheduled meetings and contributed to the Workshop on Evaluation and Participation. Most important, he served on a committee with Gaventa to prepare for the long-awaited international conference in

Nicaragua. They envisioned a focus on that country's post-literacy campaign activities and the work of popular educators generally in promoting literacy and raising civic consciousness. The committee also decided that a Planning Committee would meet at Highlander about six months prior to the Nicaragua gathering to work out a variety of organizational details.[52]

For Horton, the International Council on Adult Education meeting ended memorably. The general assembly gave special recognition to Highlander on its fiftieth anniversary and invited Horton to say a few words. Before departing, delegates from 110 countries joined hands and sang "We Shall Overcome."[53]

In March 1983, Highlander, guided by Gaventa and Horton, hosted the Planning Committee, which was responsible for drawing up an agenda that would reflect the priorities for the conference in Nicaragua, set for late August and early September and now officially dubbed "The International Popular Education Conference for Peace." All of the planners shared the same assumption, that "the problems faced by communities in Appalachia and the South are interrelated with those of developing countries."[54] Accordingly, the proposed agenda items included gaining clarity on what constitutes popular education, strengthening connections between North American and Central American popular educators, and building new partnerships among their respective organizations.[55]

The conference, held in Managua, proved a rousing success. In addition to Horton and Gaventa, Highlander sent Sue Thrasher and some of the school's new leadership, including Jane Sapp. Paulo Freire attended as well, praising Nicaragua for developing "a program of the people for educating the people." Horton also expressed admiration for Nicaragua's achievement, saying, "I don't know of any other people in the world who are so conscious of undertaking the responsibility for educating their brothers." For Highlander staff, Nicaragua's efforts to promote adult education were inseparable from the larger project of building a responsive nation. "In a pro-found way," Highlander's next report shared, "we saw that the com-mitment to an adult education process that is democratic and em-powering is but part of a broader commitment to mass participation of people in decisions about all elements of their society—their land, their culture, their work, their government."[56]

The conference helped put Highlander at the center of a North American/Central American popular education network. Sue Thrasher later singled out Horton for helping organize the 1983 exchange and for taking the lead on efforts that "led to further exchanges and the development of an international program com-mittee at Highlander." She also praised him for persistently advocat-ing "that any work around issues of social change and justice in this country had to be within an international context."[57] In a recent in-terview, Thrasher added that "amazing connections were made over the years, but none of that would have happened had Horton not pushed for that engagement."[58] Others have similarly commented, "The 1983 meeting at Highlander and the later conference in Nicara-gua served as the culmination of decades of effort by Horton and Highlander to establish networks of progressive adult education throughout the world."[59] As for Horton himself, the International Conference on Popular Education and Peace had to have been espe-cially satisfying for forging so many new connections among adult educators in the Western Hemisphere. By the late 1980s, Horton could claim that fifteen to twenty exchange visits among people in the United States and Central and South America had occurred as a direct result of the 1983 gathering in Managua.[60]

TWICE MORE IN NICARAGUA

The success of the conference set the stage for Horton to make two subsequent visits to Nicaragua. In 1984, under the auspices of a group called Witness for Peace, Horton was invited to be part of an unofficial thirty-member delegation tasked with observing the first elections held in Nicaragua since the Sandinistas had assumed power in 1979. Although the Sandinistas easily won the election, representatives of Witness for Peace reported that the elections were "fair and free." According to one observer, who represented a leading human rights group, "All seven parties were given free television and radio time and campaign expenses," and all parties vigorously campaigned without fear of reprisals. A lively press openly critiqued all of the candidates, including those running as Sandinistas.[61]

Horton's perspective on these first elections emphasized Nicaraguans' unique commitment to learning. Their approach to devising a free and fair election process involved an ambitious inquiry in which countries from around the world were asked to share their election procedures so that the best aspects of each could be incorporated into Nicaragua's approach. Like so many others who observed or took part in the 1984 elections, Horton found them to be equitable and unbiased. To him, this signified Nicaragua's struggle to continue to move toward a more open and democratic society, even as that struggle was frequently sabotaged by what Geraldine de Macías called the "incredibly stupid" policies of the United States.[62]

Still, challenges existed, as was underscored by an experience Horton had in a tiny farm community during the election process. It was not far from the Honduran border. He met a handful of popular educators who had recently buried one of their colleagues whose throat had been cut by the Contras, U.S.-backed opponents of the revolution. As he stared at the simple gravesite, Horton grew angry, "knowing that our government was really responsible for that man's death." But he also took heart from the educators' courage and resilience and from "the fact that there were people . . . who were continuing to do popular education" and who were so dedicated to perpetuating this work that "they had committed their lives to it."[63]

Horton made a final visit to Nicaragua in the winter of 1988, focusing on the city of Bluefields on the east coast, the area that had experienced much strife when the Sandinistas first came to power. Isolated and different in culture and demographics—most were black and spoke "their own brand of English"—Bluefields residents had resisted Sandinista control and sought to assert their cultural and political autonomy. During his visit, they asked Horton for help in raising funds to maintain their independence, and specifically to restore some of their historic buildings. Horton's visit once again allowed him to witness a moment in history that would have a long-term impact, one that ultimately resulted in a policy of semi-autonomy for regions on the east coast dominated by indigenous peoples and African descendants. Horton's support for the area's goals derived primarily from his commitment to democracy and to the idea that the people of any place, whether from Appalachia, Bluefields, or anywhere else, should enjoy the right to practice self-rule, self-education, and self-determination.[64]

15 *We Make the Road by Walking*

TWO KINDRED SPIRITS

Today, Myles Horton and Paulo Freire are widely acknowledged as two of the most important radical adult educators of the twentieth century. But this recognition, especially for Horton, came late in life. When Freire won praise for his book *Pedagogy of the Oppressed* in the early 1970s, many people saw the similarities between the two educators' approaches for the first time, and Horton enjoyed new recognition as Freire's peer. Numerous invitations to adult education conferences and events followed, and at one of these conferences, held in Chicago in 1973, Horton met Freire. They saw each other again a number of times in the years that followed in places like New York, California, and Nicaragua.

At a conference in California in the summer of 1987, honoring his recently deceased wife, Elza, Freire proposed that he and Horton "speak a book."[1] Horton's first reaction was skepticism, accompanied by a hearty laugh and then a quick jab at Freire's prolific output: "Well, you've got about 10 or 15 talk books already." But Freire was serious. "I want to do one with you. We've got to do one together." Still in doubt, Horton teased, "What do you want to do that for?" Freire replied, "Well, you know, you say things in different ways from the way I say them." Freire went on, "We talk about the same things and have the same philosophical background. We have the same educational ideas arrived at independently." Freire knew that a lot of his ideas had been misunderstood; this might be a way to make them more accessible. "Maybe, if we talk together," Freire joked, "I would talk more like you." Horton surrendered: "I'd be pleased to do it."[2]

Sue Thrasher, Horton's longtime colleague, recognized the historic significance of bringing them together. With the assistance of colleagues at Highlander and the nearby University of Tennessee at Knoxville, she planned a week-long meeting for the two in Tennessee in December 1987.[3] It was an especially difficult time for Freire, who continued to grieve the loss of his wife. John Peters, a professor at the University of Tennessee and one of the editors of the volume, picked Freire up at the airport in Knoxville to go to Highlander and recalled how heartbroken he still seemed.[4]

The two educators met at Horton's Highlander home to begin their extended conversation. In her remembrance, Helen Lewis set the scene: "They settled in around the fireplace, with the Great Smoky Mountains as a backdrop. Some friends and members of Highlander staff listened and acted more as clarifiers and prompters than as interviewers. Both men were great storytellers so those of us who sat with them mostly listened as they got to know each other, shared their experiences, questioned each other, compared their own development, change of ideas and educational philosophy."[5] The published "talking book" is dominated by extended monologues, especially from Horton, with relatively little back and forth questioning. But what emerges are stories and insights that do not appear in any other publication, adding a great deal to the historical record. In this sense, the finished volume, which was completed only a few days before Horton succumbed to brain cancer at the age of eighty-four, is especially important in documenting Horton's "last will and testament with respect to his ideas concerning adult education and social change."[6]

Lewis recalled that those who were present during the dialogue witnessed the flowering of a "deep and lasting friendship." Despite their occasional differences, the two men discovered striking similarities in their approaches to education and their analyses of complex social situations. The more they talked, the more their respect for one another grew, and the more they deepened their emotional ties to one another. As Lewis said, "It was like watching two old men falling in love."[7]

At the beginning of the chapter called "Formative Years," Horton led off with two important caveats. First, because his perspective would be a personal one, he recognized it might sometimes appear "that there were no other perspectives" and that somehow he worked largely alone. But, in fact, nothing could be further from the truth. Over the years, he collaborated closely with a wide range of educators and activists with their own unique points of view who added immeasurably to Highlander's success. He could never have done it alone, nor had he ever wanted to. Second, because his ideas had undergone significant change over time, what might look like inconsistencies actually reflected his commitment to continuous learning and a ceaseless pursuit of new experiences and challenges. Horton affirmed "there is a consistency in the sense that the direction is the same."[8] He also said, though, that he was as proud of his inconsistencies as he was of his consistencies, hearkening back to one of his early mentors, John Dewey, and the notion that all knowledge is "provisional," subject to change through experience. Freire signaled agreement. All human beings, Freire asserted, must act and make decisions in light of an assumption of their own incompleteness, an incompleteness that sets in motion "a permanent process of searching" and of staying curious that is absolutely indispensable for people "to continue to be or to become."[9]

Horton continued with stories of coming of age in rural Tennessee. Freire also briefly shared some of his early experiences growing up in Recife, which was and still is a large, mostly poor city on the easternmost point of Brazil. Like Horton's, Freire's family endured considerable economic hardship, especially at the beginning of the Great Depression. Like Horton, Freire too had firsthand experiences with going hungry. Freire had painful memories of desperately craving food and not having any way to alleviate his suffering. Later, he felt driven to fight for change to make it less likely that people would experience such deprivation in the future.

Freire's memories of learning to read involved mastering specific words his parents had carefully selected for him. They were words that he could relate to easily because they described his surroundings and grew directly out of his concrete childhood experiences. Later, when Freire became a teacher, he adopted the same strategy of having pre-literate students begin by mastering familiar everyday words from their immediate environment. Though he had fond memories of learning to read, Freire remembered entering secondary school rather late for his age and suffering because he had "such difficulty understanding the normal and bureaucratic lessons of my school." He felt "stupid" throughout this period of his life and only gradually gained confidence in his abilities, thanks to the support of a few sympathetic teachers.[10]

Freire's father died in 1934 when he was thirteen years old, putting additional strain on the family's finances. Just as the Hortons suffered when Perry, Horton's father, lost his job as county clerk, the Freire family was plunged into a world of economic uncertainty in which food became scarce and school was a luxury. His mother could no longer afford to pay tuition, so she searched for a free academy he could attend. It was a great day for the family when they found a school that was both free and academically strong. Soon, Freire became an avid reader whose "physical connection" to the text was so powerful that he often could not tear himself away from reading even when it was late at night and his mother implored him to put down his books and go to bed.[11]

As had been the case for Horton, what fascinated Freire most about reading good books as he got older was the moment when his reading opened up a window on reality, clarifying his understanding of the world he was experiencing. Reading books was most reward-ing when they shed light on the problems of everyday life and the larger structural context in which those problems arose. This is what he meant when he famously claimed that one of the most important goals of all education is to establish the relationship between *read-ing words and reading the world.*[12]

Freire also touched on his foundational dream of becoming a teacher, a dream he had held throughout much of his childhood. He did not know what he would teach; he just knew he loved the idea of teaching. Later, he realized this love related to a deep desire to gain knowledge and to learn, especially by asking questions. His vivid memory of playing street soccer with his *companheiros,* many of whom had virtually nothing to eat, prompted a haunting recurring question: "Why is it possible that some children eat and some others don't?"[13] Horton had noted a strikingly similar dilemma during his formative years, when he wondered how it could be that some people "work so hard and get so little, and for somebody else to have so much."[14] That question and others like it kindled Freire's interest in using critical pedagogy to create a different kind of society, one in which his friends "could eat, could study, could live free."[15]

Once he became a teacher skilled in the rudiments of Portuguese grammar and syntax, Freire worked hard to keep the freedom of the students and his own authority as a teacher in balance by practicing respect. He found that students enjoyed his classes and caught themselves learning largely because he respected "their mistakes, their errors, and their knowledge." It became essential for Freire to recognize the extent of his students' knowledge, to appreciate that knowledge, and to build on it to help them learn what they needed to know, just as Horton had striven to do at Highlander.[16]

Another striking similarity between these two radical educators concerned the influence of their spouses. Freire spoke movingly of Elza's remarkable ability as a teacher and how much he learned from her. Elza's artistic sensibility showed Freire that he had the heart of a teacher. His knack for asking interesting, searching questions and his passion for knowledge convinced her that Freire should devote his life to education. Of course, having a calling to teach did not protect Freire from making mistakes. One night after he had a long meeting with some workers from Recife, a meeting that Elza also attended, she explained that he still had a lot to learn about how to be in dialogue with the workers. The purpose of the meeting was to draw out the workers, to help them make sense of their situation, not to supply them with all the answers. He was wrong to "give the answers *and* the questions," she chided. Not only that, she added, he used the language of the university. "You cannot grasp the interest of the people while speaking with this language you spoke."[17]

In Horton's case, long before he met and married Zilphia, he knew he wanted to be an adult educator who collaborated with people and helped them develop solutions to their most pressing problems. Zilphia's love for social gatherings and her talent for music and drama rounded out Horton's teaching, endowing Highlander with a vitality and community spirit it had lacked before her arrival. Without her, Highlander might have failed. Her lively, positive spirit infused every workshop. She inspired thousands to come back for more. She probably did more than anyone to make Highlander an emotionally memorable experience as well as an intellectually stimulating one.

During Freire's visit, Highlander hosted community members one evening; Maxine Waller was among the honored invitees. In the course of the gathering, everyone was invited to draw and present pictures representing how their communities and Highlander related to each other. Waller's included a goat in a rocking chair up on the hill looking down on a Highlander workshop. She named all the parts of the picture and how they helped her community, saving the goat for last: "And this here is Myles Horton."[18] A few visitors who didn't know Horton very well feared he might be offended, but his reaction was typical: "He just died laughing; I mean, he *roared* laughing."[19] Freire was delighted to see Horton's ability to laugh at himself. Even more, he loved that using art, expression, and the analogy of a goat "occasionally butting in to push for more analysis" confirmed what he had always thought was true—"that the methods he used with peasants in Third World countries also worked in the First World, too."[20]

The two men held decidedly different views on one thing: the advantages and disadvantages of working outside the system versus working inside the system. Highlander chose to work outside the system to avoid being co-opted by official schooling and to have more freedom to experiment. The downside of this approach was that for a long time, other educators did not recognize Highlander staff as their peers. For years, people from Highlander were labeled "agitators," "activists," and "organizers," not "educators."[21]

Freire saw things differently. First, even though an educator might choose to work outside the "subsystem" of official schooling, the overall political, economic, and social system—of which the school subsystem is a part—still constrains the educator. Freedom remains limited. Second, the educator generating a "free space" outside the realm of official schooling, but still necessarily inside the system as a whole, resembles the educator attempting to work creatively within the education subsystem. That, too, can be done, and, in Freire's view, must be done to bring about meaningful change. As he put it, the ideal struggle gets carried out on two fronts, "the one internal to the schooling system and the one external to the schooling system."

Freire conceded that working outside the subsystem of school allowed more room to exercise creativity and discretion, but that "every time we can occupy some position inside of the subsystem, we should do so."[22]

Their differences stemmed partly from disagreements about how to make change and partly from contrasts in their experiences. Horton proudly remained outside the subsystem of schooling his entire life. Freire, on the other hand, endeavored, off and on, to pursue change both as an outside agitator and as an inside official for whatever elected government he was serving. He regarded fears of being co-opted as unwarranted. If the system moves to co-opt someone or something, Freire believed, that's a sign that the work is threatening the status quo. If the system ignores people, that is a sign nothing is happening. Better to be doing something transgressive and thus become, as Freire put it, "an object of co-optation."[23]

In the final section of their talking book, the two educators returned to some of the experiences that inspired them to join the social justice struggle. Horton recalled riding the Cumberland Mountain train, a pastime he loved. One day, as the train lumbered along, he spotted a desperately sad-looking teenage girl standing on the porch of her broken-down home, too poor to board the train, looking depressed and utterly resigned to a life without hope of any prospect for the future. He remembered many people in Appalachia with such despair in their eyes and no obvious way to overcome the structural barriers that had taken away their hope. These experiences made Horton want to do something for the communities of people kept down by unjust conditions. Whatever he did, Horton realized, had to address the structural barriers that prevented so many from reaching their potential. He gradually discovered that the kinds of interventions he was called to make centered on validating people's experiences, opposing racial discrimination, deepening learning, and imparting the confidence to act in concert with others.

Freire's reflections paralleled Horton's. He recalled how the love of his parents sustained him. They created "a very warm and open atmosphere" in the household where he and his siblings were able to grow and come to understand themselves more deeply. This sense of wholeness was further strengthened through exposure to Christianity, but especially a Christianity that had direct implications for how one acts and shows respect toward others. When Paolo was only six years old, he had become angry with his religiously observant grandmother for showing prejudice toward a black woman. Even at that early age he complained to his parents that her disrespectful behavior violated the teachings of the Catholic Church. His parents listened to him sympathetically as he unleashed his rage. Much later, Freire's mother revealed that when he was young, his father predicted that someday "this boy will become a subversive." Freire was proud of that prediction, because his father knew even then that his son's anger grew from a spirit of justice.[24]

Freire's last words in the talking book were about embracing both Jesus Christ and Karl Marx, two major influences on Myles Horton as well. Freire said that when he first went to work with poor people in Recife, he did so because he believed he was doing what the Church expected of him, even what Christ would have wanted. But once he got to Recife, he also saw the need to read and study Marx, because the problems of the poor were so immense, the domination and exploitation so widespread, the social and economic system so clearly structured to work against the interests of the least well off. But upon adopting Marx, he did not put aside Christ. He continued to see both as essential to his work.

While both men were anchored by deep theological and economic justice traditions, neither operated on a day-to-day basis from those lofty ideals. As Freire noted, he recognized that his relationships with people made the greatest difference to him and gave him the greatest satisfaction. He went to be with the poor people of Recife because of his affection for them. He knew it was necessary "to be-lieve in the people . . . to laugh with the people" in order to learn with them and grow with them. He "did not have any other door but to love the people."[25]

As the dialogue came to an end, Horton asked those gathered to listen to a short poem: "Go to the people. Learn from them. Live with them. Love them. Start with what they know. Build with what they have. But with the best of leaders, when the job is done, when the task is accomplished, the people will all say, 'We did it ourselves.'"

It was written by Lao Tzu, the ancient Chinese philosopher, Hor-ton noted with delight. "It's taken a long time for people to come to know these ideas, hasn't it?" He added, "The ideas are exactly what Paolo and I have been talking about."[26]

The talking book process revitalized both men. For Horton, who was then eighty-two years old and had published relatively little, the dialogue with Freire was both liberating and affirming. It provided him with a rare outlet for expressing his ideas and gave him new mo-tivation to finish his autobiographical collaboration with Judith and Herbert Kohl, eventually titled *The Long Haul.* For Freire, the talking book with Horton helped him to deal with the profound grief arising from the loss of his wife Elza. Being with a man like Myles Horton, who was Freire's senior by sixteen years but who retained vigor and lust for life, enlivened him. "At Highlander," Freire said, "I began to read and write again." Freire later returned to politics, becoming the minister of education for the city of São Paulo when a popular social-ist mayor was elected to office.[27]

A FINAL MEETING

Highlander recorded all of the words that Horton and Freire spoke; John Gaventa, Brenda Bell, and John Peters were tasked with editing the taped material and reshaping it into a narrative with coherent themes. Because the dialogue was spontaneous and did not follow any pre-set pattern, it took some time to organize the week of conversations. Nearly two years passed before the manuscript was ready for Freire's and Horton's final edits. By then, December 1989, a great deal had transpired. Horton, who had undergone surgery for colon cancer in 1987, had become very sick because the cancer had spread throughout his body and to his brain. Freire, on the other hand, was active again in Brazilian politics and had become a close supporter of presidential candidate Luiz Inácio Lula da Silva, known as Lula. If Lula won the general election, Freire would be appointed to the ministry of education and would not be able to return to Highlander to do the final edits on the talking book. As it turned out, Lula lost, which was a setback for Freire and for progressive reform in Brazil. But Freire was free to return to Tennessee, this time with his second wife, Anita. When he did, he encountered a greatly weakened Horton, for whom it was a considerable effort to speak and to participate in the final editing session. But according to those present, Horton somehow found the energy to work with Freire, and they concurred that the manuscript was ready and that they were happy with it.

John Gaventa recalls that it was always difficult to facilitate a conversation between Freire and Horton, because Freire often invoked theory and Horton typically resorted to storytelling. These difficulties multiplied as Horton's illness worsened and his words became increasingly difficult to understand. But Gaventa said that it was also "very moving to be able to bring those two people together. If there's anything I relish most from my experience with Myles, it was to play a role in making this possible. I was only one. Sue [Thrasher] and others made huge contributions, but to be part of that team was such a pleasure."[28]

Upon seeing Horton's condition, Freire became less interested in editing their book and more focused on simply spending time with his dear friend. The two ate together, admired the beautiful view of the Great Smoky Mountains, watched the birds hover around the feeder and then suddenly take flight. Freire said, "It is sad, but dying is part of living. It is wonderful that Myles may die here. Dying here is dying in the midst of life."[29]

Three days after seeing Freire for the last time, Myles Horton lost consciousness. A week later, he passed away. Freire paid tribute to his friend by speaking of the honor of being in dialogue with him. He called him "an incredible man" whose history and presence "is something which *justifies* the world."[30] A few months later, Temple University Press published their talking book with the title *We Make the Road by Walking: Conversations on Education and Social Change.*

Epilogue

REFLECTIONS

Myles Horton died on January 19, 1990, after struggling with cancer for two and a half years. Despite the tenacity of the disease, Horton refused, for a long time, to bow to its fury. According to the summer "Highlander Reports" from 1989, Horton kept a full schedule and remained forward-looking in everything he did, staying active almost to the end. In particular, he continued to link Highlander's work to the developing world by supporting exchanges between grassroots leaders in Appalachia and freedom fighters across the globe.[1]

Before finally succumbing to the cancer, Horton was helped enormously by the many gifts that came to Highlander to cover healthcare costs and to ensure that he "would finish his life at home, as productively and comfortably as possible." The contributions had made it possible to finish both of his ambitious book projects, his autobiography, *The Long Haul,* and the talking book with Paulo Freire.[2] Sue Thrasher recalled that Horton "battled cancer with the same ferocity that he had battled all of life's other injustices, and in doing so, continued to teach all of us around him about the value of life."[3] Upon returning from a trip to Montana in the late summer of 1989 that he took with Horton, John Peters recalled a rare moment of despondency when Horton suddenly volunteered, "I feel like I'm dying from the ground up."[4]

Myles Horton was buried in the Summerfield cemetery, just a few steps away from the original Highlander Folk School site. His remains were placed next to those of Zilphia, his parents, Elsie and Perry, and his paternal grandfather, Mordecai Pinkney Horton.

A plan to honor Horton with a special memorial at Highlander during the weekend of May 5–6 was announced almost immediately. People arranged to journey to Tennessee from all over the United States and the world to share their memories. At the height of what turned out to be an unseasonably cold May weekend, well over a thousand people who had known and loved Myles Horton assembled on Highlander's hill to celebrate his life and to draw on the strength of his legacy as a springboard for even bolder work ahead. They sang songs, told stories, recollected successes, shared the emboldening effects of failure, and recounted how they found the resilience to carry on in the face of racism, class hatred, and fierce opposition.

When the time came to shine the spotlight on the memory of Horton, Rosa Parks spoke of his influence on people: "He was the leader who kept us going so many times when we doubted that we would bring about a better life. . . . We will never forget Myles Horton. . . . He loved us all. We will continue to love the spirit he left behind."[5]

Close friend, noted participatory researcher, and Highlander board member Deborah Barndt recalled trying to cheer up an ailing Horton by bringing him a balloon decorated like a globe. Floating the balloon in his direction, Barndt joked, "There, now you can have the whole world in your hands." Flicking it back without missing a beat, Horton objected, "I don't want it. I want the people to have the earth in their hands."[6]

Maxine Waller, the community leader from Ivanhoe, had first come to Highlander believing that the center was doing God's work. She was surprised when there wasn't much talk about God. Perplexed, she started to do some research about Horton's background. She learned that he had started out in the church "and then found out that was where God's work wasn't being done. So Myles started doing God's work, and it was called a lot of names."[7] Waller concluded shrewdly, "Myles Horton was a man of God and he did God's work. All my life I've slept with the Bible. Now I sleep with the Bible and *The Long Haul*."[8]

Bernard Lafayette, who first encountered Horton at a pre-SNCC workshop at Highlander in 1960 and remembered him as one of the few white men in his life who taught him "to doubt your first impression, to think about what you think," inquired, "Where do we go from here?" His answer: to give birth to Highlanders all over the country. "We must transplant Highlander."[9]

AN EVEN BOLDER FUTURE

Lafayette's call to "transplant Highlander" had already been built into the weekend. Part of the program focused on how to move Highlander's traditions and practices into the next decade. Discussions centered on strategizing for a future in which the "environment, youth empowerment, leadership, culture, labor, popular education, and women's struggles" would stand at the forefront.

One of the highlights of the gathering was the announcement by the board of directors that a Myles and Zilphia Horton Fund for Education and Social Change had been established to honor the two educators and support a variety of activities and programs "to embody and promote the ideals of education for a just and democratic society" for which the couple stood. The Board also announced that it was creating the Myles and Zilphia Horton Chair for Education and Social Change to support visiting educators from around the world who espouse and practice the principles of participatory democracy and critical adult learning.[10]

In the year that Myles Horton left the earth, Highlander Center remained remarkably busy and productive. At first, people wondered what would happen to Highlander without Horton's abiding presence. Sue Thrasher said that although he "embodied the idea of Highlander more than any other individual, it is also true that Highlander was never a one-person operation. From the beginning, he worked in concert with others."[11] So the work continued.

John Gaventa, who had recently become director of the school, claimed that 1990 "was the busiest at the center in the 15 years since I've been around, with over 60 workshops and gatherings, involving some 2000 people from 40 states and a dozen countries." The projects that drew especially large numbers of participants focused on environmental concerns and included dozens of "Stop the Poisoning" study groups designed to build "a more broadbased and racially diverse movement" and to oppose the illegal dumping of toxic waste and other actions harmful to the local environment. Working with communities to help them cope with rapid change due to "global economic restructuring" became another Highlander priority. Learning how to respond to plant closings, increased unemployment, and the loss of workers' rights in low-income communities also stirred significant interest.[12]

In addition, finding ways to support youth through difficult transitions led to a series of "youth Citizenship Schools" that included workshops on how to resist and change educational systems that "disempower young people." Such grassroots leadership development remained an important part of Highlander's work and was carried out primarily through the center's innovative Southern Appalachian Leadership Training program, which worked closely with hundreds of emerging leaders. Finally, the international networks that Highlander had helped grow as a way of advancing the work of adult educators across the globe thrived in part because of the work Horton had done in the last years of his life.[13]

At the end of his famous two-hour interview with Horton, Bill Moyers asked: "How do you see yourself, Myles Horton?" Horton replied, "I'm an instrument, you know. That's why I don't take these things personally." And when Moyers asked, "An instrument of what?" Horton answered, "I tried to make Highlander an instrument of empowering people, a way to get people to understand that they can be creative and imaginative. They don't have to put up with this system the way it is. They can create a new one that would be more humane."[14] People sometimes asked about Highlander's program, but Horton regarded such details as relatively unimportant. What mattered far more was educating people by example: "You educate by your own life, who you are. I'm interested in people learning how to learn. Now the only way I can help is to share my enthusiasm and my ability to learn myself. If I quit learning, I can't share."[15] In his 1927 study of Danish folk schools, Joseph K. Hart wrote, "We have plenty of men and women who can teach what they know . . . but very few who can teach their own capacity to learn."[16] Myles Horton dedicated his life to knowing and acting on the difference.

Acknowledgments

The first person I'd like to thank is Sam Freedman. I wrote early drafts of this book in his 2017 book seminar at Columbia University, and he stood by me throughout the publication process. This book simply would not have happened without Sam's ongoing support. Naturally, he bears no responsibility for my mistakes or errors of judgment. I also want to thank the other members of the seminar for their enthusiasm about this project and their many thoughtful critiques of early drafts.

At Columbia's School for the Arts, where I graduated from the MFA Program in Nonfiction Writing in 2018, I especially want to thank Phillip Lopate, Richard Locke, and Michael Greenberg for their many insightful readings of my work. Professors Greenberg and Locke were particularly helpful as I began to sketch out preliminary chapters. I also must extend appreciation to the students in the workshops that these two instructors ran, whose suggestions contributed greatly to the final product: Synne Borgen, Allaire Conte, Tiffany Davis, Alanna Duncan, Harrison Hill, Taleen Mardirossian, Zoe Marquedant, Catherine Northington, Anne Rudiq, and Christina Schmidt.

I was also a member of a very lively writing group organized by Georgette Culucundis Mallory. I am grateful to her and the others in the group—Kalle Mattila, Trent Pollard, Dan Kagan-Kans, and Allaire Conte—for their careful reading of my work.

I am lucky to have Victoria Skurnick as an agent. She has been incredibly supportive throughout the completion of this project and often had a kind word just when I needed it.

Stephen Brookfield and David Greenwood wrote incisive reviews of the near-final manuscript and made many suggestions that I found useful. I am grateful to them for being such good friends and for helping me write better. I also want to thank Michael Morris for his friendship and his enthusiasm for Myles Horton's teaching and leadership.

David Preskill and John Preskill—my brothers—set aside time to read an early version of this book. Their positive reactions gave me new reason to believe that I was on the right track with this project. I thank them for their ongoing love and encouragement.

I want to extend special thanks to the people who agreed to be interviewed for this project. They include Sue Thrasher, John Peters, John Gaventa, Candie Carawan, Mary Thom Adams, and Peter Wood. A special shout-out to Steve Horton for helping me to arrange some of those interviews.

I am very grateful to the various librarians and archivists who assisted me in completing my research. The materials at the Wisconsin Historical Society were invaluable, and reference archivist Lee Grady and his staff were unfailingly helpful in accessing what I needed. I also thank Greta Browning, archivist at Appalachian State University, for her assistance with Highlander-related documents there. In addition, I must thank the Highlander Center staff for their hospitality and generosity. In particular, Susan Williams and Rose Carden went out of their way to make a wide variety of archival sources available to me.

At the University of California Press, Naomi Schneider's and Kate Hoffman's impressive attention to detail greatly enhanced the final version of the book. I am also grateful to editorial assistant Summer

Farah for her help during every stage of the publication process. I especially want to thank Jan Spauschus for her meticulous and painstaking efforts while editing this manuscript. She saved me from many errors and greatly improved the overall flow of the final draft.

I finished this book while sheltering in place with my son Ben, his wife Autumn, and their wonderful son Xander. I love and appreciate them all, but I am especially grateful to Xander for his boundless energy, which often rubbed off on me and pushed me to keep writing.

Finally, I am indebted to my wife Karen DeMoss, whose enthusiasm for this book and undiminished confidence in my ability kept me going when I doubted myself. In addition, her considerable editorial skills made my writing immeasurably better. I dedicate this book to her with all my love, devotion, and gratitude.

Notes

Special thanks to the Taylor and Francis Group for permission to reprint parts of a previously written chapter about Myles Horton from a book entitled *Educating for Critical Consciousness*, edited by George Yancy.

Prologue

1. Robin D. G. Kelley and Makani Themba, "Why the Highlander Attack Matters," *The Nation,* May 13, 2019, 24.

2. John Lewis, "Rep. John Lewis on the Fire at the Highlander Center," Congressional Documents and Publications, April 4, 2019, http://ezproxy.cul.columbia.edu/login?url = https://search.proquest.com/docview/22 03086345?accountid = 10226.

3. Sarah Mervosh, "White Power Symbol Was Found at Site of Fire, Civil Rights Center Says," *New York Times,* April 3, 2019, www.nytimes.com/2019/04/03/us/civil-rights-center-fire.html?searchResultPosition = 1.

4. Lucy Diavolo, "A Fire at the Highlander Center Won't Stop This Legendary Civil Rights Movement Training Organization," *Teen Vogue,* April 10, 2019, www.teenvogue.com/story/highlander-center-fire-white-power-symbol-civil-rights-movement.

Introduction

1. Anne Braden, "Doing the Impossible," *Social Policy* 21, no. 3 (Winter 1991): 27.

2. Aldon Morris, "Education for Liberation," *Social Policy* 21, no. 3 (Winter 1991): 2.

3. John Lewis and Michael D'Orso, *Walking with the Wind: A Memoir of the Movement* (New York: Simon & Schuster, 1998), 89.

4. Braden, "Doing the Impossible," 27.

5. Sara Evans and Harry Boyte, *Free Spaces: The Sources of Democratic Change in America* (Chicago: University of Chicago Press, 1992).

6. Carl T. Rowan, *South of Freedom* (New York: Knopf, 1952), 205.

7. Dale Jacobs, "Introduction," in Dale Jacobs, ed., *The Myles Horton Reader: Education for Social Change* (Knoxville: University of Tennessee Press, 2003), xxvii.

8. Keith Gilyard, *Composition and Cornel West: Notes toward a Deep Democracy* (Carbondale: Southern Illinois University Press, 2008), 111–12.

9. Darren Sands, "What Happened to Black Lives Matter?," BuzzFeed, 2017, www.buzzfeed.com/darrensands/what-happened-to-black-lives-matter.

10. Myles Horton, interview by Richard Stevens, April 1983, 25, Mss 831: Box 2, Folder 17, Myles Horton Papers.

11. Bill Moyers, "The Adventures of a Radical Hillbilly," *Bill Moyers Journal* (New Market, TN: Public Broadcasting Service, 1981).

12. Myles Horton, "A Faith Venture," in Dale Jacobs, ed., *The Myles Horton Reader: Education for Social Change* (Knoxville: University of Tennessee Press, 2003), 177.

13. M. Horton, "A Faith Venture," 177.

14. M. Horton, "A Faith Venture," 178.

15. Frank Adams, *Unearthing Seeds of Fire: The Idea of Highlander* (Winston-Salem, NC: J. F. Blair, 1975), xv.

16. John M. Glen, *Highlander: No Ordinary School, 1932–1962* (Lexington: University Press of Kentucky, 1988).

17. John M. Glen, *Highlander: No Ordinary School,* 2nd ed. (Knoxville: University of Tennessee Press, 1996).

18. Aimee Isgrig Horton, *The Highlander Folk School: A History of Its Major Programs, 1932–1961* (Brooklyn, NY: Carlson Publishing, 1989).

19. Myles Horton, *The Long Haul: An Autobiography* (New York: Doubleday, 1990).

20. Myles Horton and Paulo Freire, *We Make the Road by Walking: Conversations on Education and Social Change,* ed. Brenda Bell, John Gaventa, and John Peters (Philadelphia: Temple University Press, 1990).

21. Dale Jacobs, ed., *The Myles Horton Reader: Education for Social Change* (Knoxville: University of Tennessee Press, 2003).

22. Stephen A. Schneider, *You Can't Padlock an Idea: Rhetorical Education at the Highlander Folk School, 1932–1961* (Columbia: University of South Carolina Press, 2014).

23. Myles Horton, "Efforts to Bring About Radical Change in Education," *Cutting Edge* 4, no. 10 (1973).

24. Myles Horton, "Decision-Making Processes," in Dale Jacobs, ed., *The Myles Horton Reader: Education for Social Change* (Knoxville, Tennessee: University of Tennessee Press, 2003), 237.

25. Martha Sue Thrasher, "International Women as Popular Educators : An Inquiry into the Nature and Implications of Everyday Experience" (EdD diss., University of Massachusetts at Amherst, 1996), 42.

26. Thrasher, "International Women," 42; Deborah Barndt, *To Change This House: Popular Education under the Sandinistas* (Toronto: Between the Lines, 1991), 18–20.

27. Tom Heaney, "Resources for Popular Education," *Adult Learning* 3, no. 5 (1992): 10.

Chapter 1. Beginnings

1. Myles Horton, *The Long Haul: An Autobiography* (New York: Doubleday, 1990), 1.

2. Myles Horton, interview by Dallas Blanchard, 1984, 4, Southern Oral History Program Collection, file:///Users/stevesnew/Desktop/Dallas%20Blanchard%20Interview%20with%20MH.pdf.

3. M. Horton, interview by Dallas Blanchard, 5; Howard Zinn, *You Can't Be Neutral on a Moving Train* (Boston: Beacon Press, 2002), 165.

4. Myles Horton, "Myles Horton: Statements on the Origin of Highlander," interview by Aimee Isgrig Horton, 1966, 24, M2010: Box 11, Folder 36, Highlander Records.

5. Frank Adams, *Unearthing Seeds of Fire: The Idea of Highlander* (Winston-Salem, NC: J. F. Blair, 1975), 5.

6. "Savannah, Tennessee," in *Wikipedia*, October 18, 2019, https://en.wikipedia.org/wiki/Savannah,_Tennessee.

7. M. Horton, *Long Haul*, 4.

8. M. Horton, *Long Haul*, 2.

9. M. Horton, *Long Haul*, 2.

10. M. Horton, *Long Haul*, 2.

11. M. Horton, *Long Haul*, 2.

12. Adams, *Unearthing Seeds of Fire,* 5.

13. M. Horton, *Long Haul,* 7.

14. M. Horton, *Long Haul,* 7.

15. Thomas Bledsoe, *Or We'll All Hang Separately: The Highlander Idea* (Boston: Beacon Press, 1969), 34; Myles Horton, interview by Dana Thomas, March 9, 1959, 11, M2010 : Box 2, Folder 16, Highlander Records.

16. Cynthia Stokes Brown, "Giving Aunt Donnie Her Due," *Social Policy* 21, no. 3 (Winter 1991): 21.

17. C. Brown, "Giving Aunt Donnie Her Due," 21.

18. Myles Horton and Paulo Freire, *We Make the Road by Walking: Conversations on Education and Social Change,* ed. Brenda Bell, John Gaventa, and John Peters (Philadelphia: Temple University Press, 1990), 19.

19. Horton and Freire, *We Make the Road,* 19.

20. Horton and Freire, *We Make the Road,* 228-29.

21. Horton and Freire, *We Make the Road,* 14-15.

22. Myles Horton, "Myles Horton Speaks to the Unitarian Fellowship of Memphis," February 2, 1969, 4, Mss 831: Box 3, Folder 14, Myles Horton Papers; Horton and Freire, *We Make the Road,* 17-18.

23. Horton and Freire, *We Make the Road,* 20.

24. Frank Adams, *James A. Dombrowski: An American Heretic,* 1897-1983 (Knoxville: University of Tennessee Press, 1992), 73-74; M. Horton, *Long Haul,* 80; James Dombrowski, "James Dombrowski to Lilian Johnson," January 2, 1935, M2010: Box 2, Folder 6, Highlander Records.

25. M. Horton, *Long Haul,* 79-81.

26. Jeanne Theoharis, *A More Beautiful and Terrible History: The Uses and Misuses of Civil Rights History* (Beacon Press, 2018), 193.

27. Horton and Freire, *We Make the Road,* 27.

28. Adams, *Unearthing Seeds of Fire,* 6; Winstead Bone, *A History of Cumberland University,* 1842-1935 (Lebanon, TN: self-pub., 1935).

29. Adams, *Unearthing Seeds of Fire,* 6; Bone, *A History of Cumberland University.*

30. M. Horton, *Long Haul,* 11.

31. Myles Horton, "Autobiographical Notes, Box Factory" (n.d.), Mss 831: Box 1, Folder 3, Myles Horton Papers.

32. Adams, *Unearthing Seeds of Fire,* 7.

33. Bledsoe, *Or We'll All Hang Separately,* 35.

34. Bledsoe, *Or We'll All Hang Separately,* 36.

35. M. Horton, *Long Haul,* 17-18.

36. Myles Horton, "Story about Race," Madison, Wisconsin, 1929, Mss 831: Box 4, Folder 6, Myles Horton Papers, http://digital.library.wisc.edu/1711.dl /wiarchives.uw-whs-mss00831.

37. M. Horton, *Long Haul,* 16.

38. John M. Glen, *Highlander: No Ordinary School,* 2nd ed. (Knoxville: University of Tennessee Press, 1996), 12; M. Horton, interview with Dana Thomas, 13.

39. Bledsoe, *Or We'll All Hang Separately,* 35; M. Horton, interview with Dana Thomas, 13.

40. Horton and Freire, *We Make the Road,* 39–40.

41. M. Horton, *Long Haul,* 25.

42. Benjamin Hunnicutt, *Work without End: Abandoning Shorter Hours for the Right to Work* (Philadelphia: Temple University Press, 1988), 41.

43. M. Horton, *Long Haul,* 25.

44. Horton and Freire, *We Make the Road,* 231.

45. Adams, *Unearthing Seeds of Fire,* 8–9.

Chapter 2. The Lessons of Ozone

1. Michelle Alexander, *The New Jim Crow: Mass Incarceration in the Age of Colorblindness* (New York: New Press, 2012).

2. Douglas A. Blackmon, *Slavery by Another Name: The Re-Enslavement of Black Americans from the Civil War to World War II,* repr. (New York: Anchor, 2009); Frank Adams, *Unearthing Seeds of Fire: The Idea of Highlander* (Winston-Salem, NC: J. F. Blair, 1975), 3; Karin A. Shapiro, *A New South Rebellion: The Battle against Convict Labor in the Tennessee Coalfields,* 1871–1896 (Chapel Hill: University of North Carolina Press, 1998).

3. Adams, *Unearthing Seeds of Fire,* 2.

4. Myles Horton, interview by Dana Thomas, March 9, 1959, M2010: Box 2, Folder 16, Highlander Records.

5. Michael E. Birdwell and W. Calvin Dickinson, eds., *Rural Life and Culture in the Upper Cumberland* (Lexington: University Press of Kentucky, 2004), 218.

6. Birdwell and Dickinson, *Rural Life,* 218; Myles Horton, *The Long Haul: An Autobiography* (New York: Doubleday, 1990), 20–21.

7. Birdwell and Dickinson, *Rural Life,* 218; Harry F. Ward, *Our Economic Morality and the Ethic of Jesus* (New York: Macmillan, 1929).

8. Thomas Bledsoe, *Or We'll All Hang Separately: The Highlander Idea* (Boston: Beacon Press, 1969), 30; M. Horton, interview by Dana Thomas, 7.

9. "U.S. Census Records, 1930 Data," Censusrecords.com, accessed December 22, 2019, https://www.censusrecords.com/Search?State = tennessee&Census Year=1930&County=Cumberland&o=CityTownship&_=1577045464604&page = 6; "The Demographic Statistical Atlas of the United States," Statisticalatlas.com, accessed December 22, 2019, https://statisticalatlas.com/county-subdivision/Tennessee/Cumberland-County/Cumberland-District-6/Population.

10. Adams, *Unearthing Seeds of Fire*, 1–3; M. Horton, *Long Haul*, 21–22.

11. M. Horton, *Long Haul*, 22.

12. Myles Horton and Paulo Freire, *We Make the Road by Walking: Conversations on Education and Social Change*, ed. Brenda Bell, John Gaventa, and John Peters (Philadelphia: Temple University Press, 1990), 48.

13. Adams, *Unearthing Seeds of Fire*, 3.

14. Adams, *Unearthing Seeds of Fire*, 3.

15. M. Horton, *Long Haul*, 23.

16. Horton and Freire, *We Make the Road*, 49.

17. Horton and Freire, *We Make the Road*, 49.

18. M. Horton, *Long Haul*, 21–23.

19. Frank Adams, "In the Company of a Listener," *Social Policy* 21, no. 3 (Winter 1991): 31.

20. Adams, *Unearthing Seeds of Fire*, 3.

21. M. Horton, *Long Haul*, 23.

22. Aimee Isgrig Horton, *The Highlander Folk School: A History of Its Major Programs, 1932–1961* (Brooklyn, NY: Carlson Publishing, 1989), 16; Horton, *Long Haul*, 23.

23. A. Horton, *Highlander Folk School*, 16; M. Horton, interview by Dana Thomas.

24. M. Horton, interview by Dana Thomas.

25. M. Horton, *Long Haul*, 23–24; Horton and Freire, *We Make the Road*, 50.

26. Myles Horton, interview by Dallas Blanchard, 1984, 9, Southern Oral History Program Collection, file:///Users/stevesnew/Desktop/Dallas%20Blanchard%20Interview%20with%20MH.pdf.

27. M. Horton, *Long Haul*, 24; Horton and Freire, *We Make the Road*, 51.

28. Adams, *Unearthing Seeds of Fire*, 9.

29. Myles Horton, "Myles Horton: Statements on the Origin of Highlander," interview by Aimee Isgrig Horton, 1966, 4, M2010: Box 11, Folder 36, Highlander Papers.

30. M. Horton, interview by Dana Thomas, 6.

31. Myles Horton, "The Adventures of a Radical Hillbilly, Part 1," in Dale Jacobs, ed., *The Myles Horton Reader* (Knoxville: University of Tennessee Press, 2003), 127.

32. Adams, *Unearthing Seeds of Fire*, 10.

1. Robert Handy, *A History of Union Theological Seminary in New York* (New York: Columbia University Press, 1987).

2. Harry F. Ward, *Our Economic Morality and the Ethic of Jesus* (New York: Macmillan, 1929).

3. Myles Horton, *The Long Haul: An Autobiography* (New York: Doubleday, 1990), 32.

4. David Duke, *In the Trenches with Jesus and Marx: Harry F. Ward and the Struggle for Social Justice,* 2nd ed. (Tuscaloosa: University of Alabama Press, 2003); "Harry Ward Dies; Led ACLU to '40," *New York Times,* December 10, 1966, sec. Deaths.

5. Doug Rossinow, "The Radicalization of the Social Gospel: The Search for a New Social Order, 1898-1936," *Religion and American Culture: A Journal of Interpretation* 15, no. 1 (2005): 68.

6. Rossinow, "Radicalization of the Social Gospel," 89.

7. Frank Adams, *James A. Dombrowski: An American Heretic, 1897-1983* (Knoxville: University of Tennessee Press, 1992), 39.

8. Reinhold Niebuhr, *Moral Man and Immoral Society* (New York: Scribner's, 1932), 34.

9. Niebuhr, *Moral Man,* 15.

10. M. Horton, *Long Haul,* 35.

11. Richard Fox, *Reinhold Niebuhr* (New York: Pantheon, 1985), 136.

12. Daniel A. Morris, "Unnoticed Consensus: Dewey, Niebuhr, and the Politics of Sovereignty," *Journal of Religion* 93, no. 3 (2013): 219.

13. M. Horton, *Long Haul,* 38.

14. M. Horton, *Long Haul,* 34.

15. Myles Horton, "The Adventures of a Radical Hillbilly, Part 1," in Dale Jacobs, ed., *The Myles Horton Reader* (Knoxville: University of Tennessee Press, 2003), 127-28.

16. M. Horton, *Long Haul,* 35.

17. Tom Heaney, "Adult Education for Social Change: From Center Stage to the Wings and Back Again," Information Series No. 365, ERIC Clearinghouse for Adult, Continuing and Vocational Education, 1996, 33.

18. Myles Horton, interview by Dana Thomas, March 9, 1959, 8, M2010: Box 2, Folder 16, Highlander Records.

19. M. Horton, *Long Haul,* 36.

20. Aimee Isgrig Horton, *The Highlander Folk School: A History of Its Major Programs, 1932-1961* (Brooklyn, NY: Carlson Publishing, 1989), 20.

21. M. Horton, *Long Haul,* 44–45.

22. George S. Counts and Wayne J. Urban, *Dare the School Build a New Social Order?* (Carbondale: Southern Illinois University Press, 1978).

23. Eduard Lindeman, *The Meaning of Adult Education* (New Republic Press, 1926), 6–11.

24. John Peters and Brenda Bell, "Horton of Highlander," in *Twentieth Century Thinkers in Adult and Continuing Education,* ed. Peter Jarvis, 2nd ed. (London: Kogan Page, 2001), 245.

25. Stephen D. Brookfield, *The Power of Critical Theory: Liberating Adult Learning and Teaching* (San Francisco: Jossey-Bass, 2005), 270–71.

26. M. Horton, *Long Haul,* 36.

27. M. Horton, *Long Haul,* 38.

28. A. Horton, *Highlander Folk School,* 23–24.

29. M. Horton, *Long Haul,* 24.

30. William Darity, "Robert E. Park," in *International Encyclopedia of the Social Sciences,* 2nd ed. (New York: Macmillan, 2008; Gale eBooks).

31. M. Horton, *Long Haul,* 47.

32. Myles Horton, interview by Richard Stevens, April 1983, 13, Mss 831: Box 2, Folder 17, Myles Horton Papers.

33. Allen F. Davis, *American Heroine: The Life and Legend of Jane Addams* (Chicago: Ivan R. Dee, 2000), 198.

34. Louise Knight, *Citizen: Jane Addams and the Struggle for Democracy* (Chicago: University of Chicago Press, 2006).

35. M. Horton, *Long Haul,* 48.

36. M. Horton, *Long Haul,* 48–49.

37. M. Horton, *Long Haul,* 49.

38. M. Horton, *Long Haul,* 49.

39. Frank Adams, *Unearthing Seeds of Fire: The Idea of Highlander* (Winston-Salem, NC: J. F. Blair, 1975), 19.

40. Myles Horton, "Highlander," in Dale Jacobs, ed., *The Myles Horton Reader: Education for Social Change* (Knoxville: University of Tennessee Press, 2003), 15.

41. *Interview with Myles Horton by John Peters and Brenda Bell (Part 2),* DVD (Highlander Center, 1987).

42. John M. Glen, *Highlander: No Ordinary School,* 2nd ed. (Knoxville: University of Tennessee Press, 1996), 18.

43. Myles Horton, "Influences on Highlander Research and Education Center, New Market, Tennessee, USA," in Dale Jacobs, ed., *The Myles Horton*

Reader: Education for Social Change (Knoxville: University of Tennessee Press, 2003), 29.

44. M. Horton, *Long Haul,* 51; M. Horton, "Influences on Highlander," 29.

45. M. Horton, "Influences on Highlander," 29.

46. M. Horton, "Influences on Highlander," 30.

47. M. Horton, *Long Haul,* 51–52; Myles Horton, "Building in the Democracy Mountains: The Legacy of the Highlander Center," in Dale Jacobs, ed., *The Myles Horton Reader: Education for Social Change* (Knoxville: University of Tennessee Press, 2003), 18.

48. M. Horton, "Influences on Highlander," 30.

49. M. Horton, *Long Haul,* 52–53; M. Horton, "Influences on Highlander," 30–31.

50. Joseph Hart, *Light from the North: The Danish Folk Highschools, Their Meanings for America* (New York: Henry Holt, 1927), 149.

51. Adams, *James A. Dombrowski,* 64.

52. Alice Cobb, "Alice Cobb to Myles Horton," n.d., Mss 265: Box 2, Folder 3, Highlander Records.

53. Adams, *Unearthing Seeds of Fire,* 24.

54. Thomas Bledsoe, *Or We'll All Hang Separately: The Highlander Idea* (Boston: Beacon Press, 1969), 19–20.

55. Reinhold Niebuhr and Myles Horton, "Fundraising Letter," May 27, 1932, Mss 831: Box 12, Folder 5, Myles Horton Papers.

56. Adams, *James A. Dombrowski,* 65.

Chapter 4. Highlander's Beginnings

1. Eliot Wigginton, *Refuse to Stand Silently By: An Oral History of Grass Roots Social Activism in America,* 1921–64 (New York: Doubleday, 1992), 75.

2. Hulan Thomas, "A History of the Highlander Folk School, 1932–1941" (master's thesis, Vanderbilt University, 1964), 8.

3. James J. Lorence, *A Hard Journey: The Life of Don West* (Urbana: University of Illinois Press, 2007), 27–28.

4. M. Sharon Herbers, "Progressive Era Roots of Highlander Folk School: Lilian Wyckoff Johnson's Legacy," in *Tennessee Women: Their Lives and Times,* ed. Beverly Greene Bond and Sarah Wilkerson Freeman, vol. 2 (Athens: University of Georgia Press, 2015), 346.

5. Lorence, *A Hard Journey,* 28; Wigginton, *Refuse to Stand Silently By,* 77.

6. Don West, interview by Sue Thrasher, 1974, 51, 50th Anniversary Interview Archive, Highlander Research and Education Center, New Market, TN; Wigginton, *Refuse to Stand Silently By*, 77.

7. Frank Adams, *James A. Dombrowski: An American Heretic*, 1897–1983 (Knoxville: University of Tennessee Press, 1992), 73–74; James Dombrowski, "James Dombrowski to Lilian Johnson," January 2, 1935, M2010: Box 2, Folder 6, Highlander Records.

8. Frank Adams, *Unearthing Seeds of Fire: The Idea of Highlander* (Winston-Salem, NC: J. F. Blair, 1975), 64.

9. West, interview by Sue Thrasher, 38–39.

10. Lorence, *A Hard Journey*, 27.

11. Wigginton, *Refuse to Stand Silently By*, 77.

12. Wigginton, *Refuse to Stand Silently By*, 78.

13. Thomas Bledsoe, *Or We'll All Hang Separately: The Highlander Idea* (Boston: Beacon Press, 1969), 173.

14. John M. Glen, *Highlander: No Ordinary School*, 2nd ed. (Knoxville: University of Tennessee Press, 1996), 32.

15. Myles Horton, "Study the Power Structure," in Dale Jacobs, ed., *The Myles Horton Reader: Education for Social Change* (Knoxville: University of Tennessee Press, 2003), 100.

16. Adams, *Unearthing Seeds of Fire*, 27.

17. Wigginton, *Refuse to Stand Silently By*, 78.

18. Lorence, *A Hard Journey*, 30.

19. Michael Price, "The New Deal in Tennessee: Highlander Folk School and Worker Response in Grundy County," *Tennessee Historical Quarterly* 43, no. 2 (Summer 1984): 101.

20. Adams, *Unearthing Seeds of Fire*, 28–30.

21. Myles Horton and Paulo Freire, *We Make the Road by Walking: Conversations on Education and Social Change*, ed. Brenda Bell, John Gaventa, and John Peters (Philadelphia: Temple University Press, 1990), 54.

22. Perry Cotham, *Toil, Turmoil, and Triumph: A Portrait of the Tennessee Labor Movement* (Franklin, TN: Hillsboro Press, 1995), 196.

23. Adams, *James A. Dombrowski*, 66.

24. Adams, *Unearthing Seeds of Fire*, 32.

25. Bledsoe, *Or We'll All Hang Separately*, 174–75.

26. Bledsoe, *Or We'll All Hang Separately*, 174.

27. Anthony Dunbar, *Against the Grain: Southern Radicals and Prophets*, 1929–1959 (Charlottesville: University Press of Virginia, 1981), 4.

28. Myles Horton, "Building in the Democracy Mountains: The Legacy of the Highlander Center," in Dale Jacobs, ed., *The Myles Horton Reader: Education for Social Change* (Knoxville: University of Tennessee Press, 2003), 133.

29. Cotham, *Toil, Turmoil, and Triumph*, 118.

30. Adams, *Unearthing Seeds of Fire*, 32–35; Myles Horton, *The Long Haul: An Autobiography* (New York: Doubleday, 1990), 40–41.

31. Glen, *Highlander*, 31.

32. Fellowship of Reconciliation, United States, "FORUSA: Advocating Peace & Justice through Nonviolence," accessed December 23, 2019, https://www.forusa.org/.

33. Myles Horton, interview by Dallas Blanchard, 1984, 11, Southern Oral History Program Collection, file:///Users/stevesnew/Desktop/Dallas%20Blanchard%20Interview%20with%20MH.pdf.

34. Dunbar, *Against the Grain*, 21.

35. Dunbar, *Against the Grain*, 29.

36. Robert Martin, *Howard Kester and the Struggle for Social Justice in the South, 1904-77* (Charlottesville: University Press of Virginia, 1991), 47.

37. Martin, *Howard Kester*, 47.

38. Martin, *Howard Kester*, 49.

39. Dunbar, *Against the Grain*, 9.

40. Martin, *Howard Kester*, 50.

41. Dunbar, *Against the Grain*, 23.

42. Adams, *Unearthing Seeds of Fire*, 37.

43. Adams, *Unearthing Seeds of Fire*, 37.

44. Price, "The New Deal in Tennessee," 102.

45. Stephen A. Schneider, *You Can't Padlock an Idea: Rhetorical Education at the Highlander Folk School, 1932-1961* (Columbia: University of South Carolina Press, 2014), 62.

46. Schneider, *You Can't Padlock an Idea*, 64.

47. Schneider, *You Can't Padlock an Idea*, 65.

48. Adams, *Unearthing Seeds of Fire*, 38.

Chapter 5. Building a More Stable Highlander

1. M. Sharon Herbers, "Progressive Era Roots of Highlander Folk School: Lilian Wyckoff Johnson's Legacy," in *Tennessee Women: Their Lives and Times*, ed. Beverly Greene Bond and Sarah Wilkerson Freeman, vol. 2 (Athens: University of Georgia Press, 2015), 254.

2. Frank Adams, *Unearthing Seeds of Fire: The Idea of Highlander* (Winston-Salem, NC: J. F. Blair, 1975), 44.

3. James J. Lorence, *A Hard Journey: The Life of Don West* (Urbana: University of Illinois Press, 2007), 35; Don West, interview by Sue Thrasher, 1974, 50th Anniversary Interview Archive, Highlander Research and Education Center, New Market, TN.

4. Lorence, *A Hard Journey,* 34.

5. Lorence, *A Hard Journey,* 35–36.

6. Myles Horton, interview by Richard Stevens, April 1983, 3, Mss 831: Box 2, Folder 17, Myles Horton Papers.

7. John Egerton, "Highlander in the Thirties: An Appalachian Seedbed for Social Change," *Appalachian Heritage* 22, no. 1 (1994): 5–9; Myles Horton, *The Long Haul: An Autobiography* (New York: Doubleday, 1990), 65.

8. Frank Adams, *James A. Dombrowski: An American Heretic,* 1897–1983 (Knoxville: University of Tennessee Press, 1992), 71.

9. John Fish, "The Christian Commonwealth Colony: A Georgia Experiment, 1896–1900," *Georgia Historical Review* 57, no. 2 (1973): 215.

10. Adams, *James A. Dombrowski,* 71.

11. Adams, *James A. Dombrowski,* 76.

12. Adams, *James A. Dombrowski,* 60.

13. John Daniel, "From Looking After: A Son's Memoir," *Northwest Review* 34, no. 3 (1996): 9.

14. Daniel, "From Looking After," 9.

15. Eliot Wigginton, *Refuse to Stand Silently By: An Oral History of Grass Roots Social Activism in America,* 1921–64 (New York: Doubleday, 1992), 92–93.

16. Wigginton, *Refuse to Stand Silently By,* 94–95.

17. John M. Glen, *Highlander: No Ordinary School* (Knoxville: University of Tennessee Press, 1996), 41.

18. Adams, *Unearthing Seeds of Fire,* 41, 44; Glen, *Highlander,* 40.

19. Wigginton, *Refuse to Stand Silently By,* 94–95.

20. Adams, *James A. Dombrowski,* 59.

21. Zilla Hawes, "Zilla Hawes to Jim Dombrowski," February 28, 1937, Mss 265: Box 14, Folder 29, Highlander Records.

22. Hawes, "Zilla Hawes to Jim Dombrowski."

23. James Dombrowski, "James Dombrowski to Zilla Hawes," March 3, 1937, Mss 265: Box 14, Folder 29, Highlander Records.

24. Glen, *Highlander,* 92; M. Horton, *Long Haul,* 121–22; Myles Horton and Paulo Freire, *We Make the Road by Walking: Conversations on Education and Social*

Change, ed. Brenda Bell, John Gaventa, and John Peters (Philadelphia: Temple University Press, 1990), 110–11.

25. Thomas Bledsoe, *Or We'll All Hang Separately: The Highlander Idea* (Boston: Beacon Press, 1969), 177.

26. M. Horton, *Long Haul,* 121–22.

27. Horton and Freire, *We Make the Road,* 110–11.

28. M. Horton, *Long Haul,* 180.

29. Myles Horton, "Building in the Democracy Mountains: The Legacy of the Highlander Center," in Dale Jacobs, ed., *The Myles Horton Reader: Education for Social Change* (Knoxville: University of Tennessee Press, 2003), 43.

30. Myles Horton, "Profile of Huey Long," September 9, 1934, HREC 2010 Addition: Box 11, Folder 10, Highlander Research and Education Center, New Market, TN.

31. Barbara Ransby, *Ella Baker and the Black Freedom Movement: A Radical Democratic Vision* (Chapel Hill: University of North Carolina Press, 2003), 188.

32. Septima Clark, *Ready from Within: Septima Clark and the Civil Rights Movement; A First Person Narrative,* ed. Cynthia Stokes Brown (Navarro, CA: Wild Trees Press, 1986), 77–78.

33. M. Horton, *Long Haul,* 126–27.

34. M. Horton, *Long Haul,* 130–43.

35. M. Horton, *Long Haul,* 137.

36. M. Horton, *Long Haul,* 153.

37. Gary Conti and Robert Fellenz, "Ideas That Have Withstood the Test of Time," in Dale Jacobs, ed., *The Myles Horton Reader: Education for Social Change* (Knoxville: University of Tennessee Press, 2003), 50; Myles Horton, "Influences on Highlander Research and Education Center, New Market, Tennessee, USA," in Dale Jacobs, ed., *The Myles Horton Reader: Education for Social Change* (Knoxville: University of Tennessee Press, 2003), 27.

38. Myles Horton, "Highlander," in Dale Jacobs, ed., *The Myles Horton Reader: Education for Social Change* (Knoxville: University of Tennessee Press, 2003), 13.

39. Myles Horton, "Highlander's Educational Program," in Dale Jacobs, ed., *The Myles Horton Reader: Education for Social Change* (Knoxville, Tennessee: University of Tennessee Press, 2003), 269.

40. Myles Horton, "A Circle of Learners," in Dale Jacobs, ed., *The Myles Horton Reader: Education for Social Change* (Knoxville: University of Tennessee Press, 2003), 274.

41. M. Horton, "A Circle of Learners," 272.

42. Frank Adams, "In the Company of a Listener," *Social Policy* 21, no. 3 (Winter 1991): 31.

43. Adams, "In the Company of a Listener," 32.

44. Adams, "In the Company of a Listener," 32.

45. Myles Horton, "The Adventures of a Radical Hillbilly, Part 1," in Dale Jacobs, ed., *The Myles Horton Reader* (Knoxville: University of Tennessee Press, 2003), 132.

46. M. Horton, "A Circle of Learners," 276.

Chapter 6. Zilphia Horton and Highlander's "Singing Army"

1. Chelsea Hodge, "The Coal Operator's Daughter: Zilphia Horton, Folk Music, and Labor Activism," *Arkansas Historical Quarterly* 76, no. 4 (2017): 292–93.

2. Eric Gellman and Jarod Roll, *The Gospel of the Working Class: Labor's Southern Prophets in New Deal America* (Urbana: University of Illinois Press, 2011), 41.

3. Chelsea Hodge, "'A Song Workers Everywhere Sing': Zilphia Horton and the Creation of Labor's Musical Canon" (master's thesis, University of Arkansas, 2014), 8.

4. Hodge, "'A Song,'" 9.

5. Gellman and Roll, *Gospel of the Working Class,* 42.

6. Gellman and Roll, *Gospel of the Working Class,* 44.

7. Gellman and Roll, *Gospel of the Working Class,* 45.

8. Hodge, "The Coal Operator's Daughter," 295.

9. Gellman and Roll, *Gospel of the Working Class,* 57.

10. Gellman and Roll, *Gospel of the Working Class,* 57.

11. Howard Kester, "Letter to Zilphia Mae Johnson," January 24, 1935, Mss 831: Box 15, Folder 13, Myles Horton Papers.

12. Thomas Bledsoe, *Or We'll All Hang Separately: The Highlander Idea* (Boston: Beacon Press, 1969), 151–52.

13. Hodge, "The Coal Operator's Daughter," 296.

14. Myles Horton, "Family" (n.d.), Mss 831: Box 1, Folder 2, Myles Horton Papers.

15. John M. Glen, *Highlander: No Ordinary School,* 2nd ed. (Knoxville: University of Tennessee Press, 1996), 43.

16. Myles Horton, "Myles Horton to Zilphia Horton," January 22, 1936, Mss 831: Box 15, Folder 13, Myles Horton Papers.

17. Frank Adams, *Unearthing Seeds of Fire: The Idea of Highlander* (Winston-Salem, NC: J. F. Blair, 1975), 76.

18. Hodge, "The Coal Operator's Daughter," 297.

19. Hodge, "The Coal Operator's Daughter," 298.

20. Zilphia Horton, "An Experiment in Drama at the Highlander Folk School," 1940, Microfilm 12479: Reel 24, Frame 799, 1, Grassroots Social Activism Records of the Highlander Folk School and Highlander Education and Research Center, 1932–1978 [microform], https://clio.columbia.edu/catalog/SCSB-1576272?counter=3.

21. Glen, *Highlander,* 46.

22. Z. Horton, "An Experiment in Drama," 1.

23. Stephen A. Schneider, *You Can't Padlock an Idea: Rhetorical Education at the Highlander Folk School,* 1932–1961 (Columbia: University of South Carolina Press, 2014), 64–65.

24. Schneider, *You Can't Padlock an Idea,* 67.

25. Adams, *Unearthing Seeds of Fire,* 72.

26. Eliot Wigginton, *Refuse to Stand Silently By: An Oral History of Grass Roots Social Activism in America,* 1921–64 (New York: Doubleday, 1992), 114.

27. Julia Pirro-Schmidt and Karen McCurdy, "Employing Music in the Cause of Social Justice: Ruth Crawford Seeger and Zilphia Horton," *Voices* 31, no. 1/2 (Spring 2005): 35.

28. Alicia R. Massie-Legg, "Zilphia Horton: A Voice for Change" (PhD diss., University of Kentucky, 2014), 37.

29. Massie-Legg, "Zilphia Horton," 88.

30. Adams, *Unearthing Seeds of Fire,* 76.

31. Hodge, "The Coal Operator's Daughter," 298.

32. Zilphia Horton, "People Like to Sing," *Food for Thought* 8, no. 6 (March 1948): 17–20.

33. Z. Horton, "People Like to Sing," 18.

34. Z. Horton, "People Like to Sing," 18.

35. Z. Horton, "People Like to Sing," 20.

36. Aleine Austin, interview by Sue Thrasher, August 19, 1982, 14, 50th Anniversary Interview Archive, Highlander Research and Education Center, New Market, TN.

37. Austin, interview by Sue Thrasher, 15.

38. Hodge, "The Coal Operator's Daughter," 291–92.

39. Vicki Carter, "The Singing Heart of Highlander Folk School," *New Horizons in Adult Education and Human Resource Development* 8, no. 2 (Spring 1994): 4–24.

40. Lucy Massie Phenix and Veronica Solver, *You Got to Move: Stories of Change in the South,* DVD (Milliarium Zero, 1985).

41. Hodge, "The Coal Operator's Daughter," 298.

42. Pete Seeger, *Where Have All the Flowers Gone? A Singalong Memoir,* rev. ed. (W. W. Norton, 2009), 32.

43. Schneider, *You Can't Padlock an Idea,* 159; Seeger, *Where Have All the Flowers Gone?,* 32–35.

44. Adams, *Unearthing Seeds of Fire,* 72–76; https://en.wikipedia.org/wiki/We_Shall_Overcome.

45. Fred Brown, "Listen World: They're Playing Her Song," *Knoxville News-Sentinel,* January 14, 1990.

46. Massie-Legg, "Zilphia Horton."

Chapter 7. Racial Equality within the Union Movement

1. John M. Glen, *Highlander: No Ordinary School,* 2nd ed. (Knoxville: University of Tennessee Press, 1996), 105.

2. Myles Horton, "Building in the Democracy Mountains: The Legacy of the Highlander Center," in Dale Jacobs, ed., *The Myles Horton Reader: Education for Social Change* (Knoxville: University of Tennessee Press, 2003), 36.

3. Frank Adams, *Unearthing Seeds of Fire: The Idea of Highlander* (Winston-Salem, NC: J. F. Blair, 1975), 90–91.

4. John P. C. Daves, "Raising Black Dreams: Representations of Six Generations of a Family's Local Racial-Activist Traditions" (PhD diss., University of Maryland, 2007); Glen, *Highlander,* 38.

5. Myles Horton, "Letter to Arthur Raper," May 21, 1940, Mss 265: Box 23, Folder 22, Highlander Records.

6. Cynthia Stokes Brown, "Giving Aunt Donnie Her Due," *Social Policy* 21, no. 3 (Winter 1991): 25.

7. Glen, *Highlander,* 113; Aimee Isgrig Horton, *The Highlander Folk School: A History of Its Major Programs, 1932–1961* (Brooklyn, NY: Carlson Publishing, 1989), 114.

8. Glen, *Highlander,* 113.

9. Glen, *Highlander,* 114.

10. Bob Jones, "Highlander 1944 Annual Report," 1945, Mss 265: Box 1, Folder 5, Highlander Records.

11. Glen, *Highlander,* 115.

12. "Bob Jones Speaks His Mind," *Highlander Fling,* November 1945, Mss 265: Box 84, Folder 7, Highlander Records.

13. "Bob Jones Speaks His Mind"; Jones, "Highlander 1944 Annual Report."

14. "Bob Jones Speaks His Mind"; Jones, "Highlander 1944 Annual Report."

15. Glen, *Highlander,* 118–19.

16. Glen, *Highlander,* 120.

17. Glen, *Highlander,* 121.

18. Adams, *Unearthing Seeds of Fire,* 101.

19. A. Horton, *Highlander Folk School,* 197.

20. A. Horton, *Highlander Folk School,* 198.

21. Glen, *Highlander,* 123.

22. Glen, *Highlander,* 124.

23. Glen, *Highlander,* 123–24.

24. Glen, *Highlander,* 147.

25. Bruce Fehn, "'The Only Hope We Had': United Packinghouse Workers Local 46 and the Struggle for Racial Equality in Waterloo, Iowa, 1848–1960," *Annals of Iowa* 54 (Summer 1995): 194.

26. Jeffrey Zacharakis-Jutz, "Seizing the Moment: Highlander Folk School and the Packinghouse Workers Union," *Convergence* 26, no. 4 (1993).

27. Glen, *Highlander,* 147.

28. Cyril Robinson, *Marching with Dr. King: Ralph Helstein and the United Packinghouse Workers of America* (Santa Barbara, CA: Praeger, 2011), 154–55.

29. Shelton Stromquist, *Solidarity and Survival: An Oral History of Iowa Labor in the Twentieth Century* (Iowa City: University of Iowa Press, 1993), 256.

30. Stromquist, *Solidarity and Survival,* 259.

31. Roger Horowitz, "The Path Not Taken: A Social History of Industrial Unionism in Meatpacking, 1930–1960" (PhD diss., University of Wisconsin at Madison, 1990), 671.

32. Rick Halpern and Roger Horowitz, *Meatpackers: An Oral History of Black Packinghouse Workers and Their Struggle for Racial and Economic Equality* (New York: Twayne, 1996), 19; Horowitz, "The Path Not Taken," 664.

33. Fehn, "'The Only Hope We Had,'" 198.

34. Myles Horton, "Report of Myles Horton, Education Director, UPWA Convention," 1952, Mss 265: Box 74, Folder 1, Highlander Records; also Microfilm 12479: Reel 39, Frames 652–61, Grassroots Social Activism Records of the Highlander Folk School and Highlander Education and Research Center, 1932–1978 [microform], https://clio.columbia.edu/catalog/SCSB-1576272?counter=3.

35. Myles Horton, "1952 Progress Report to UPWA," 1952, Mss 265: Box 74, Folder 1, Highlander Records; also Microfilm 12479: Reel 39, Frame 693, Grassroots Social Activism Records of the Highlander Folk School and Highlander Education and Research Center, 1932–1978 [microform], https://clio.columbia.edu/catalog/SCSB-1576272?counter=3.

36. Kenneth Eby, "The 'Drip' Theory in Labor Unions," *Antioch Review,* March 1, 1953, 97.

37. C. Robinson, *Marching with Dr. King,* 153.

38. Zacharakis-Jutz, "Seizing the Moment."

39. Glen, *Highlander,* 149.

40. Halpern and Horowitz, *Meatpackers,* 126–27.

41. Thomas Bledsoe, *Or We'll All Hang Separately: The Highlander Idea* (Boston: Beacon Press, 1969), 206.

42. Zacharakis-Jutz, "Seizing the Moment"; Jeffrey Zacharakis-Jutz, "Straight to the Heart of a Union, Straight to the Heart of a Movement: Workers' Education in the United Packinghouse Workers of America between 1951 and 1953" (EdD diss., Northern Illinois University, 1991), 253–54.

43. Zacharakis-Jutz, "Straight to the Heart of a Union," 16.

44. Bledsoe, *Or We'll All Hang Separately,* 206.

45. C. Robinson, *Marching with Dr. King,* 154.

46. Adams, *Unearthing Seeds of Fire,* 87.

47. C. Robinson, *Marching with Dr. King,* 154.

48. M. Horton, "Building in the Democracy Mountains," 37.

Chapter 8. The White Supremacist versus the Social Egalitarian

1. Federal Bureau of Investigation, Highlander Folk School Records, Folder 14, The Vault, https://vault.fbi.gov/Highlander%20Folk%20School.

2. Dorothy M. Zellner, "Red Roadshow: Eastland in New Orleans, 1954," *Louisiana History: The Journal of the Louisiana Historical Association* 33, no. 1 (1992): 31–60.

3. Christopher Asch, *The Senator and the Sharecropper: The Freedom Struggles of James O. Eastland and Fannie Lou Hamer* (New York: New Press, 2008), 143–45; Zellner, "Red Roadshow," 32–36.

4. Asch, *The Senator and the Sharecropper,* 35.

5. J. Lee Annis, *Big Jim Eastland: The Godfather of Mississippi* (Jackson: University Press of Mississippi, 2016).

6. Asch, *The Senator and the Sharecropper,* 34–47.

7. John Dollard, *Caste and Class in a Southern Town,* 2nd ed. (Madison: University of Wisconsin Press, 1989), 66.

8. Dollard, *Caste and Class,* 69.

9. Asch, *The Senator and the Sharecropper,* 149.

10. Frank Adams, *James A. Dombrowski: An American Heretic, 1897–1983* (Knoxville: University of Tennessee Press, 1992), 223–24.

11. Adams, *James A. Dombrowski,* 225.

12. Adams, *James A. Dombrowski,* 224–25.

13. Adams, *James A. Dombrowski,* 225.

14. Adams, *James A. Dombrowski,* 225.

15. Adams, *James A. Dombrowski,* 226; United States Congress, Senate Committee on the Judiciary, *Southern Conference Educational Fund, Inc.: Hearings before the Subcommittee to Investigate the Administration of the Internal Security Act and Other Internal Security Laws of the Committee on the Judiciary, United States Senate, Eighty-Third Congress, Second Session, on Subversive Influence in Southern Conference Educational Fund, Inc.,* March 18–20, 1954 (hereafter *SCEF Hearings*) (Washington, DC: US Government Printing Office, 1955), 133.

16. Adams, *James A. Dombrowski,* 226.

17. Adams, *James A. Dombrowski,* 227.

18. Zellner, "Red Roadshow," 38.

19. United States Congress, Senate Committee on the Judiciary, *SCEF Hearings,* 2.

20. United States Congress, Senate Committee on the Judiciary, *SCEF Hearings,* 38.

21. United States Congress, Senate Committee on the Judiciary, *SCEF Hearings,* 55.

22. United States Congress, Senate Committee on the Judiciary, *SCEF Hearings,* 55–56.

23. Zellner, "Red Roadshow," 42–43.

24. United States Congress, Senate Committee on the Judiciary, *SCEF Hearings,* 74.

25. United States Congress, Senate Committee on the Judiciary, *SCEF Hearings,* 87.

26. Zellner, "Red Roadshow," 48.

27. United States Congress, Senate Committee on the Judiciary, *SCEF Hearings,* 104.

28. United States Congress, Senate Committee on the Judiciary, *SCEF Hearings,* 104.

29. United States Congress, Senate Committee on the Judiciary, *SCEF Hearings,* 107.

30. United States Congress, Senate Committee on the Judiciary, *SCEF Hearings,* 150.

31. United States Congress, Senate Committee on the Judiciary, *SCEF Hearings,* 150.

32. United States Congress, Senate Committee on the Judiciary, *SCEF Hearings,* 150.

33. United States Congress, Senate Committee on the Judiciary, *SCEF Hearings,* 150–51.

34. Zellner, "Red Roadshow," 56.

35. United States Congress, Senate Committee on the Judiciary, *SCEF Hearings,* 151.

36. Adams, *James A. Dombrowski,* 231.

37. "Probe Witness Ousted on Order by Eastland," *Times-Picayune,* March 21, 1954, sec. 1.

38. "Witness Ejected at Hearing; Ex-Red's Story Starts Fight," *New York Times,* March 21, 1954, https://timesmachine.nytimes.com/timesmachine/1954/03/21/92554257.html?pageNumber=1.

39. Myles Horton, "Letter to Arthur Carstens," March 22, 1954, Mss 265: Box 33, Folder 9, Highlander Records.

40. Frank Adams, *Unearthing Seeds of Fire: The Idea of Highlander* (Winston-Salem, NC: J.F. Blair, 1975), 199.

41. "Witness Ejected."

42. Adams, *Unearthing Seeds of Fire,* 200.

43. "Ejected Witness Denies He Is a Red; Never Was, Horton Asserts—Says Removal by Eastland Prevented Testimony," *New York Times,* March 23, 1954, https://timesmachine.nytimes.com/timesmachine/1954/03/23/92821515.pdf?pdf_redirect=true&ip=0.

44. John M. Glen, *Highlander: No Ordinary School,* 2nd ed. (Knoxville: University of Tennessee Press, 1996), 214.

45. Adams, *Unearthing Seeds of Fire,* 200.

46. Zellner, "Red Roadshow."

47. Gregory S. Taylor, *The Life and Lies of Paul Crouch: Communist, Opportunist, Cold War Snitch* (Gainesville: University Press of Florida, 2014), 172.

48. H.T. Swartz, "Letter from H.T. Swartz," February 20, 1957, Mss 265: Box 34, Folder 4, Highlander Records.

49. Aimee Isgrig Horton, *The Highlander Folk School: A History of Its Major Programs,* 1932–1961 (Brooklyn, NY: Carlson Publishing, 1989), 214.

50. "Protest against Revocation of Tax Exempt Status," May 8, 1957, Box 8, Folder 4, Highlander Folk School Manuscript Collection, 1932–1966, Tennessee State Library and Archives, Nashville; H.T. Swartz, "Second Letter from H.T. Swartz," December 18, 1957, Mss 265: Box 34, Folder 4, Highlander Records.

Chapter 9. Mrs. Parks Goes to Highlander

1. Danielle L. McGuire, *At the Dark End of the Street: Black Women, Rape, and Resistance—A New History of the Civil Rights Movement from Rosa Parks to the Rise of Black Power*, repr. (New York: Knopf, 2010).

2. Jeanne Theoharis, *The Rebellious Life of Mrs. Rosa Parks* (Boston: Beacon Press, 2013), 33–34; Eliot Wigginton, *Refuse to Stand Silently By: An Oral History of Grass Roots Social Activism in America, 1921–64* (New York: Doubleday, 1992), 230.

3. Virginia Foster Durr, *Outside the Magic Circle: The Autobiography of Virginia Foster Durr*, ed. Hollinger F. Barnard (Tuscaloosa: University of Alabama Press, 1990), 278–79.

4. Phillip Hoose, *Claudette Colvin: Twice toward Justice* (New York: Square Fish, 2010), 44–45.

5. Hoose, *Claudette Colvin*, 35.

6. Hoose, *Claudette Colvin*, 35.

7. Hoose, *Claudette Colvin*, 57.

8. Hoose, *Claudette Colvin*, 52.

9. McGuire, *At the Dark End of the Street*, 75.

10. Hoose, *Claudette Colvin*, 65.

11. Rosa Parks, Myles Horton, and E. D. Nixon, interview by Studs Terkel, 1973, 11, HREC 0002: Box 5, Folder 90, Highlander Research and Education Center, New Market, TN.

12. Theoharis, *The Rebellious Life of Mrs. Rosa Parks*, 37–38.

13. Parks, Horton, and Nixon, interview by Studs Terkel, 7.

14. John M. Glen, *Highlander: No Ordinary School*, 2nd ed. (Knoxville: University of Tennessee Press, 1996), 160–61.

15. Parks, Horton, and Nixon, interview by Studs Terkel, 7–8.

16. Septima Clark, *Ready from Within: Septima Clark and the Civil Rights Movement; A First Person Narrative*, ed. Cynthia Stokes Brown (Navarro, CA: Wild Trees Press, 1986), 17.

17. Julius Lester, "Laughing All the Way," *Social Policy* 21, no. 3 (Winter 1991): 10–12.

18. Durr, *Outside the Magic Circle*, 279.

19. Rosa Parks, *Rosa Parks: My Story* (New York: Puffin Books, 1999), 106–7.

20. Wigginton, *Refuse to Stand Silently By*, 240.

21. Theoharis, *The Rebellious Life of Mrs. Rosa Parks*, 29.

22. Stephen Preskill and Stephen D. Brookfield, *Learning as a Way of Leading: Lessons from the Struggle for Social Justice* (San Francisco: Jossey-Bass, 2009), 71.

23. S. Clark, *Ready from Within*, 16–17.

24. Douglas Brinkley, *Rosa Parks: A Life,* repr. (New York: Penguin Books, 2005), 67.

25. S. Clark, *Ready from Within*, 16–17.

26. Glen, *Highlander,* 160–61.

27. Theoharis, *The Rebellious Life of Mrs. Rosa Parks,* 40.

28. Theoharis, *The Rebellious Life of Mrs. Rosa Parks,* 40.

29. Theoharis, *The Rebellious Life of Mrs. Rosa Parks,* 41.

30. Durr, *Outside the Magic Circle,* 279.

31. Parks, Horton, and Nixon, interview by Studs Terkel, 12.

32. Parks, *Rosa Parks,* 78–79.

33. Legacy Museum and National Memorial for Peace and Justice, "The Legacy Museum and National Memorial for Peace and Justice," accessed January 5, 2020, https://museumandmemorial.eji.org/news/2019-05-20/peace-and-justice-center-monument.

34. McGuire, *At the Dark End of the Street,* 12, 78–79; Parks, *Rosa Parks,* 115–16; Theoharis, *The Rebellious Life of Mrs. Rosa Parks,* 62–63.

35. Parks, *Rosa Parks,* 116.

36. Parks, Horton, and Nixon, interview by Studs Terkel, 13; Theoharis, *The Rebellious Life of Mrs. Rosa Parks,* 1.

37. Katherine Mellen Charron, *Freedom's Teacher: The Life of Septima Clark* (Chapel Hill: University of North Carolina Press, 2009), 235.

38. Parks, Horton, and Nixon, interview by Studs Terkel, 10.

39. Virginia Foster Durr, *Freedom Writer: Virginia Foster Durr, Letters from the Civil Rights Years,* ed. Patricia A. Sullivan (Athens: University of Georgia Press, 2006), 103–4.

40. "Highlander Research and Education Center," n.d., 9, HREC 0002: Box 5, Folder 90, Highlander Research and Education Center, New Market, TN.

41. Theoharis, *The Rebellious Life of Mrs. Rosa Parks,* 43.

42. S. Clark, *Ready from Within*, 17–18.

43. "Meeting at Highlander," March 3, 1956, 1, Box 7, Folder 9, Highlander Folk School Manuscript Collection, 1932-1966, Tennessee State Library and Archives, Nashville.

44. "Meeting at Highlander," 25.

45. Hoose, *Claudette Colvin,* 94, 108.

46. David Emblidge, ed., *My Day: The Best of Eleanor Roosevelt's Acclaimed Newspaper Columns,* 1936–1962 (Boston: Da Capo Press, 2001), 234; "Meeting at Highlander."

47. Emblidge, *My Day,* 234; "Meeting at Highlander."

Chapter 10. The Citizenship School on Johns Island

1. "UN Workshop," 1954, Mss 265: Box 78, Folder 6, Highlander Records.

2. Eliot Wigginton, *Refuse to Stand Silently By: An Oral History of Grass Roots Social Activism in America,* 1921–64 (New York: Doubleday, 1992), 248.

3. Wigginton, *Refuse to Stand Silently By,* 248.

4. Wigginton, *Refuse to Stand Silently By,* 248–49.

5. Wigginton, *Refuse to Stand Silently By,* 249.

6. "UN Workshop"; Bernice Robinson, "Letter to Highlander from Bernice Robinson," July 19, 1955, Box 5, Folder 5, Highlander Folk School Manuscript Collection, 1932–1966, Tennessee State Library and Archives, Nashville; "Sea Islands: General Reports," 1954–1957, Mss 265: Box 67, Folder 3, Highlander Records.

7. Peter Ling, "Local Leadership in the Early Civil Rights Movement: The South Carolina Citizenship Education Program of the Highlander Folk School," *Journal of American Studies* 20, no. 3 (1995): 399–422.

8. Guy Carawan and Candie Carawan, *Ain't You Got a Right to the Tree of Life: The People of Johns Island, South Carolina,* rev. ed. (Athens: University of Georgia Press, 1989), 172–73.

9. B. Robinson, "Letter to Highlander"; Bernice Robinson, interview by Sue Thrasher and Eliot Wigginton, 1980, 50th Anniversary Interview Archive, Highlander Research and Education Center, New Market, TN.

10. Carl Tjerandsen, *Education for Citizenship: A Foundation's Experience* (Santa Cruz, CA: Emil Schwarzhaupt Foundation, 1980), chap. 4.

11. Katherine Mellen Charron, *Freedom's Teacher: The Life of Septima Clark* (Chapel Hill: University of North Carolina Press, 2009), 285.

12. Susan Kates, "Literacy, Voting Rights, and the Citizenship Schools in the South, 1957–1970," *College Composition and Communication* 57, no. 3 (February 2006): 479–502; Spencer Smith, "Septima Clark Yelled: A Revisionist History of Citizenship Schools," *American Educational History Journal* 46, no. 2 (2019): 95–110; Clare Russell, "A Beautician without Teacher Training," *The Sixties: A Journal of History, Politics, and Culture* 4, no. 1 (June 2011): 31–50.

13. John M. Glen, *Highlander: No Ordinary School,* 2nd ed. (Knoxville: University of Tennessee Press, 1996), 188.

14. Tjerandsen, *Education for Citizenship,* 146.

15. Aimee Isgrig Horton, *The Highlander Folk School: A History of Its Major Programs, 1932–1961* (Brooklyn, NY: Carlson Publishing, 1989), 217.

16. Glen, *Highlander,* 185.

17. A. Horton, *Highlander Folk School,* 204.

18. Septima Clark, *Ready from Within: Septima Clark and the Civil Rights Movement; A First Person Narrative,* ed. Cynthia Stokes Brown (Navarro, CA: Wild Trees Press, 1986), 30.

19. Charron, *Freedom's Teacher,* 222–23.

20. Septima Clark, "Septima Clark to Myles Horton," July 22, 1954, Mss 265: Box 9, Folder 12, Highlander Records.

21. Septima Poinsette Clark and LeGette Blythe, *Echo in My Soul* (New York: Dutton, 1962), 121.

22. Glen, *Highlander,* 188; Charron, *Freedom's Teacher,* 225.

23. Esau Jenkins, "About Esau Jenkins and the Sea Islands of South Carolina," 1966, Microfilm 12479: Reel 22, Frames 786–826, Grassroots Social Activism Records of the Highlander Folk School and Highlander Education and Research Center, 1932–1978 [microform], https://clio.columbia.edu/catalog/SCSB-1576272?counter=3.

24. Ling, "Local Leadership," 405.

25. Ling, "Local Leadership," 406.

26. Carawan and Carawan, *Ain't You Got a Right to the Tree of Life,* 149.

27. Tjerandsen, *Education for Citizenship,* 152.

28. "UN Workshop."

29. Clark and Blythe, *Echo in My Soul,* 137.

30. Carawan and Carawan, *Ain't You Got a Right to the Tree of Life,* 141.

31. Guy Carawan and Candie Carawan, interview by Sue Thrasher, 1982, 172–73, 50th Anniversary Interview Archive, Highlander Research and Education Center, New Market, TN.

32. Esau Jenkins, "Esau Jenkins to Myles Horton 1954," September 20, 1954, Mss 265: Box 67, Folder 3, Highlander Records.

33. Tinsley Yarbrough, *A Passion for Justice: J. Waties Waring and Civil Rights* (Oxford: Oxford University Press, 1987).

34. Zilphia Horton, "Notes on Johns Island," November 1954, Mss 265: Box 67, Folder 3, Highlander Records.

35. David Levine, "Citizenship Schools" (PhD diss., University of Wisconsin at Madison, 1999), 106.

36. Myles Horton, "Myles Horton Field Trip Report on Johns Island" (December 1954), Mss 265: Box 67, Folder 3, Highlander Records.

37. Charron, *Freedom's Teacher,* 228.

38. Charron, *Freedom's Teacher,* 228.

39. Tjerandsen, *Education for Citizenship,* 156.

40. Myles Horton, "Conference on Leadership Training," March 19, 1955, Box 3, Folder 2, Highlander Folk School Manuscript Collection, 1932-1966, Tennessee State Library and Archives, Nashville; Tjerandsen, *Education for Citizenship,* 156.

41. Tjerandsen, *Education for Citizenship,* 154.

42. Tjerandsen, *Education for Citizenship,* 155.

43. Tjerandsen, *Education for Citizenship,* 160.

44. Gary Conti and Robert Fellenz, "Ideas That Have Withstood the Test of Time," in Dale Jacobs, ed., *The Myles Horton Reader: Education for Social Change* (Knoxville: University of Tennessee Press, 2003), 56-57.

45. Clark and Blythe, *Echo in My Soul,* 141.

46. S. Clark, *Ready from Within,* 53.

47. S. Clark, *Ready from Within,* 52-53; David Levine, "The Birth of the Citizenship Schools: Entwining the Struggles for Liberty and Freedom," *History of Education Quarterly* 44, no. 3 (Autumn 2004): 398.

48. S. Clark, *Ready from Within,* 53.

49. Charron, *Freedom's Teacher,* 248.

50. Tjerandsen, *Education for Citizenship,* 160.

51. S. Clark, *Ready from Within,* 48-49.

52. B. Robinson, interview by Sue Thrasher and Eliot Wigginton, 90-91.

53. Russell, "A Beautician without Teacher Training."

54. Frank Adams, "In the Company of a Listener," *Social Policy* 21, no. 3 (Winter 1991): 31-34.

55. Charron, *Freedom's Teacher,* 250.

56. Septima Clark, interview by Sandra Oldendorf, 1986, 18, Mss 831: Box 5, Folder 5, Myles Horton Papers.

57. Glen, *Highlander,* 194.

58. B. Robinson, interview by Sue Thrasher and Eliot Wigginton, 92.

59. B. Robinson, interview by Sue Thrasher and Eliot Wigginton, 92.

60. Stephen A. Schneider, *You Can't Padlock an Idea: Rhetorical Education at the Highlander Folk School,* 1932-1961 (Columbia: University of South Carolina Press, 2014), 129.

61. Bernice Robinson, "Citizenship Training Schools," November 1979, M2004: Box 2, Folder 36, Highlander Records.

62. Myles Horton, *The Long Haul: An Autobiography* (New York: Doubleday, 1990), 131.

63. Deanna M. Gillespie, "'They Walk, Talk, and Act Like New People': Black Women and the Citizenship Education Program, 1957–1970" (PhD diss., State University of New York at Binghamton, 2008), 52; Clark and Blythe, *Echo in My Soul,* 149.

64. Levine, "Citizenship Schools," 133–34.

65. Levine, "Citizenship Schools," 134.

66. B. Robinson, "Citizenship Training Schools."

67. Charron, *Freedom's Teacher,* 251.

68. Russell, "A Beautician without Teacher Training," 38.

69. A. Horton, *Highlander Folk School,* 224–25.

70. B. Robinson, "Citizenship Training Schools."

71. Gillespie, "'They Walk, Talk, and Act Like New People,'" 56.

72. Levine, "Citizenship Schools," 136.

73. Tjerandsen, *Education for Citizenship,* 164.

74. Glen, *Highlander,* 198.

75. Glen, *Highlander,* 199.

76. Glen, *Highlander,* 200.

77. Tjerandsen, *Education for Citizenship,* 174.

78. Tjerandsen, *Education for Citizenship,* 181.

79. Kates, "Literacy, Voting Rights, and the Citizenship Schools in the South," 492; Tjerandsen, *Education for Citizenship,* 181.

80. Charron, *Freedom's Teacher,* 295–99, 310, 316.

81. Dorothy Cotton, *If Your Back's Not Bent: The Role of the Citizenship Education Program in the Civil Rights Movement* (New York: Atria Books, 2012), 112.

82. A. Horton, *Highlander Folk School,* 237–38.

83. Amy Blanton, "Liberty's Hidden History: The Dorchester Center and Citizenship Education in Southeast Georgia during the 1960s" (EdD diss., Georgia Southern University, 2017), https://digitalcommons.georgiasouthern.edu/etd/1633.

84. Cotton, *If Your Back's Not Bent,* 145.

85. Glen, *Highlander,* 218.

86. Federal Bureau of Investigation, Highlander Folk School Records, Folder 14, The Vault, https://vault.fbi.gov/Highlander%20Folk%20School.

87. Glen, *Highlander,* 231.

88. Glen, *Highlander,* 238.

89. Myles Horton, "The Adventures of a Radical Hillbilly, Part 1," in Dale Jacobs, ed., *The Myles Horton Reader* (Knoxville: University of Tennessee Press, 2003), 119.

90. "In Memoriam: Aimee Horton and Lawrence Guyot," Highlander Research and Education Center, accessed November 30, 2019, www.highlander-center.org/in-memoriam-aimee-horton; Norma Nerstrom and Sue Himplemann, "Aimee Isgrig Horton," *Adult Learning Unleashed: ALU Consulting* (blog), November 30, 2019, www.alu-c.com/aimee-horton.

91. David Garrow, "Series Editor's Preface," in Aimee Isgrig Horton, *The Highlander Folk School: A History of Its Major Programs,* 1932–1961 (Brooklyn, NY: Carlson Publishing, 1989).

92. A. Horton, *Highlander Folk School,* xii.

93. A. Horton, *Highlander Folk School,* xiii.

Chapter 11. Highlander and SNCC

1. John Lewis and Michael D'Orso, *Walking with the Wind: A Memoir of the Movement* (New York: Simon & Schuster, 1998), 71.

2. Lewis and D'Orso, *Walking with the Wind,* 83.

3. Lewis and D'Orso, *Walking with the Wind,* 83–84.

4. Lewis and D'Orso, *Walking with the Wind,* 84.

5. Lewis and D'Orso, *Walking with the Wind,* 84, 86.

6. Lewis and D'Orso, *Walking with the Wind,* 110.

7. Lewis and D'Orso, *Walking with the Wind,* 88.

8. Aldon Morris, *The Origins of the Civil Rights Movement: Black Communities Organizing for Change* (New York: Free Press, 1984), 147.

9. A. Morris, *Origins of the Civil Rights Movement,* 200.

10. David Halberstam, *The Children* (New York: Fawcett Books, 1998), 102.

11. Pete Seeger and Bob Reiser, *Everybody Says Freedom: A History of the Civil Rights Movement in Songs and Pictures* (New York: W. W. Norton, 1989), 30.

12. Halberstam, *The Children,* 216.

13. Myles Horton, "Class on Nashville Sit-Ins," Highlander Social Needs and Social Resources Workshop, March 1960, Mss 831: Box 13, Folder 24, Myles Horton Papers; also HREC 0002: Box 7 Folder 119, Highlander Research and Education Center, New Market, TN.

14. *Seventh Annual College Workshop: The New Generation Fights for Equality,* Highlander Folk School, 1960, Mss 265: Box 78, Folder 9, Highlander Records.

15. Seeger and Reiser, *Everybody Says Freedom,* 34–35.

16. A. Morris, *Origins of the Civil Rights Movement,* 147–48.

17. Julius Lester, "Laughing All the Way," *Social Policy* 21, no. 3 (Winter 1991): 10.

18. Candie Carawan, interview by Stephen Preskill, May 23, 2018.

19. Lewis and D'Orso, *Walking with the Wind,* 90.

20. Taylor Branch, *Parting the Waters: America in the King Years, 1954–63* (New York: Simon & Schuster, 1988), 263.

21. Marshall Surratt, "Myles Horton: Activism and Gospel," *Christianity and Crisis* 50, no. 18 (December 17, 1990): 400.

22. Seeger and Reiser, *Everybody Says Freedom,* 35.

23. Myles Horton, *The Long Haul: An Autobiography* (New York: Doubleday, 1990), 184.

24. Septima Clark, "Report of the 7th Annual Highlander Folk School College Workshop," Highlander Folk School, April 1, 1960, Mss 265: Box 78, Folder 9, Highlander Records.

25. *Seventh Annual College Workshop.*

26. Rudy Abramson, "Sit-In Group Opens Seminar," Nashville *Tennessean,* April 3, 1960, 12A; *Seventh Annual College Workshop.*

27. Lewis and D'Orso, *Walking with the Wind,* 89.

28. Branch, *Parting the Waters,* 264.

29. Lewis and D'Orso, *Walking with the Wind,* 90.

30. C. Carawan, interview by Stephen Preskill.

31. Stephen A. Schneider, *You Can't Padlock an Idea: Rhetorical Education at the Highlander Folk School, 1932–1961* (Columbia: University of South Carolina Press, 2014), 168.

32. *Seventh Annual College Workshop.*

33. Lewis and D'Orso, *Walking with the Wind,* 90.

34. Charles Payne, *I've Got the Light of Freedom: The Organizing Tradition and the Mississippi Freedom Struggle* (Berkeley: University of California Press, 1995), 68.

35. Barbara Ransby, *Ella Baker and the Black Freedom Movement: A Radical Democratic Vision* (Chapel Hill: University of North Carolina Press, 2003), 243.

36. Ransby, *Ella Baker and the Black Freedom Movement,* 242.

37. Gerda Lerner, *Black Women in White America: A Documentary History* (New York: Vintage, 1972), 347, 352; Payne, *I've Got the Light of Freedom,* 93.

38. Ransby, *Ella Baker and the Black Freedom Movement,* 360.

39. Ransby, *Ella Baker and the Black Freedom Movement,* 360.

40. Ransby, *Ella Baker and the Black Freedom Movement,* 358–59.

41. Stephen Preskill and Stephen D. Brookfield, *Learning as a Way of Leading: Lessons from the Struggle for Social Justice* (San Francisco: Jossey-Bass, 2009), 123.

42. Myles Horton and Paulo Freire, *We Make the Road by Walking: Conversations on Education and Social Change,* ed. Brenda Bell, John Gaventa, and John Peters (Philadelphia: Temple University Press, 1990), 147.

43. Gary Conti and Robert Fellenz, "Ideas That Have Withstood the Test of Time," in Dale Jacobs, ed., *The Myles Horton Reader: Education for Social Change* (Knoxville: University of Tennessee Press, 2003), 53.

44. Ransby, *Ella Baker and the Black Freedom Movement,* 362.

45. Ransby, *Ella Baker and the Black Freedom Movement,* 363.

46. Ransby, *Ella Baker and the Black Freedom Movement,* 363.

47. Aimee Isgrig Horton, *The Highlander Folk School: A History of Its Major Programs,* 1932-1961 (Brooklyn, NY: Carlson Publishing, 1989), 250.

48. John M. Glen, *Highlander: No Ordinary School,* 2nd ed. (Knoxville: University of Tennessee Press, 1996), 178.

49. Judith Gregory, "A Weekend at Highlander," *Catholic Worker,* November 1960, Microfilm 12479: Reel 43, Frame 938, Grassroots Social Activism Records of the Highlander Folk School and Highlander Education and Research Center, 1932–1978 [microform], https://clio.columbia.edu/catalog/SCSB-1576272?counter=3.

50. Gregory, "A Weekend at Highlander."

51. Gregory, "A Weekend at Highlander."

52. A. Morris, *Origins of the Civil Rights Movement,* 218.

53. Lewis and D'Orso, *Walking with the Wind,* 181.

54. Ransby, *Ella Baker and the Black Freedom Movement,* 269.

55. Robert Moses and Charles Cobb, *Radical Equations: Civil Rights from Mississippi to the Algebra Project* (Boston: Beacon Press, 2001), 44.

56. J. Todd Moye, *Ella Baker: Community Organizer of the Civil Rights Movement* (New York: Rowman and Littlefield, 2013), 132-33.

57. Ransby, *Ella Baker and the Black Freedom Movement,* 270.

58. M. Horton, *Long Haul,* 184.

59. Francesca Polletta, *Freedom Is an Endless Meeting: Democracy in American Social Movements* (Chicago: University of Chicago Press, 2002), 64-67.

60. Polletta, *Freedom Is an Endless Meeting,* 74-75.

61. Polletta, *Freedom Is an Endless Meeting,* 76.

Chapter 12. From Civil Rights to Appalachia

1. John M. Glen, "Like a Flower Slowly Blooming: Highlander and the Nurturing of an Appalachian Movement," in *Fighting Back in Appalachia: Traditions of*

Resistance and Change, ed. Stephen L. Fisher (Philadelphia: Temple University Press, 1993), 34.

2. "Leadership Development Workshops for Emerging Leaders," July 1980, 2, M90: Box48, Folder 7, Highlander Records.

3. Glen, "Like a Flower Slowly Blooming," 31.

4. "Leadership Development Workshops," 3.

5. Myles Horton, "Letter to Board of Directors," November 9, 1965, Mss 265: Box 100, Folder 8, Highlander Records.

6. "Appalachian Workshop, March 12–14, 1964," Highlander Research and Education Center, Mss 831: Box 9, Folder 12, Myles Horton Papers.

7. Frank Adams, *Unearthing Seeds of Fire: The Idea of Highlander* (Winston-Salem, NC: J. F. Blair, 1975), 181.

8. Adams, *Unearthing Seeds of Fire,* 181.

9. "Appalachian Workshop."

10. Myles Horton, "Appalachian Community Leadership Workshop," October 26, 1968, Mss 265: Box 109, Folder 14, Highlander Records.

11. Myles Horton, "Highlander Center Appalachian Project," 1965, Mss 265: Box 100, Folder 8, Highlander Records; Myles Horton, "Appalachian Project Staff Memo 2," September 14, 1965, Mss 265: Box 32, Folder 9, Highlander Records; M. Horton, "Appalachian Community Leadership Workshop."

12. Myles Horton, "Notes on Top-Downism," October 10, 1968, Mss 265: Box 100, Folder 11, Highlander Records.

13. M. Horton, "Highlander Center Appalachian Project."

14. *Meeting of the Appalachian Project,* 1965, Audio 515A/18, Highlander Records; *Meeting of the Community Development Project,* 1965, Audio 515A/17, Highlander Records; Myles Horton, "Letter from Myles Horton to Appalachian Project Staff," April 22, 1965, Mss 265: Box 108, Folder 8, Highlander Records.

15. Myles Horton, "Proposed Highlander Center Project for Appalachian Poor," Summer 1966, Mss 265: Box 32, Folder 9, Highlander Records.

16. Myles Horton, "Appalachian Self-Education Program," 1968, Mss 265: Box 100, Folder 10, Highlander Records.

17. Mike Clark, "A Talk to Vista Workers," October 1969, Mss 265: Box 100, Folder 1, Highlander Records.

18. M. Clark, "A Talk to Vista Workers."

19. M. Clark, "A Talk to Vista Workers."

20. Mike Clark and Colin Greer, "A Culture of Politics," *Social Policy* 21, no. 3 (Winter 1991): 35.

21. Adams, *Unearthing Seeds of Fire,* 185.

22. Mike Clark, "Poor People Develop Poor People's Power," March 20, 1969, M90: Box 50, Folder 51, Highlander Records.

23. M. Clark, "Poor People Develop Poor People's Power."

24. M. Clark, "Poor People Develop Poor People's Power."

25. Adams, *Unearthing Seeds of Fire,* 186.

26. M. Clark, "Poor People Develop Poor People's Power."

27. M. Clark, "Poor People Develop Poor People's Power."

28. Bill Osinski, "Highlander Center: A Half-Century on the Cutting Edge of Change," Louisville, Kentucky *Courier-Journal Magazine,* 1982.

29. Myles Horton, "Decision-Making Processes," in Dale Jacobs, ed., *The Myles Horton Reader: Education for Social Change* (Knoxville, Tennessee: University of Tennessee Press, 2003), 244.

30. M. Horton, "Decision-Making Processes," 245.

31. Gordon Mantler, *Power to the Poor: Black-Brown Coalition and the Fight for Economic Justice,* 1960-1974 (Chapel Hill: University of North Carolina Press, 2013), 100.

32. Mantler, *Power to the Poor,* 109-10.

33. Mantler, *Power to the Poor,* 110-11.

34. Adams, *Unearthing Seeds of Fire,* 180.

35. John M. Glen, *Highlander: No Ordinary School,* 2nd ed. (Knoxville: University of Tennessee Press, 1996), 260-61.

36. Ashley Halsey, "An Oasis for Social Change Celebrates Its Past, Future," *Philadelphia Inquirer,* October 21, 1982.

37. John Gaventa, interview by Stephen Preskill, December 18, 2018.

38. Appalachian Land Ownership Task Force, *Who Owns Appalachia? Landownership and Its Impact* (Lexington: University Press of Kentucky, 1983), xi.

39. Appalachian Land Ownership Task Force, *Who Owns Appalachia?,* xxix.

40. Appalachian Land Ownership Task Force, *Who Owns Appalachia?,* xi.

41. Appalachian Land Ownership Task Force, *Who Owns Appalachia?,* 41-42.

42. John Egerton, "Appalachia's Absentee Landlords," *The Progressive,* June 1981.

43. Egerton, "Appalachia's Absentee Landlords."

44. Shaunna Scott, "The Appalachian Land Ownership Study Revisited," *Appalachian Journal* 35, no. 3 (2008): 236-52.

45. Shaunna Scott, "Discovering What the People Knew: The 1979 Appalachian Land Ownership Study," *Action Research* 7, no. 2 (2009): 185-205.

46. Egerton, "Appalachia's Absentee Landlords."

47. Egerton, "Appalachia's Absentee Landlords."

48. Myles Horton, *The Long Haul: An Autobiography* (New York: Doubleday, 1990), 208–9.

49. M. Horton, *Long Haul,* 208.

50. M. Horton, *Long Haul,* 209.

51. M. Horton, *Long Haul,* 209.

Chapter 13. Leadership and Research in Ivanhoe

1. Mary Ann Hinsdale, Helen M. Lewis, and S. Maxine Waller, *It Comes from the People: Community Development and Local Theology* (Philadelphia: Temple University Press, 1995).

2. Hinsdale, Lewis, and Waller, *It Comes from the People,* xv.

3. Hinsdale, Lewis, and Waller, *It Comes from the People,* 2.

4. Helen Lewis, *Helen Mathews Lewis: Living Social Justice in Appalachia* (Lexington: University Press of Kentucky, 2012), 5–6.

5. Sue Thrasher, interview by Stephen Preskill, September 19, 2018.

6. H. Lewis, *Helen Mathews Lewis,* 151, 153.

7. Hinsdale, Lewis, and Waller, *It Comes from the People,* 171.

8. Hinsdale, Lewis, and Waller, *It Comes from the People,* 54–55.

9. Maxine Waller et al., "'It Has to Come from the People': Responding to Plant Closings in Ivanhoe, Virginia," in *Communities in Economic Crisis: Appalachia and the South,* ed. John Gaventa, Barbara Ellen Smith, and Alex Willingham (Philadelphia: Temple University Press, 1990), 22.

10. Hinsdale, Lewis, and Waller, *It Comes from the People,* 81.

11. Waller et al., "'It Has to Come from the People,'" 23–24; Hinsdale, Lewis, and Waller, *It Comes from the People,* 82.

12. Guy Carawan and Candie Carawan, *Voices from the Mountains* (New York: Knopf, 1975), 26.

13. Carawan and Carawan, *Voices from the Mountains,* 82.

14. Helen Lewis, Linda Johnson, and Donald Askins, *Colonialism in Modern America: The Appalachian Case* (Boone, NC: Appalachian State Press, 1978).

15. Waller et al., "'It Has to Come from the People,'" 25; Hinsdale, Lewis, and Waller, *It Comes from the People,* 84.

16. Waller et al., "'It Has to Come from the People,'" 24.

17. Waller et al., "'It Has to Come from the People,'" 26; Hinsdale, Lewis, and Waller, *It Comes from the People,* 82–83.

18. Waller et al., "'It Has to Come from the People,'" 26; Hinsdale, Lewis, and Waller, *It Comes from the People,* 83.

19. Waller et al., "'It Has to Come from the People,'" 27.

20. Carawan and Carawan, *Voices from the Mountains,* 216.

21. Waller et al., "'It Has to Come from the People,'" 28.

22. Hinsdale, Lewis, and Waller, *It Comes from the People,* 86.

23. Hinsdale, Lewis, and Waller, *It Comes from the People,* 86-87.

24. Hinsdale, Lewis, and Waller, *It Comes from the People,* 89-90.

25. Hinsdale, Lewis, and Waller, *It Comes from the People,* 88.

26. Hinsdale, Lewis, and Waller, *It Comes from the People,* 86.

27. Hinsdale, Lewis, and Waller, *It Comes from the People,* 89.

28. Hinsdale, Lewis, and Waller, *It Comes from the People,* 96.

29. Maxine Waller, "Local Organizing: Ivanhoe, Virginia," *Social Policy* 21, no. 3 (Winter 1991): 65.

30. Hinsdale, Lewis, and Waller, *It Comes from the People,* 98.

31. Hinsdale, Lewis, and Waller, *It Comes from the People,* 98-99.

32. Waller, "Local Organizing," 63.

33. Waller, "Local Organizing," 64.

34. Hinsdale, Lewis, and Waller, *It Comes from the People,* 134-35.

35. Hinsdale, Lewis, and Waller, *It Comes from the People,* 332.

36. Hinsdale, Lewis, and Waller, *It Comes from the People,* 134-35.

37. Hinsdale, Lewis, and Waller, *It Comes from the People,* 138.

38. Hinsdale, Lewis, and Waller, *It Comes from the People,* 332.

39. Thrasher, interview by Stephen Preskill.

40. Waller, "Local Organizing," 67.

41. Hinsdale, Lewis, and Waller, *It Comes from the People,* 148.

42. Hinsdale, Lewis, and Waller, *It Comes from the People,* 336.

Chapter 14. Myles Horton, Internationalist

1. Myles Horton, *The Long Haul: An Autobiography* (New York: Doubleday, 1990), 212.

2. Myles Horton, "Myles Horton to Geraldine Macías," August 15, 1977, Mss 831: Box 8, Folder 5, Myles Horton Papers.

3. Myles Horton, "Letter to Margot Machado," April 21, 1959, Mss 265: Box 38, Folder 7, Highlander Records; M. Horton, *Long Haul,* 202.

4. Aimee Isgrig Horton, "Adult Education for Hemisphere Development: A Report on the First Inter-American Adult Education Seminar, Cuautla, Morelos, Mexico, December 16-21, 1962," Mss 831: Box 8, Folder 2, Myles Horton Papers.

5. M. Horton, *Long Haul,* 203.

6. Geraldine Macías, "Geraldine Macías to Myles Horton," October 5, 1977, Mss 831: Box 8, Folder 5, Myles Horton Papers.

7. Geraldine O'Leary-Macías, *Lighting My Fire: Memoirs* (Bloomington, IN: Trafford Publishing, 2013).

8. Macías, "Geraldine Macías to Myles Horton," October 5, 1977.

9. Macías, "Geraldine Macías to Myles Horton," October 5, 1977.

10. Myles Horton, "Myles Horton to Geraldine Macías," December 14, 1977, Mss 831: Box 8, Folder 5, Myles Horton Papers.

11. M. Horton, "Myles Horton to Geraldine Macías," December 14, 1977.

12. M. Horton, "Myles Horton to Geraldine Macías," December 14, 1977.

13. Geraldine Macías, "Geraldine Macías to Myles Horton," March 16, 1978, Mss 831: Box 8, Folder 5, Myles Horton Papers.

14. Macías, "Geraldine Macías to Myles Horton," March 16, 1978.

15. Geraldine Macías, "Geraldine Macías to Myles Horton," May 27, 1978, Mss 831: Box 8, Folder 5, Myles Horton Papers.

16. Merle Wolin, "Nicaragua's Revolution," *New York Times,* June 30, 1979.

17. Geraldine Macías, "Geraldine Macías to Myles Horton," October 23, 1979, Mss 831: Box 8, Folder 5, Myles Horton Papers.

18. Myles Horton, "Myles Horton to Geraldine Macías," December 14, 1979, Mss 831: Box 8, Folder 5, Myles Horton Papers.

19. Deborah Barndt, *To Change This House: Popular Education under the Sandinistas* (Toronto: Between the Lines, 1991), 5.

20. Geraldine Macías, "Geraldine Macías to Myles Horton," January 14, 1980, Mss 831: Box 8, Folder 5, Myles Horton Papers.

21. Macías, "Geraldine Macías to Myles Horton," January 14, 1980.

22. Robert Arnove, *Education and Revolution in Nicaragua* (Westport, CT: Praeger, 1986), 28.

23. Arnove, *Education and Revolution,* 19.

24. Valerie Miller, *Between Struggle and Hope: The Nicaraguan Literacy Crusade* (Boulder, CO: Westview Press, 1985), 170; 212.

25. Miller, *Between Struggle and Hope.* Miller's book would eventually become the definitive account of the literacy crusade.

26. M. Horton, *Long Haul,* 202–3.

27. Miller, *Between Struggle and Hope,* 191–92.

28. Miller, *Between Struggle and Hope,* 194.

29. Barndt, *To Change This House,* 5.

30. Myles Horton, "A Trip to Nicaragua to Learn About and Celebrate the Year of the Literacy Crusade, August 21–August 30, 1980," M2004: Box 7, Folder 52, Highlander Records.

31. M. Horton, "A Trip to Nicaragua."

32. Allison Haley Gose, "A Failed Dream: Literacy Education in the Global South" (honors thesis, University of Tennessee, 2015), 44, http://trace.tennessee.edu/utk_chanhonoproj/1768.

33. M. Horton, "A Trip to Nicaragua."

34. Miller, *Between Struggle and Hope,* 205.

35. Miller, *Between Struggle and Hope,* 205.

36. Miller, *Between Struggle and Hope,* 232.

37. M. Horton, *Long Haul,* 202.

38. Myles Horton, "Letter to Georgia McFadden," September 11, 1980, Mss 831: Box 8, Folder 5, Myles Horton Papers.

39. Myles Horton, "Myles Horton to Geraldine Macías," September 19, 1980, Mss 831: Box 8, Folder 5, Myles Horton Papers.

40. Geraldine Macías, "Geraldine Macías to Myles Horton," October 13, 1980, Mss 831: Box 8, Folder 5, Myles Horton Papers.

41. Betty James, "Betty J. James to Myles Horton," February 18, 1981, Mss 831: Box 8, Folder 6, Myles Horton Papers.

42. Mary Midyette, "Mary Midyette to Myles Horton," March 11, 1981, Mss 831: Box 8, Folder 6, Myles Horton Papers.

43. Deborah Barndt, "Deborah Barndt to Myles Horton," January 20, 1981, Mss 831: Box 8, Folder 6, Myles Horton Papers.

44. Myles Horton, "Myles Horton to John McFadden," May 12, 1981, Mss 831: Box 8, Folder 6, Myles Horton Papers.

45. Gose, "A Failed Dream," 52–53.

46. Geraldine Macías, "Geraldine Macías to Myles Horton," March 15, 1982, Mss 831: Box 8, Folder 6, Myles Horton Papers.

47. Myles Horton, "Myles Horton to Geraldine Macías," April 8, 1982, Mss 831: Box 8, Folder 6, Myles Horton Papers.

48. Geraldine Macías, "Newsletter from Geraldine Macías," July 14, 1982, Mss 831: Box 8, Folder 6, Myles Horton Papers.

49. O'Leary-Macías, *Lighting My Fire,* 233–34.

50. John Gaventa, "From John Gaventa," December 1982, Mss 831: Box 12, Folder 21, Myles Horton Papers.

51. Budd Hall, "Letter from Budd Hall to Myles Horton," July 6, 1982, Mss 831: Box 12, Folder 19, Myles Horton Papers.

52. Myles Horton, "Letter from Myles Horton to Paulette Irving," December 22, 1982, Mss 831: Box 12, Folder 19, Myles Horton Papers.

53. M. Horton, "Letter from Myles Horton to Paulette Irving."

54. Gose, "A Failed Dream," 56.

55. Ernesto Vallecillo, "Letter from Ernesto Vallecillo," August 11, 1983, Mss 831: Box 8, Folder 6, Myles Horton Papers.

56. "Highlander Reports: Highlander Co-Sponsors International Conference," October 1983, M2010: Box 2, Folder 23, Highlander Records.

57. Sue Thrasher, "Degrees of Change: Myles Horton's Lifetime Commitment to Radical Education," *Sojourners* 19, no. 3 (April 1990): 29.

58. Sue Thrasher, interview by Stephen Preskill, September 19, 2018.

59. Gose, "A Failed Dream," 5.

60. M. Horton, *Long Haul*, 205.

61. Lois Whitman, "Nicaraguan Vote: 'Free, Fair, Hotly Contested,'" *New York Times*, November 16, 1984.

62. M. Horton, *Long Haul*, 205–6.

63. Myles Horton and Paulo Freire, *We Make the Road by Walking: Conversations on Education and Social Change*, ed. Brenda Bell, John Gaventa, and John Peters (Philadelphia: Temple University Press, 1990), 224.

64. Luciano Baracco, "The Historical Roots of Autonomy in Nicaragua's Caribbean Coast: From British Colonialism to Indigenous Autonomy," *Bulletin of Latin American Research* 35, no. 3 (2016): 291–305; Myles Horton, "From Myles Horton to Marilyn Fedelchak," April 7, 1988, Mss 831: Box 8, Folder 6, Myles Horton Papers.

Chapter 15. We Make the Road by Walking

1. Myles Horton and Paulo Freire, *We Make the Road by Walking: Conversations on Education and Social Change*, ed. Brenda Bell, John Gaventa, and John Peters (Philadelphia: Temple University Press, 1990), vii.

2. Myles Horton, "A Different Kettle of Fish," interview by Susan Walker and Ike Coleman, 1989, Mss 831: Box 2, Folder 21, Myles Horton Papers.

3. Horton and Freire, *We Make the Road*, viii.

4. John Peters, interview by Stephen Preskill, May 20, 2018.

5. Helen Lewis, "Paulo Freire at Highlander," in *Memories of Paulo*, ed. Tom Wilson, Peter Park, and Anaida Colón-Muñiz (Rotterdam: Sense Publishers, 2010), 121.

6. Peter Mayo, review of Myles Horton and Paulo Freire, *We Make the Road by Walking*, *Convergence* 24, no. 4 (1992): 77–80.

7. H. Lewis, "Paulo Freire at Highlander," 121.

8. Horton and Freire, *We Make the Road*, 10–11.

9. Horton and Freire, *We Make the Road*, 11.

10. Horton and Freire, *We Make the Road*, 24–25.

11. Horton and Freire, *We Make the Road*, 27.

12. Horton and Freire, *We Make the Road*, 31.

13. Horton and Freire, *We Make the Road*, 57–58.

14. Myles Horton, *The Long Haul: An Autobiography* (New York: Doubleday, 1990), 2.

15. Horton and Freire, *We Make the Road*, 57–58.

16. Horton and Freire, *We Make the Road*, 61.

17. Horton and Freire, *We Make the Road*, 65.

18. Maxine Waller, "Local Organizing: Ivanhoe, Virginia," *Social Policy* 21, no. 3 (Winter 1991): 64.

19. Waller, "Local Organizing," 64.

20. H. Lewis, "Paulo Freire at Highlander," 122.

21. Horton and Freire, *We Make the Road*, 200–201.

22. Horton and Freire, *We Make the Road*, 203.

23. Horton and Freire, *We Make the Road*, 206.

24. Horton and Freire, *We Make the Road*, 243.

25. Horton and Freire, *We Make the Road*, 247.

26. Horton and Freire, *We Make the Road*, 247–48.

27. Horton and Freire, *We Make the Road*, xxxi.

28. John Gaventa, interview by Stephen Preskill.

29. Horton and Freire, *We Make the Road*, xxxiii.

30. Horton and Freire, *We Make the Road*, xxxiii.

Epilogue

1. "Highlander Reports: An Update with Myles," Summer 1989, M2010: Box 2, Folder 23, Highlander Records.

2. "Highlander Reports: Building for the Long Haul: The Horton Fund," Winter 1991, M2000: Box 4, Folder 29, Highlander Records.

3. Sue Thrasher, "Degrees of Change: Myles Horton's Lifetime Commitment to Radical Education," *Sojourners* 19, no. 3 (April 1990): 29.

4. John Peters, interview by Stephen Preskill, May 20, 2018.

5. "Highlander Reports," Summer 1990, M2000: Box 4, Folder 30, Highlander Records.

6. "Highlander Reports."

7. Marshall Surratt, "Myles Horton: Activism and Gospel," *Christianity and Crisis* 50, no. 18 (December 17, 1990): 402.

8. William Ayers, "A Curriculum of Civil Rights: Teaching the Taboo and Trudging toward Freedom," in *Critical Times in Curriculum Thought: People, Politics and Perspectives,* ed. Marcella Kysilka (Greenwich, CT: Information Age, 2014), 127.

9. Ayers, "A Curriculum of Civil Rights," 128.

10. "Highlander Reports."

11. Thrasher, "Degrees of Change."

12. John Gaventa, "Carrying On . . .," *Social Policy* 21, no. 3 (Winter 1991): 69.

13. Gaventa, "Carrying On . . .," 70.

14. Myles Horton, "The Adventures of a Radical Hillbilly, Part 2," in Dale Jacobs, ed., *The Myles Horton Reader: Education for Social Change* (Knoxville: University of Tennessee Press, 2003), 207.

15. M. Horton, "The Adventures of a Radical Hillbilly, Part 2," 207.

16. Joseph Hart, *Light from the North: The Danish Folk Highschools, Their Meanings for America* (New York: Henry Holt, 1927), 148–49.

Works Cited

Both the Myles Horton Papers and the Highlander Records (Highlander Research and Education Center Records, 1917–2005) are housed at the Wisconsin Historical Society in Madison, Wisconsin.

Abramson, Rudy. "Sit-In Group Opens Seminar." Nashville *Tennessean,* April 3, 1960.

Adams, Frank. "In the Company of a Listener." *Social Policy* 21, no. 3 (Winter 1991): 31–34.

———. *James A. Dombrowski: An American Heretic, 1897–1983.* Knoxville: University of Tennessee Press, 1992.

———. *Unearthing Seeds of Fire: The Idea of Highlander.* Winston-Salem, NC: J. F. Blair, 1975.

Alexander, Michelle. *The New Jim Crow: Mass Incarceration in the Age of Colorblindness.* New York: New Press, 2012.

Annis, J. Lee. *Big Jim Eastland: The Godfather of Mississippi.* Jackson: University Press of Mississippi, 2016.

Appalachian Land Ownership Task Force. *Who Owns Appalachia? Landownership and Its Impact.* Lexington: University Press of Kentucky, 1983.

"Appalachian Workshop, March 12–14, 1964." Highlander Research and Education Center. Mss 831: Box 9, Folder 12, Myles Horton Papers.

Arnove, Robert. *Education and Revolution in Nicaragua.* Westport, CT: Praeger, 1986.

Asch, Christopher. *The Senator and the Sharecropper: The Freedom Struggles of James O. Eastland and Fannie Lou Hamer.* New York: New Press, 2008.

Austin, Aleine. Interview by Sue Thrasher, August 19, 1982. 50th Anniversary Interview Archive, Highlander Research and Education Center, New Market, TN.

Ayers, William. "A Curriculum of Civil Rights: Teaching the Taboo and Trudging toward Freedom." In *Critical Times in Curriculum Thought: People, Politics, and Perspectives,* ed. Marcella Kysilka, 115–41. Greenwich, CT: Information Age, 2014.

Baracco, Luciano. "The Historical Roots of Autonomy in Nicaragua's Caribbean Coast: From British Colonialism to Indigenous Autonomy." *Bulletin of Latin American Research* 35, no. 3 (2016): 291–305.

Barndt, Deborah. "Deborah Barndt to Myles Horton," January 20, 1981. Mss 831: Box 8, Folder 6, Myles Horton Papers.

———. *To Change This House: Popular Education under the Sandinistas.* Toronto: Between the Lines, 1991.

Birdwell, Michael E., and W. Calvin Dickinson, eds. *Rural Life and Culture in the Upper Cumberland.* Lexington: University Press of Kentucky, 2004.

Blackmon, Douglas A. *Slavery by Another Name: The Re-Enslavement of Black Americans from the Civil War to World War II.* Reprint. New York: Anchor, 2009.

Blanton, Amy. "Liberty's Hidden History: The Dorchester Center and Citizenship Education in Southeast Georgia during the 1960s." EdD diss., Georgia Southern University, 2017, https://digitalcommons.georgiasouthern.edu/etd/1633.

Bledsoe, Thomas. *Or We'll All Hang Separately: The Highlander Idea.* Boston: Beacon Press, 1969.

"Bob Jones Speaks His Mind." *Highlander Fling,* November 1945. Mss 265: Box 84, Folder 7, Highlander Records.

Bone, Winstead. *A History of Cumberland University,* 1842–1935. Lebanon, TN: self-published, 1935.

Braden, Anne. "Doing the Impossible." *Social Policy* 21, no. 3 (Winter 1991): 26–30.

Branch, Taylor. *Parting the Waters: America in the King Years,* 1954–63. New York: Simon & Schuster, 1988.

Brinkley, Douglas. *Rosa Parks: A Life.* Reprint. New York: Penguin, 2005.

Brookfield, Stephen D. *The Power of Critical Theory: Liberating Adult Learning and Teaching.* San Francisco: Jossey-Bass, 2005.

Brown, Cynthia Stokes. "Giving Aunt Donnie Her Due." *Social Policy* 21, no. 3 (Winter 1991): 19–25.

Brown, Fred. "Listen World: They're Playing Her Song." *Knoxville News-Sentinel,* January 14, 1990.

Carawan, Candie. Interview by Stephen Preskill, May 23, 2018.

Carawan, Guy, and Candie Carawan. *Ain't You Got a Right to the Tree of Life: The People of Johns Island, South Carolina.* Rev. ed. Athens: University of Georgia Press, 1989.

———. Interview by Sue Thrasher, 1982. 50th Anniversary Interview Archive, Highlander Research and Education Center, New Market, TN.

———. *Voices from the Mountains.* New York: Knopf, 1975.

Carter, Vicki. "The Singing Heart of Highlander Folk School." *New Horizons in Adult Education and Human Resource Development* 8, no. 2 (Spring 1994): 4–24.

Charron, Katherine Mellen. *Freedom's Teacher: The Life of Septima Clark.* Chapel Hill: University of North Carolina Press, 2009.

Clark, Mike. "Poor People Develop Poor People's Power," March 20, 1969. M90: Box 50, Folder 51, Highlander Records.

———. "A Talk to Vista Workers," October 1969. Mss 265: Box 100, Folder 1, Highlander Records.

Clark, Mike, and Colin Greer. "A Culture of Politics." *Social Policy* 21, no. 3 (Winter 1991): 33–37.

Clark, Septima. Interview by Sandra Oldendorf, 1986. Mss 831: Box 5, Folder 5, Myles Horton Papers.

———. *Ready from Within: Septima Clark and the Civil Rights Movement; A First Person Narrative,* ed. Cynthia Stokes Brown. Navarro, CA: Wild Trees Press, 1986.

———. "Report of the 7th Annual Highlander Folk School College Workshop." Highlander Folk School, April 1, 1960. Mss 265: Box 78, Folder 9, Highlander Records.

———. "Septima Clark to Myles Horton," July 22, 1954. Mss 265: Box 9, Folder 12, Highlander Records.

Clark, Septima Poinsette, and Legette Blythe. *Echo in My Soul.* New York: Dutton, 1962.

Cobb, Alice. "Alice Cobb to Myles Horton," n.d. Mss 265: Box 2, Folder 3, Highlander Records.

Conti, Gary, and Robert Fellenz. "Ideas That Have Withstood the Test of Time." In Dale Jacobs, ed., *The Myles Horton Reader: Education for Social Change,* 44–58. Knoxville: University of Tennessee Press, 2003.

Cotham, Perry. *Toil, Turmoil, and Triumph: A Portrait of the Tennessee Labor Movement.* Franklin, TN: Hillsboro Press, 1995.

Cotton, Dorothy. *If Your Back's Not Bent: The Role of the Citizenship Education Program in the Civil Rights Movement.* New York: Atria, 2012.

Counts, George S., and Wayne J. Urban. *Dare the School Build a New Social Order?* Carbondale: Southern Illinois University Press, 1978.

Daniel, John. "From Looking After: A Son's Memoir." *Northwest Review* 34, no. 3 (1996): 6–10.

Darity, William. "Robert E. Park." In *International Encyclopedia of the Social Sciences.* 2nd ed., 6:140–42. New York: Macmillan, 2008. Gale eBooks.

Daves, John P. C. "Raising Black Dreams: Representations of Six Generations of a Family's Local Racial-Activist Traditions." PhD diss., University of Maryland, 2007.

Davis, Allen F. *American Heroine: The Life and Legend of Jane Addams.* Chicago: Ivan R. Dee, 2000.

Diavolo, Lucy. "A Fire at the Highlander Center Won't Stop This Legendary Civil Rights Movement Training Organization." *Teen Vogue,* April 10, 2019. www.teenvogue.com/story/highlander-center-fire-white-power-symbol-civil-rights-movement.

Dollard, John. *Caste and Class in a Southern Town.* 2nd ed. Madison: University of Wisconsin Press, 1989.

Dombrowski, James. "James Dombrowski to Lilian Johnson," January 2, 1935. M2010: Box 2, Folder 6, Highlander Records.

———. "James Dombrowski to Zilla Hawes," March 3, 1937. Mss 265: Box 14, Folder 29, Highlander Records.

Duke, David. *In the Trenches with Jesus and Marx: Harry F. Ward and the Struggle for Social Justice.* 2nd ed. Tuscaloosa: University of Alabama Press, 2003.

Dunbar, Anthony. *Against the Grain: Southern Radicals and Prophets, 1929–1959.* Charlottesville: University Press of Virginia, 1981.

Durr, Virginia Foster. *Freedom Writer: Virginia Foster Durr, Letters from the Civil Rights Years.* Ed. Patricia A. Sullivan. Athens: University of Georgia Press, 2006.

———. *Outside the Magic Circle: The Autobiography of Virginia Foster Durr,* ed. Hollinger F. Barnard. Tuscaloosa: University of Alabama Press, 1990.

Eby, Kenneth. "The 'Drip' Theory in Labor Unions." *Antioch Review,* March 1, 1953.

Egerton, John. "Appalachia's Absentee Landlords." *The Progressive,* June 1981.

———. "Highlander in the Thirties: An Appalachian Seedbed for Social Change." *Appalachian Heritage* 22, no. 1 (1994): 5–9.

"Ejected Witness Denies He Is a Red; Never Was, Horton Asserts—Says Removal by Eastland Prevented Testimony." *New York Times,* March 23, 1954.

Emblidge, David, ed. *My Day: The Best of Eleanor Roosevelt's Acclaimed Newspaper Columns, 1936–1962.* Boston: Da Capo Press, 2001.

Evans, Sara, and Harry Boyte. *Free Spaces: The Sources of Democratic Change in America.* Chicago: University of Chicago Press, 1992.

Federal Bureau of Investigation. Highlander Folk School Records, Folder 14, The Vault, https://vault.fbi.gov/Highlander%20Folk%20School.

Fehn, Bruce. "'The Only Hope We Had': United Packinghouse Workers Local 46 and the Struggle for Racial Equality in Waterloo, Iowa, 1848–1960." *Annals of Iowa* 54 (Summer 1995): 185–216.

Fellowship of Reconciliation, United States. "FORUSA: Advocating Peace & Justice through Nonviolence." Accessed December 23, 2019. www.forusa.org/.

Fish, John. "The Christian Commonwealth Colony: A Georgia Experiment, 1896–1900." *Georgia Historical Review* 57, no. 2 (1973): 213–26.

Fox, Richard. *Reinhold Niebuhr.* New York: Pantheon, 1985.

Garrow, David. "Series Editor's Preface." In Aimee Isgrig Horton, *The Highlander Folk School: A History of Its Major Programs, 1932–1961.* Brooklyn, NY: Carlson Publishing, 1989.

Gaventa, John. "Carrying On . . . " *Social Policy* 21, no. 3 (Winter 1991): 68–70.

———. "From John Gaventa," December 1982. Mss 831: Box 12, Folder 21, Myles Horton Papers.

———. Interview by Stephen Preskill, December 18, 2018.

Gellman, Eric, and Jarod Roll. *The Gospel of the Working Class: Labor's Southern Prophets in New Deal America.* Urbana: University of Illinois Press, 2011.

Gillespie, Deanna M. "'They Walk, Talk, and Act Like New People': Black Women and the Citizenship Education Program, 1957–1970." PhD Diss., State University of New York at Binghamton, 2008.

Gilyard, Keith. *Composition and Cornel West: Notes toward a Deep Democracy.* Carbondale: Southern Illinois University Press, 2008.

Glen, John M. *Highlander: No Ordinary School, 1932–1962.* Lexington: University Press of Kentucky, 1988.

———. *Highlander: No Ordinary School.* 2nd ed. Knoxville: University of Tennessee Press, 1996.

———. "Like a Flower Slowly Blooming: Highlander and the Nurturing of an Appalachian Movement." In *Fighting Back in Appalachia: Traditions of Resistance and Changes,* ed. Stephen L. Fisher, 31–55. Philadelphia: Temple University Press, 1993.

Gose, Allison Haley. "A Failed Dream: Literacy Education in the Global South." Honors thesis, University of Tennessee, 2015, http://trace.tennessee.edu/utk_chanhonoproj/1768.

Gregory, Judith. "A Weekend at Highlander." *Catholic Worker,* November 1960. Microfilm 12479: Reel 43, Frame 938, Grassroots Social Activism Records of the Highlander Folk School and Highlander Education and Research Center, 1932-1978 [microform], https://clio.columbia.edu/catalog/SCSB-1576272? counter=3.

Halberstam, David. *The Children.* New York: Fawcett, 1998.

Hall, Budd. "Letter from Budd Hall to Myles Horton," July 6, 1982. Mss 831: Box 12, Folder 19, Myles Horton Papers.

Halpern, Rick, and Roger Horowitz. *Meatpackers: An Oral History of Black Packinghouse Workers and Their Struggle for Racial and Economic Equality.* New York: Twayne, 1996.

Halsey, Ashley. "An Oasis for Social Change Celebrates Its Past, Future." *Philadelphia Inquirer,* October 21, 1982.

Handy, Robert. *A History of Union Theological Seminary in New York.* New York: Columbia University Press, 1987.

"Harry Ward Dies; Led ACLU to '40." *New York Times,* December 10, 1966, sec. Deaths.

Hart, Joseph. *Light from the North: The Danish Folk Highschools, Their Meanings for America.* New York: Henry Holt, 1927.

Hawes, Zilla. "Zilla Hawes to Jim Dombrowski," February 28, 1937. Mss 265: Box 14, Folder 29, Highlander Records.

Heaney, Tom. "Adult Education for Social Change: From Center Stage to the Wings and Back Again," Information Series No. 365, ERIC Clearinghouse for Adult, Continuing and Vocational Education, 1996.

——. "Resources for Popular Education." *Adult Learning* 3, no. 5 (1992): 10.

Herbers, M. Sharon. "Progressive Era Roots of Highlander Folk School: Lilian Wyckoff Johnson's Legacy." In *Tennessee Women: Their Lives and Times,* ed. Beverly Greene Bond and Sarah Wilkerson Freeman, 2:337-59. Athens: University of Georgia Press, 2015.

"Highlander Reports," Summer 1990. M2000: Box 4, Folder 30, Highlander Records.

"Highlander Reports: An Update with Myles," Summer 1989. M2010: Box 2, Folder 23, Highlander Records.

"Highlander Reports: Building for the Long Haul: The Horton Fund," Winter 1991. M2000: Box 4, Folder 29, Highlander Records.

"Highlander Reports: Highlander Co-Sponsors International Conference," October 1983. M2010: Box 2, Folder 23, Highlander Records.

"Highlander Research and Education Center," n.d. HREC 0002: Box 5, Folder 90, Highlander Research and Education Center, New Market, TN.

Hinsdale, Mary Ann, Helen M. Lewis, and S. Maxine Waller. *It Comes from the People: Community Development and Local Theology.* Philadelphia: Temple University Press, 1995.

Hodge, Chelsea. "The Coal Operator's Daughter: Zilphia Horton, Folk Music, and Labor Activism." *Arkansas Historical Quarterly* 76, no. 4 (2017): 291–307.

———. "'A Song Workers Everywhere Sing': Zilphia Horton and the Creation of Labor's Musical Canon." Master's thesis, University of Arkansas, 2014.

Hoose, Phillip. *Claudette Colvin: Twice toward Justice.* New York: Square Fish, 2010.

Horowitz, Roger. "The Path Not Taken: A Social History of Industrial Unionism in Meatpacking, 1930–1960." PhD diss., University of Wisconsin at Madison, 1990.

Horton, Aimee Isgrig. "Adult Education for Hemisphere Development: A Report on the First Inter-American Adult Education Seminar, Cuautla, Morelos, Mexico, December 16–21, 1962." Mss 831: Box 8, Folder 2, Myles Horton Papers.

———. *The Highlander Folk School: A History of Its Major Programs, 1932–1961.* Brooklyn, NY: Carlson Publishing, 1989.

Horton, Myles. "The Adventures of a Radical Hillbilly, Part 1." In Dale Jacobs, ed., *The Myles Horton Reader: Education for Social Change,* 117–38. Knoxville: University of Tennessee Press, 2003.

———. "The Adventures of a Radical Hillbilly, Part 2." In Dale Jacobs, ed., *The Myles Horton Reader: Education for Social Change,* 189–208. Knoxville: University of Tennessee Press, 2003.

———. "Appalachian Community Leadership Workshop," October 26, 1968. Mss 265: Box 109, Folder 14, Highlander Records.

———. "Appalachian Project Staff Memo 2," September 14, 1965. Mss 265: Box 32, Folder 9, Highlander Records.

———. "Appalachian Self-Education Program," 1968. Mss 265: Box 100, Folder 10, Highlander Records.

———. "Autobiographical Notes, Box Factory," n.d. Mss 831: Box 1, Folder 3, Myles Horton Papers.

———. "Building in the Democracy Mountains: The Legacy of the Highlander Center." In Dale Jacobs, ed., *The Myles Horton Reader: Education for Social Change,* 33–44. Knoxville: University of Tennessee Press, 2003.

———. "A Circle of Learners." In Dale Jacobs, ed., *The Myles Horton Reader: Education for Social Change,* 272–78. Knoxville: University of Tennessee Press, 2003.

———. "Class on Nashville Sit-Ins." Highlander Social Needs and Social Resources Workshop, March 1960. Mss 831: Box 13, Folder 24, Myles Horton Papers; also HREC 0002: Box 7, Folder 119, Highlander Research and Education Center, New Market, TN.

———. "Conference on Leadership Training," March 19, 1955. Box 3, Folder 2, Highlander Folk School Manuscript Collection, 1932–1966, Tennessee State Library and Archives, Nashville.

———. "Decision-Making Processes." In Dale Jacobs, ed., *The Myles Horton Reader: Education for Social Change,* 233–50. Knoxville: University of Tennessee Press, 2003.

———. "A Different Kettle of Fish." Interview by Susan Walker and Ike Coleman, 1989. Mss 831: Box 2, Folder 21, Myles Horton Papers.

———. "Efforts to Bring About Radical Change in Education." *Cutting Edge* 4, no. 10 (1973).

———. "A Faith Venture." In Dale Jacobs, ed., *The Myles Horton Reader: Education for Social Change,* 177–80. Knoxville: University of Tennessee Press, 2003.

———. "Family," n.d. Mss 831: Box 1, Folder 2, Myles Horton Papers.

———. "From Myles Horton to Marilyn Fedelchak," April 7, 1988. Mss 831: Box 8, Folder 6, Myles Horton Papers.

———. "Highlander." In Dale Jacobs, ed., *The Myles Horton Reader: Education for Social Change,* 11–20. Knoxville: University of Tennessee Press, 2003.

———. "Highlander Center Appalachian Project," 1965. Mss 265: Box 100, Folder 8, Highlander Records.

———. "Highlander's Educational Program." In Dale Jacobs, ed., *The Myles Horton Reader: Education for Social Change,* 257–69. Knoxville: University of Tennessee Press, 2003.

———. "Influences on Highlander Research and Education Center, New Market, Tennessee, USA." In Dale Jacobs, ed., *The Myles Horton Reader: Education for Social Change,* 20–32. Knoxville: University of Tennessee Press, 2003.

———. Interview by Dallas Blanchard, 1984. Southern Oral History Program Collection, file:///Users/stevesnew/Desktop/Dallas%20Blanchard%20Interview%20with%20MH.pdf.

———. Interview by Dana Thomas, March 9, 1959. M2010: Box 2, Folder 16, Highlander Records.

———. Interview by Richard Stevens, April 1983. Mss 831: Box 2, Folder 17, Myles Horton Papers.

———. *Interview with Myles Horton by John Peters and Brenda Bell (Part 2)*. DVD. Highlander Center, 1987.

———. "Letter from Myles Horton to Appalachian Project Staff," April 22, 1965. Mss 265: Box 108, Folder 8, Highlander Records.

———. "Letter from Myles Horton to Paulette Irving," December 22, 1982. Mss 831: Box 12, Folder 19, Myles Horton Papers.

———. "Letter to Arthur Carstens," March 22, 1954. Mss 265: Box 33, Folder 9, Highlander Records.

———. "Letter to Arthur Raper," May 21, 1940. Mss 265: Box 23, Folder 22, Highlander Records.

———. "Letter to Board of Directors," November 9, 1965. Mss 265: Box 100, Folder 8, Highlander Records.

———. "Letter to Georgia McFadden," September 11, 1980. Mss 831: Box 8, Folder 5, Myles Horton Papers.

———. "Letter to Margot Machado," April 21, 1959. Mss 265: Box 38, Folder 7, Highlander Records.

———. *The Long Haul: An Autobiography*. New York: Doubleday, 1990.

———. "Myles Horton Field Trip Report on Johns Island," December 1954. Mss 265: Box 67, Folder 3, Highlander Records.

———. "Myles Horton Speaks to the Unitarian Fellowship of Memphis," February 2, 1969. Mss 831: Box 3, Folder 14, Myles Horton Papers.

———. "Myles Horton: Statements on the Origin of Highlander." Interview by Aimee Isgrig Horton, 1966. M2010: Box 11, Folder 36, Highlander Records.

———. "Myles Horton to Geraldine Macías," August 15, 1977. Mss 831: Box 8, Folder 5, Myles Horton Papers.

———. "Myles Horton to Geraldine Macías," December 14, 1977. Mss 831: Box 8, Folder 5, Myles Horton Papers.

———. "Myles Horton to Geraldine Macías," December 14, 1979. Mss 831: Box 8, Folder 5, Myles Horton Papers.

———. "Myles Horton to Geraldine Macías," September 19, 1980. Mss 831: Box 8, Folder 5, Myles Horton Papers.

———. "Myles Horton to Geraldine Macías," April 8, 1982. Mss 831: Box 8, Folder 6, Myles Horton Papers.

———. "Myles Horton to John McFadden," May 12, 1981, Mss 831: Box 8, Folder 6, Myles Horton Papers.

———. "Myles Horton to Zilphia Horton," January 22, 1936. Mss 831: Box 15, Folder 13, Myles Horton Papers.

———. "1952 Progress Report to UPWA." Mss 265: Box 74, Folder 1, Highlander Records; also Microfilm 12479: Reel 39, Frame 693, Grassroots Social Activism Records of the Highlander Folk School and Highlander Education and Research Center, 1932–1978 [microform], https://clio.columbia.edu/catalog/SCSB-1576272?counter=3.

———. "Notes on Top-Downism," October 10, 1968. Mss 265: Box 100, Folder 11, Highlander Records.

———. "Profile of Huey Long." September 9, 1934. HREC 2010 Addition: Box 11, Folder 10, Highlander Research and Education Center, New Market, TN.

———. "Proposed Highlander Center Project for Appalachian Poor," Summer 1966. Mss 265: Box 32, Folder 9, Highlander Records.

———. "Report of Myles Horton, Education Director, UPWA Convention," 1952. Mss 265: Box 74, Folder 1, Highlander Records; also Microfilm 12479: Reel 39, Frames 652–61, Grassroots Social Activism Records of the Highlander Folk School and Highlander Education and Research Center, 1932–1978 [microform], https://clio.columbia.edu/catalog/SCSB-1576272?counter=3.

———. "Story about Race." Madison, Wisconsin, 1929. Mss 831: Box 4, Folder 6, Myles Horton Papers.

———. "Study the Power Structure." In Dale Jacobs, ed., *The Myles Horton Reader: Education for Social Change,* 99–108. Knoxville: University of Tennessee Press, 2003.

———. "A Trip to Nicaragua to Learn About and Celebrate the Year of the Literacy Crusade, August 21-August 30, 1980." M2004: Box 7, Folder 52, Highlander Records.

Horton, Myles, and Paulo Freire. *We Make the Road by Walking: Conversations on Education and Social Change,* ed. Brenda Bell, John Gaventa, and John Peters. Philadelphia: Temple University Press, 1990.

Horton, Zilphia. "An Experiment in Drama at the Highlander Folk School," 1940. Microfilm 12479: Reel 24, Frame 799, Grassroots Social Activism Records of the Highlander Folk School and Highlander Education and Research Center, 1932–1978 [microform], https://clio.columbia.edu/catalog/SCSB-1576272?counter=3.

———. "Notes on Johns Island," November 1954. Mss 265: Box 67, Folder 3, Highlander Records.

——. "People Like to Sing." *Food for Thought* 8, no. 6 (March 1948): 17–20.

Hunnicutt, Benjamin. *Work without End: Abandoning Shorter Hours for the Right to Work*. Philadelphia: Temple University Press, 1988.

"In Memoriam: Aimee Horton and Lawrence Guyot." Highlander Research and Education Center. Accessed November 30, 2019. www.highlandercenter. org/in-memoriam-aimee-horton.

Jacobs, Dale, ed. *The Myles Horton Reader: Education for Social Change*. Knoxville: University of Tennessee Press, 2003.

James, Betty. "Betty J. James to Myles Horton," February 18, 1981. Mss 831: Box 8, Folder 6, Myles Horton Papers.

Jenkins, Esau. "About Esau Jenkins and the Sea Islands of South Carolina," 1966. Microfilm 12479: Reel 22, Frames 786–826, Grassroots Social Activism Records of the Highlander Folk School and Highlander Education and Research Center, 1932–1978 [microform], https://clio.columbia.edu/catalog /SCSB-1576272?counter=3.

——. "Esau Jenkins to Myles Horton 1954," September 20, 1954. Mss 265: Box 67, Folder 3, Highlander Records.

Jones, Bob. "Highlander 1944 Annual Report," 1945. Mss 265: Box 1, Folder 5, Highlander Records.

Kates, Susan. "Literacy, Voting Rights, and the Citizenship Schools in the South, 1957–1970." *College Composition and Communication* 57, no. 3 (February 2006): 479–502.

Kelley, Robin D. G., and Makani Themba. "Why the Highlander Attack Matters." *The Nation*, May 13, 2019.

Kester, Howard. "Letter to Zilphia Mae Johnson," January 24, 1935. Mss 831: Box 15, Folder 13, Myles Horton Papers.

Knight, Louise. *Citizen: Jane Addams and the Struggle for Democracy*. Chicago: University of Chicago Press, 2006.

"Leadership Development Workshops for Emerging Leaders," July 1980. M90: Box 48, Folder 7, Highlander Records.

Legacy Museum and National Memorial for Peace and Justice. "The Legacy Museum and National Memorial for Peace and Justice." Accessed January 5, 2020. https://museumandmemorial.eji.org/news/2019–05–20/peace-and-justice-center-monument.

Lerner, Gerda. *Black Women in White America: A Documentary History*. New York: Vintage, 1972.

Lester, Julius. "Laughing All the Way." *Social Policy* 21, no. 3 (Winter 1991): 8–12.

Levine, David. "The Birth of the Citizenship Schools: Entwining the Struggles for Liberty and Freedom." *History of Education Quarterly* 44, no. 3 (Autumn 2004): 388–414.

———. "Citizenship Schools." PhD diss., University of Wisconsin at Madison, 1999.

Lewis, Helen. *Helen Mathews Lewis: Living Social Justice in Appalachia.* Lexington, KY: University Press of Kentucky, 2012.

———. "Paulo Freire at Highlander." In *Memories of Paulo,* ed. Tom Wilson, Peter Park, and Anaida Colón-Muñiz. Rotterdam: Sense Publishers, 2010.

Lewis, Helen, Linda Johnson, and Donald Askins. *Colonialism in Modern America: The Appalachian Case.* Boone, NC: Appalachian State Press, 1978.

Lewis, John. "Rep. John Lewis on the Fire at the Highlander Center." Congressional Documents and Publications, April 4, 2019. http://ezproxy.cul.columbia.edu/login?url=https://search.proquest.com/docview/22 03086345?accountid= 10226.

Lewis, John, and Michael D'Orso. *Walking with the Wind: A Memoir of the Movement.* New York: Simon & Schuster, 1998.

Lindeman, Eduard. *The Meaning of Adult Education.* New York: New Republic Press, 1926.

Ling, Peter. "Local Leadership in the Early Civil Rights Movement: The South Carolina Citizenship Education Program of the Highlander Folk School." *Journal of American Studies* 20, no. 3 (1995): 399–422.

Lorence, James J. *A Hard Journey: The Life of Don West.* Urbana: University of Illinois Press, 2007.

Macías, Geraldine. "Geraldine Macías to Myles Horton," October 5, 1977. Mss 831: Box 8, Folder 5, Myles Horton Papers.

———. "Geraldine Macías to Myles Horton," March 16, 1978. Mss 831: Box 8, Folder 5, Myles Horton Papers.

———. "Geraldine Macías to Myles Horton," May 27, 1978. Mss 831: Box 8, Folder 5, Myles Horton Papers.

———. "Geraldine Macías to Myles Horton," October 23, 1979. Mss 831: Box 8, Folder 5, Myles Horton Papers.

———. "Geraldine Macías to Myles Horton," January 14, 1980. Mss 831: Box 8, Folder 5, Myles Horton Papers.

———. "Geraldine Macías to Myles Horton," October 13, 1980. Mss 831: Box 8, Folder 5, Myles Horton Papers.

———. "Geraldine Macías to Myles Horton," March 15, 1982. Mss 831: Box 8, Folder 6, Myles Horton Papers.

———. "Newsletter from Geraldine Macías," July 14, 1982. Mss 831: Box 8, Folder 6, Myles Horton Papers.

Mantler, Gordon. *Power to the Poor: Black-Brown Coalition and the Fight for Economic Justice, 1960–1974.* Chapel Hill: University of North Carolina Press, 2013.

Martin, Robert. *Howard Kester and the Struggle for Social Justice in the South, 1904–77.* Charlottesville: University Press of Virginia, 1991.

Massie-Legg, Alicia R. "Zilphia Horton: A Voice for Change." PhD diss., University of Kentucky, 2014.

Mayo, Peter. Review of Myles Horton and Paulo Freire, *We Make the Road by Walking, Convergence* 24, no. 4 (1992): 77–80.

McGuire, Danielle L. *At the Dark End of the Street: Black Women, Rape, and Resistance—A New History of the Civil Rights Movement from Rosa Parks to the Rise of Black Power.* Reprint. New York: Knopf, 2010.

"Meeting at Highlander," March 3, 1956. Box 7, Folder 9, Highlander Folk School Manuscript Collection, 1932–1966, Tennessee State Library and Archives, Nashville.

Meeting of the Appalachian Project, 1965. Audio 515A/18, Highlander Records.

Meeting of the Community Development Project, 1965. Audio 515A/17, Highlander Records.

Mervosh, Sarah. "White Power Symbol Was Found at Scene of Fire, Civil Rights Center Says." *New York Times,* April 3, 2019. www.nytimes.com/2019/04/03 /us/civil-rights-center-fire.html?searchResultPosition=1.

Midyette, Mary. "Mary Midyette to Myles Horton," March 11, 1981. Mss 831: Box 8, Folder 6, Myles Horton Papers.

Miller, Valerie. *Between Struggle and Hope: The Nicaraguan Literacy Crusade.* Boulder, CO: Westview Press, 1985.

Morris, Aldon. "Education for Liberation." *Social Policy* 21, no. 3 (Winter 1991): 2–6.

———. *The Origins of the Civil Rights Movement: Black Communities Organizing for Change.* New York: Free Press, 1984.

Morris, Daniel A. "Unnoticed Consensus: Dewey, Niebuhr, and the Politics of Sovereignty." *Journal of Religion* 93, no. 3 (2013): 319–40.

Moses, Robert, and Charles Cobb. *Radical Equations: Civil Rights from Mississippi to the Algebra Project.* Boston: Beacon Press, 2001.

Moye, J. Todd. *Ella Baker: Community Organizer of the Civil Rights Movement.* New York: Rowman and Littlefield, 2013.

Moyers, Bill. "The Adventures of a Radical Hillbilly." *Bill Moyers Journal.* New Market, TN: Public Broadcasting Service, 1981.

Nerstrom, Norma, and Sue Himplemann. "Aimee Isgrig Horton." *Adult Learning Unleashed: ALU Consulting* (blog), November 30, 2019. www.alu-c.com/aimee-horton.

Niebuhr, Reinhold. *Moral Man and Immoral Society.* New York: Scribner's, 1932.

Niebuhr, Reinhold, and Myles Horton. "Fundraising Letter," May 27, 1932. Mss 831: Box 12, Folder 5, Myles Horton Papers.

O'Leary-Macías, Geraldine. *Lighting My Fire Memoirs: Between Two Worlds: The Passionate Journey of a Young American Woman.* Bloomington, IN: Trafford Publishing, 2013.

Osinski, Bill. "Highlander Center: A Half-Century on the Cutting Edge of Change." Louisville, Kentucky *Courier-Journal Magazine,* 1982.

Parks, Rosa. *Rosa Parks: My Story.* New York: Puffin, 1999.

Parks, Rosa, Myles Horton, and E. D. Nixon. Interview by Studs Terkel, 1973. HREC 0002: Box 5, Folder 90, Highlander Research and Education Center, New Market, TN.

Payne, Charles. *I've Got the Light of Freedom: The Organizing Tradition and the Mississippi Freedom Struggle.* Berkeley: University of California Press, 1995.

Peters, John. Interview by Stephen Preskill, May 20, 2018.

Peters, John, and Brenda Bell. "Horton of Highlander." In *Twentieth Century Thinkers in Adult and Continuing Education,* ed. Peter Jarvis. 2nd ed. London: Kogan Page, 2001.

Phenix, Lucy Massie, and Veronica Solver. *You Got to Move: Stories of Change in the South.* DVD. Milliarium Zero, 1985.

Pirro-Schmidt, Julia, and Karen McCurdy. "Employing Music in the Cause of Social Justice: Ruth Crawford Seeger and Zilphia Horton." *Voices* 31, no. 1/2 (Spring 2005): 32–36.

Polletta, Francesca. *Freedom Is an Endless Meeting: Democracy in American Social Movements.* Chicago: University of Chicago Press, 2002.

Preskill, Stephen, and Stephen D. Brookfield. *Learning as a Way of Leading: Lessons from the Struggle for Social Justice.* San Francisco: Jossey-Bass, 2009.

Price, Michael. "The New Deal in Tennessee: Highlander Folk School and Worker Response in Grundy County." *Tennessee Historical Quarterly* 43, no. 2 (Summer 1984): 99–120.

"Probe Witness Ousted on Order by Eastland." *Times-Picayune.* March 21, 1954, sec. 1.

"Protest against Revocation of Tax Exempt Status," May 8, 1957. Box 8, Folder 4, Highlander Folk School Manuscript Collection, 1932–1966, Tennessee State Library and Archives, Nashville.

Ransby, Barbara. *Ella Baker and the Black Freedom Movement: A Radical Democratic Vision.* 1st ed. Chapel Hill: University of North Carolina Press, 2003.

Robinson, Bernice. "Citizenship Training Schools," November 1979. M2004: Box 2, Folder 36, Highlander Records.

———. Interview by Sue Thrasher and Eliot Wigginton, 1980. 50th Anniversary Interview Archive, Highlander Research and Education Center, New Market, TN.

———. "Letter to Highlander from Bernice Robinson," July 19, 1955. Box 5, Folder 5, Highlander Folk School Manuscript Collection, 1932–1966, Tennessee State Library and Archives, Nashville.

Robinson, Cyril. *Marching with Dr. King: Ralph Helstein and the United Packinghouse Workers of America.* Santa Barbara, CA: Praeger, 2011.

Rossinow, Doug. "The Radicalization of the Social Gospel: The Search for a New Social Order, 1898–1936." *Religion and American Culture: A Journal of Interpretation* 15, no. 1 (2005): 63–106.

Rowan, Carl T. *South of Freedom.* New York: Knopf, 1952.

Russell, Clare. "A Beautician without Teacher Training." *The Sixties: A Journal of History, Politics, and Culture* 4, no. 1 (June 2011): 31–50.

Sands, Darren. "What Happened to Black Lives Matter?," BuzzFeed, 2017. www.buzzfeed.com/darrensands/what-happened-to-black-lives-matter.

Schneider, Stephen A. *You Can't Padlock an Idea: Rhetorical Education at the Highlander Folk School, 1932–1961.* Columbia: University of South Carolina Press, 2014.

Scott, Shaunna. "The Appalachian Land Ownership Study Revisited." *Appalachian Journal* 35, no. 3 (2008): 236–52.

———. "Discovering What the People Knew: The 1979 Appalachian Land Ownership Study." *Action Research* 7, no. 2 (2009): 185–205.

"Sea Islands: General Reports," 1954–1957. Mss265: Box 67, Folder 3, Highlander Records.

Seeger, Pete. *Where Have All the Flowers Gone? A Singalong Memoir.* Rev. ed. New York: W. W. Norton, 2009.

Seeger, Pete, and Bob Reiser. *Everybody Says Freedom: A History of the Civil Rights Movement in Songs and Pictures.* New York: W. W. Norton, 1989.

Seventh Annual College Workshop: The New Generation Fights for Equality. Highlander Folk School, 1960. Mss 265: Box 78, Folder 9, Highlander Records.

Shapiro, Karin A. *A New South Rebellion: The Battle against Convict Labor in the Tennessee Coalfields, 1871–1896.* Chapel Hill: University of North Carolina Press, 1998.

Smith, Spencer. "Septima Clark Yelled: A Revisionist History of Citizenship Schools." *American Educational History Journal* 46, no. 2 (2019): 95–110.

Stromquist, Shelton. *Solidarity and Survival: An Oral History of Iowa Labor in the Twentieth Century.* Iowa City: Iowa State Press, 1993.

Surratt, Marshall. "Myles Horton: Activism and Gospel." *Christianity and Crisis* 50, no. 18 (December 17, 1990): 398–402.

Swartz, H. T. "Letter from H. T. Swartz," February 20, 1957. Mss 265: Box 34, Folder 4, Highlander Records.

———. "Second Letter from H. T. Swartz," December 18, 1957. Mss 265: Box 34, Folder 4, Highlander Records.

Taylor, Gregory S. *The Life and Lies of Paul Crouch: Communist, Opportunist, Cold War Snitch.* Gainesville: University Press of Florida, 2014.

Theoharis, Jeanne. *A More Beautiful and Terrible History: The Uses and Misuses of Civil Rights History.* Boston: Beacon Press, 2018.

———. *The Rebellious Life of Mrs. Rosa Parks.* Boston: Beacon Press, 2013.

Thomas, Hulan. "A History of the Highlander Folk School, 1932–1941." Master's thesis, Vanderbilt University, 1964.

Thrasher, Martha Sue. "International Women as Popular Educators : An Inquiry into the Nature and Implications of Everyday Experience." EdD diss., University of Massachusetts at Amherst, 1996.

Thrasher, Sue. "Degrees of Change: Myles Horton's Lifetime Commitment to Radical Education." *Sojourners* 19, no. 3 (April 1990).

———. Interview by Stephen Preskill, September 19, 2018.

Tjerandsen, Carl. *Education for Citizenship: A Foundation's Experience.* Santa Cruz, CA: Emil Schwarzhaupt Foundation, 1980.

United States Congress, Senate Committee on the Judiciary. *Southern Conference Educational Fund, Inc.: Hearings before the Subcommittee to Investigate the Administration of the Internal Security Act and Other Internal Security Laws of the Committee on the Judiciary, United States Senate, Eighty-Third Congress, Second Session, on Subversive Influence in Southern Conference Educational Fund, Inc.,* March 18–20, 1954. Washington, DC: US Government Printing Office, 1955.

"UN Workshop," 1954. Mss 265: Box 78, Folder 6, Highlander Records.

Vallecillo, Ernesto. "Letter from Ernesto Vallecillo," August 11, 1983. Mss 831: Box 8, Folder 6, Myles Horton Papers.

Waller, Maxine. "Local Organizing: Ivanhoe, Virginia." *Social Policy* 21, no. 3 (Winter 1991): 62–67.

Waller, Maxine, Helen Lewis, Clare McBrien, and Carroll Wessinger. "'It Has to Come from the People': Responding to Plant Closings in Ivanhoe, Virginia."

In *Communities in Economic Crisis: Appalachia and the South,* ed. John
Gaventa, Barbara Ellen Smith, and Alex Willingham. Philadelphia: Temple
University Press, 1990.

Ward, Harry F. *Our Economic Morality and the Ethic of Jesus.* New York: Macmillan, 1929.

West, Don. Interview by Sue Thrasher, 1974. 50th Anniversary Interview
Archive, Highlander Research and Education Center, New Market, TN.

Whitman, Lois. "Nicaraguan Vote: 'Free, Fair, Hotly Contested.'" *New York
Times,* November 16, 1984.

Wigginton, Eliot. *Refuse to Stand Silently By: An Oral History of Grass Roots Social
Activism in America, 1921–64.* New York: Doubleday, 1992.

"Witness Ejected at Hearing; Ex-Red's Story Starts Fight." *New York Times,*
March 21, 1954, www.nytimes.com/1954/03/21/archives/witness-ejected-at-
hearing-exreds-story-starts-fight-2-at-hearing.html.

Wolin, Merle. "Nicaragua's Revolution." *New York Times,* June 30, 1979.

Yarbrough, Tinsley. *A Passion for Justice: J. Waties Waring and Civil Rights.*
Oxford: Oxford University Press, 1987.

Zacharakis-Jutz, Jeffrey. "Seizing the Moment: Highlander Folk School and the
Packinghouse Workers Union." *Convergence* 26, no. 4 (1993).

———. "Straight to the Heart of a Union, Straight to the Heart of a Movement:
Workers' Education in the United Packinghouse Workers of America
Between 1951 and 1953." EdD diss., Northern Illinois University, 1991.

Zellner, Dorothy M. "Red Roadshow: Eastland in New Orleans, 1954."
Louisiana History: The Journal of the Louisiana Historical Association 33, no. 1
(1992): 31–60.

Zinn, Howard. *You Can't Be Neutral on a Moving Train.* Boston: Beacon Press,
2002.

Index

Page references in italics indicate an illustration, and those followed by a t indicate a table. MH refers to Myles Horton, and MLK refers to Martin Luther King, Jr.

demagogues/charismatic leaders, 89–90, 250–52
democracy: Addams on, 56–57; democratic education, 49, 219–20; developmental, 220; Highlander's democratic principles/goals, 2, 90–91, 177, 236; MH on, 4, 139–40; Park on, 53–54
Democratic Union of Liberation (Nicaragua), 259
Dewey, John, 4, 46, 49–51, 278
Dollard, John: *Caste and Class in a Southern Town*, 128
Dombrowski, James: arthritis suffered by, 133; Christian Commonwealth Colony studied by, 81–82; as a Christian radical, 82; as a Communist supporter, alleged, 131; on crisis intervention, 85; education of, 80–81; fundraising by, 82; Highlander co-founded by, 45–46; Highlander organized by, 80–82; at SISS hearing, 129–33; and Ward, 81
Dorchester Center (Midway, Ga.), 194
Du Bois, W. E. B., 111–12
Dunford, Linda, 250
Durr, Clifford, 129, 137, 139, 168
Durr, Virginia, 129–30, 134–35, 156, 164, 166

Early, Kay, 249–50
Eastland, James O., 125–41; background/upbringing of, 126–27; on civil rights activism as Communist agitation, 126; as the "godfather of Mississippi politics," 127; law practice of, 127; personality of, 128; role in IRS finding on Highlander, 141; as a segregationist, 126, 128; at the University of Mississippi, 127; as a white supremacist, 125–27

—SISS HEARINGS, 128–29; aftermath, 140–42; censorship during, 139; commencement and location, 130–31; defense strategy, 129–30; Dombrowski's testimony, 131–33; Virgina Durr's testimony, 134–35; Eastland's demeanor, 131; media coverage, 139–40; MH's testimony, 136–40; subpoenas issued to civil rights activists, 125–26; Aubrey Williams's testimony, 135
Eastland, Woods, 127
Edgerton, John, 28–30
education: about labor, 120–21 (*see also under* Highlander Research and Education Center); adult, international network for, 271–73, 292; adult, theories of, 51–52, 60, 185, 188; adult literacy (*see* citizenship school); democratic, 49, 219–20; Dewey on, 49–50; "drip" vs. "percolator" style of, 120–21; experience's role in, 50, 52; Paulo Freire on, 189, 213, 258, 280, 282–83; indoctrination in, 51; institutionalized, 20–21, 42; vs. organizing, 86–90; popular, 9–10, 255, 268–69, 272–74; progressive, 49–50; in Tennessee, 14, 20 (*see also* Highlander Research and Education Center)
El Nuevo Éxodo (New Exodus), 271
evolutionary theory, 24

FBI, 196
Fellowship of Reconciliation, 73–74, 201
Fentress Coal and Coke, 70–72
Field Foundation, 194
Flint, Robert, 225–26
folk songs, 105

5, 11–14, 18–19; children of, 101, 225; circles of learners role of, 92–94; citizenship school role of, 171–75, 184, 186–87, 191; on citizenship schools, 259; on communism, 139–40; as a Communist, alleged, 122; on conflict, 54, 85, 207; in the CPC, 15, 22, 31; on crisis intervention, 85; on decision-making, 230–31; on democracy, 4, 139–40; in Denmark, 58–61; early employment, 18–19, 23; effectiveness as an adult educator, 9; exclusion opposed by, 25; football played by, 22–23, 143; on free speech and equal treatment, 118–19; and Paulo Freire, 276–78, 286–87; gravesite of, 290; and Hawes, 84–86; Highlander co-founded by, 1, 61–63, 136–37, viii; as Highlander director, 2, 253, viii; on Highlander's vision, 6–7; illness and death of, 4, 109, 286–87, 289–90, viii; on individualism vs. cooperation, 91–92; influence of, 290; influences on, 4, 284 (*see also* Counts, George S.; Dewey, John; Lindeman, Eduard; Niebuhr, Reinhold; Nightingale, Abram); on the injustice of the wage/labor system, 15, 19–20; on institutionalized education, 20–21, 42; integrity of, 48; at the International Council on Adult Education conference, 271–72; international travel by, 255–57; *It Comes from the People* dedicated to, 240; and Jenkins, 180–83; on Johns Island, 182–83; and Lacayo, 268; laughter/ sense of humor of, 159–60; leadership of, 253; legacy of, ix; listening skills of, 39, 93–94; *The Long Haul,* 8, 207, 251, 255, 285, 289; on love and trustworthiness, 16; marriage to Aimee, 198; marriage to Zilphia (*see* Horton, Zilphia Mae); memorial for, 290–91; on MLK, 90; Moyers's interview with, 6, 197, 293; in New York City, 52–53; in Nicaragua, 263–67, 273–75; on Nicaraguan elections, 273–74; on the Nicaraguan revolution, 269; and Nightingale, 33–35, 38, 41–44; and O'Leary, 255–63, 267, 269–70; Ozone's importance to, 41–42; and Parks, 147, 159–60, 164, 166–67, 290; personality of, 3–4, 65; photos of, 143, 145–50, 152–53; popular education, interest in, 255, 268–69, 272–74; pragmatism of, 80; questioning/devil's advocate played by, 206–7, 213, 246; on racial equality, 27–28; racism, writings on, 26–27; radicalization of, 30, 53; reaction to Highlander's closing, 197; reading habits of, 17–18, 21, 23; religious life of, 31; retirement of, 255; on the SCEF board, 129; at SISS hearing, 125–26, 129–30, 136–40; on the sit-in movement, 204; storytelling by, 20, 87, 286; as a strike organizer, 86–88; structure and organization, aversion to, 80–81; on the struggle for justice's impact on participants, 219; on student protesters' independence from organizations, 204, 210; suspicion about educational purposes of, 125; as a teacher, 206–7, 213, 219–20, 281; unionizing attempt by, 29–30; as UPWA education director, 118, 120–23; voice and manner of, 205–6; on

Horton, Myles *(continued)*
Waller, 250–51; and Don West, 64–66; on whites' role in supporting black colleagues, 214–15; on working outside vs. inside the system, 282–83; YMCA work of, 24–27, 42, 56. See also *We Make the Road by Walking*
—EDUCATION: Cumberland University, 22–23, 28, 30, 52–53, 56, 143; early, 12–13, 18, 20–21; Union Theological Seminary, 42–49; University of Chicago, 53–54, 57–58
Horton, Perry (MH's father), 11–13, 17–18, 28, 279, 290
Horton, Thorsten (MH's son), 101, 225–26
Horton, Zilphia Mae (*née* Johnson): activism of, 101; arrival at Highlander, 100; childhood and upbringing of, 96–97; death of, 109; gravesite of, 290; influence on "We Shall Overcome," 108–9; on Jenkins, 181–82; marriage to MH, 100–101, 146; as a musician, 96–97, 105–6; personality of, 106–7; role in Highlander's music and drama programs, 101–8, 173, 248, 281; as a social justice thespian, 101–3; on unions, 123; and Claude Williams, 97–99
House Un-American Activities Committee, 125
Hull House (Chicago), 54–57
Humboldt (Tennessee), 12

"I'm Going to Sit at the Welcome Table," 209
Industrial Workers of the World (IWW), 97–98

INPRHU (Institute for Human Development), 258, 262
integration: Highlander's promotion of, 2, 111–17, 141, 148, 162–63, 177, 195, 202; in unions, 118–19; white supremacists' fear of, 110
Inter-American Adult Education Seminar (Cuautla, Mexico, 1962), 256
International Council of Adult Education (Yugoslavia, 1980), 271
International Council on Adult Education (Paris, 1982), 271–72
International Popular Education Conference for Peace (Managua, Nicaragua, 1983), 272–73
International Popular Education Conference for Peace (Nicaragua, 1983), 272–73
IRS (Internal Revenue Service), 141–42
It Comes from the People (Hinsdale, Waller, and H. Lewis), 240, 254
Ivanhoe (Virginia): community renewal in, 239; decision-making power in, 245; female leadership in, 240; "Hands across Ivanhoe" campaign, 242–43; health needs of, 248; industrial pollution in, 250; Ivanhoe History Project, 248–50; Ivanhoe Tech, 247–49; population of, 242; poverty in, 245; townspeople's priorities, 246–47
Ivanhoe Civic League, 242, 252–54
IWW (Industrial Workers of the World), 97–98

Jacobs, Dale: *Myles Horton Reader,* 8
Jenkins, Esau, 149; citizenship school role of, 174–75, 183–84, 191; and

Septima Clark, 172, 177-78, 180, 183-84; commitment to the citizenship school, 173, 180-81; Highlander workshop attended by, 170-71, 180; on literacy, 170-71, 179; and MH, 180-83; in the NAACP, 178; runs for school board trustee, 180-81; on segregated education/racial discrimination, 178; transportation of African Americans provided by, 178-79

Jim Crow. *See* segregation

John C. Campbell Folk School (Brasstown, N.C.), 83

Johns Island (South Carolina), 172, 175-78. *See also* citizenship school

Johnson, Charles, 112

Johnson, Lilian, 64-67, 78-79, 137, 144

Johnson, Linda: *Colonialism in Modern America,* 244

Johnson, Lyndon, 223

Johnson, Robert Guy, 96-99

Johnson, Zilphia Mae. *See* Horton, Zilphia Mae

Jones, Bob, 113-14

Kazan, Elia: *People of the Cumberland,* 268

"Keep Your Eyes on the Prize," 209

Kelly, Anna D., 176-77

Kennedy administration, 217

Kester, Alice, 73-75

Kester, Howard ("Buck"), 73-75, 99

Kinco, 64

King, Martin Luther, Jr.: assassination of, 90, 232; attempts to capture the youth movement, 211; civil rights movement influenced by, 89-90; as a Communist, alleged, 151; as a freedom fighter, 3; at Highlander anniversary, 150-51, 195-96; letter to MH, 154; on the Poor People's Campaign, 231-32; SCLC led by, 89, 162, 193

King, Mary, 212

knowledge, 233-34, 238

Knoxville College, 111

Kodak (Tennessee), 175

Kohl, Judith and Herbert: *The Long Haul,* 8, 207, 251, 255, 285, 289

Kohn, John P., 134

Ku Klux Klan, 156

labor movement, 2. *See also* unions

Lacayo, Francisco ("Chico"), 268

Lafayette, Bernard, 202, 205-8, 291

Lamb, Brian, 3

Lao Tzu, 285

Lawson, James, 201-3, 206

leadership: and change, 251; charismatic, 89-90, 250-52; collaborative, 253-54; group-centered, 213-14

learning, 213-14, 230-31. *See also* education

Lerner, Gerda, 212

Lester, Julius, 159-60

Levine, David, 191

Lewis, Helen: *Colonialism in Modern America,* 244; *It Comes from the People,* 240, 254; in Ivanhoe, 239, 241, 246-48; Ivanhoe History Project supervised by, 248; on leadership, 241, 254; on MH and Freire's collaboration, 277-78; as a participatory researcher, 239-41, 246-47; role in international network of adult educators, 271

Lewis, John (congressman): at ABT, 200; and Bevel, 200–201; and Septima Clark, 208–9; on the Highlander fire, vii; on Highlander's purpose, 210; Highlander workshop attended by, 205–6; on integration at Highlander, 2; and Lawson, 201; and MH, 208; on nonviolence, 207; nonviolent-resistance workshops attended by, 201–2; preaching skills of, 200; on the Voter Education Project, 217; on "We Shall Overcome," 209

Lewis, John L. (United Mine Workers president), 104

Lindeman, Eduard, 49, 51–52, 60

Ling, Peter, 173

literacy: Septima Clark on, 191; importance of, 189, 191; Jenkins on, 170–71, 179; Robinson on, 171; tests for, 179, 184, 186

Lomax, Alan, 107

Long, Huey, 89

The Long Haul (MH and the Kohls), 8, 207, 251, 255, 285, 289

Lula (Luiz Inácio Lula da Silva), 286

Lyons, Bob, 38–39

Lyons, George, 250

Macías, Edgard de, 257–62, 267–68, 270–71

Macías, Geraldine O. de. *See* O'Leary, Geraldine

Macías O'Leary, Alana Libertad, 260, 262–63, 267

Macías O'Leary, Genevieve Paz, 267

Marshall, Thurgood, 153

Marx, Karl, 4, 284

McCarthyism/Red Scare, 118, 125–26, 129. *See also* SISS

McFadden, Georgia and John, 263

Mencken, H. L., 24

Merrifield, Juliet, 241, 271

Mexican Americans, 232

Miller, Valerie, 264, 266–67

Mineral Springs (Tennessee), 228–30

mining, 32–33, 70–72

Minority Group Conference (Atlanta, 1968), 231

Mississippi planter society, 126–28

Montgomery (Alabama): bus boycott in, 21, 147, 155, 158, 166–68; discrimination/segregation in, 164–66; integration of bus system in, 168; sued over segregated transportation, 168

Moore, Amzie, 217–18

"Mopping Up" (Hawes), 103

morality, 46–47

Moral Man and Immoral Society (Niebuhr), 46–47

Morris, Aldon, 1

Moses, Bob, 217–18

Moyers, Bill, 6, 197, 293

Myles and Zilphia Horton Fund for Education and Social Change, 109, 291

Myles Horton Reader (Jacobs), 8

NAACP (National Association for the Advancement of Colored People), 204; Baker's leadership of, 162; desegregation efforts of, 157–58; goals of, 156; lawsuit against Montgomery, 168; Parks's role in, 156–57, 160; Youth Council, 156–57, 160, 166–67

Nash, Diane, 202, 217

Nashville sit-ins, 203–4, 208

National Association for the Advancement of Colored People. *See* NAACP

National Association of Manufacturers, 28-29

National Carbide, 242, 244

National Youth Administration, 129

Native American fishing rights, 232

New Deal, 129

New Jersey Zinc, 242, 244

New York Times, 139-40

Nicaragua, 255; earthquake in (1972), 257; elections in (1984), 273-74; Highlander's connection with, 268; Nicaraguan National Literacy Crusade, 263-67; repression after the revolution in, 269-70; the Sandinistas, 261, 269, 274-75; scarcity and unemployment in, 263; social movements in, 260; under Somoza, 257-62; U.S. involvement in, 258, 262, 269-70, 274; violence in, 259, 261

Niebuhr, Reinhold, 41, 45-49, 53-54, 57-58, 62, 140; *Moral Man and Immoral Society,* 46-47

Nightingale, Abram, 33-35, 38, 41-44

Nixon, E. D., 156-58, 161, 166-67

nonviolent resistance/protests, 202-4

Nuevo Éxodo (New Exodus), 271

O'Leary, Geraldine, 255-63, 267-71, 274

opinion vs. knowledge, 233-34

organizations' role in empowerment, 56

organizing vs. education, 86-90

Our Economic Morality and the Ethic of Jesus (Ward), 33, 44-45

Ozone (Tennessee): Bible school in, 31-33, 36; community meetings in, 35-41, 230; economy of, 32; importance to MH, 41-42; location/views of, 31-32

pacifism, 201

Padgett, Early, 228-30

Palmer (A. Mitchell) Raids, 45

Park, Robert, 53-54, 57-58

Parks, Rosa, 155-69; activism of, 156, 161, 163, 169; arrest of, 129, 155, 167; and Baker, 161-62, 167; and Septima Clark, 158, 160-62, 164, 166-67; and Colvin, 157; as a freedom fighter, 3; on the Freedom Train, 160-61; on gradualism, 163; at Highlander anniversary, 150; Highlander workshop attended by, 155-56, 158-60, 162-64, 166-67, 169; integrated meetings attended by, 160; leadership of, 240-41; and MH, 147, 159-60, 164, 166-67, 290; and the Montgomery bus boycott, 147, 155, 167-68; at Montgomery Fair, 164; NAACP role of, 156-57, 160; refuses to give up bus seat, 164-67, 169; and Eleanor Roosevelt, 168; whites in support of, 129; on whites' role in desegregation efforts, 215

participatory research, 233-34, 236-41, 246-47

Participatory Research Group, 262

Patterson, Frederick, 94-95

Payne, Charles, 211

Pedagogy of the Oppressed (Freire), 276

People of the Cumberland (Kazan), 268

Perkins, Frances, 76-77

Peters, John, 277, 285-86, 289-90

Phenix, Lucy: *You've Got to Move,* 107-8

134–35. *See also under* Eastland, James O.

sit-in movement, 202–4, 208, 216

SNCC (Student Nonviolent Coordinating Committee): debate over goals (direct action vs. voting rights), 216–19; democratic education of participants, 219–20; factions within, 218; founding of, 162, 211–16; meeting held at Highlander, 216, 218; White Student Project, 222–23

social justice: Highlander's commitment to, 3, 141–42; "the ought to be" concept of, 60, 110–11; the struggle's impact on participants, 219; *We Make the Road by Walking* on joining the struggle, 283–84

social movements: black freedom movement, 109, 219 (*see also* SNCC); Black Lives Matter movement, 3; citizenship school movement, 175–76, 192–93, 256, 259, 292 (*see also* citizenship school (Johns Island, S.C.)); impetus for, 53, 176; preconditions for success, 163; women's movement, 241. *See also* civil rights movement

Solver, Veronica: *You've Got to Move*, 107–8

Somoza regime, 257–62

song's power to unite, 209–10

Southern Appalachian Training Program, 243, 292

Southern Christian Leadership Conference. *See* SCLC

Southern Conference Education Fund. *See* SCEF

Southern Jim Crow segregation, 1–2, 27, 110, 149. *See also* segregation

Stephens, A. T., 121–23

stock market crash (1929), 43

Stokely, Jim, 148

Student Nonviolent Coordinating Committee. *See* SNCC

Summerfield (Tennessee), 63, 68

Supreme Court: *Browder v. Gale* upheld by, 168; *Brown v. Board of Education*, 94, 126, 159, 177

Swartz, H. T., 141

Taitt-Magubane, Lenora, 212

Taylor, Alva W., 65–66, 74–75

Tefferteller, Ralph, 99, 104

Tennessee: agriculture in, 13; attitude toward African Americans in, 16; education in, 14, 20 (*see also* Highlander Research and Education Center); liquor sales prohibited in, 196–97; segregation in, 110

Tennessee Products, 76–77

textile workers' strike (Lumberton, N.C.), 86–88

Theoharis, Jeanne, 21

Thomas, Henry, 76–77

Thomas, Hulan Glyn, 63

Thomas, Norman, 70

Thompson, Dorothy, 66

Thompson, John B., 66–67, 70–71

Thrasher, Sue, 9, 241, 271–73, 277, 286, 289, 292

Tiller, John, 244

UAW (United Auto Workers), 113–16

Ulloa de Alaniz, Maria, 264–65

Unearthing Seeds of Fire (Adams), 7, 260

unions: AFL, 78, 123; Amalgamated Clothing Workers of America, 85; business vs. social unionism, 119; CIO, 78, 85–86, 118, 123;

unions *(continued)*
    conservatism of, 118, 123; hostility
    toward, 86; integration in, 118–19;
    MH's early interest in, 28; miners'
    strike in Wilder, 70–75; plays about
    union experiences, 102–3; UAW,
    113–16; United Mine Workers, 70,
    223; UPWA, 118–24, 147
Union Theological Seminary (New
    York City), 42–49
United Auto Workers (UAW), 113–16
United Mine Workers, 70, 223
United Packinghouse Workers
    Association (UPWA), 118–24, 147
University of Chicago, 53–54, 57–58
University of Mississippi, 127
UPWA (United Packinghouse
    Workers Association), 118–24, 147

Virginia Coal and Iron, 223
Voter Education Project, 217
voter registration, 156, 171, 176, 179,
    187, 192–94, 217–18

Waller, Maxine: education of, 245–47,
    249–50; on Highlander and MH,
    281–82; Highlander visits by,
    243–45; *It Comes from the People,* 240,
    254; on Ivanhoe's history, 249–50;
    leadership of, 239, 241–43, 250–54;
    on MH, 290–91
Ward, Harry: ACLU founded by, 45;
    anti-war activism of, 44; on
    capitalism, 44–45; and Dom-
    browski, 81; *Our Economic Morality
    and the Ethic of Jesus,* 33, 44–45; at
    Union Theological Seminary, 45–46
Waring, J. Waties and Elizabeth, 181
war on poverty, 223, 232
Washington, Lucille, 252

wealth inequality, 14–15, 20, 235
Wellstone, Paul, 3–5
We Make the Road by Walking (MH and
    P. Freire), 276–87; on apparent
    inconsistencies, 278; on collabora-
    tions, 278; "Formative Years,"
    278–79; on human incompleteness,
    278; idea for, 276–77; on joining the
    social justice struggle, 283–84;
    manuscript preparation, 285–86;
    publication of, 8, 287; as revitalizing
    both authors, 285
"We Shall Overcome," 108–9, 209,
    272
West, Connie, 66, 79–80
West, Cornel, 3
West, Don: on Appalachia as a colony,
    244; appearance and personality of,
    65; departure from Highlander,
    79–80; Highlander co-founded by,
    63–65, 136–37, viii; on Highlander's
    first year, 67; and MH, 64–66;
    radicalism of, 80; and Taylor,
    65–66; at Vanderbilt University,
    65–66
White, Mildred, 137
white supremacy: giving credit to
    white men, 174; integrationists
    feared by, 110; MH on, 25, 27; in
    Mississippi, 127–28; Parks's fight
    against, 156, 169; permanence of,
    171; and whites' duty to end racism,
    116. *See also* Eastland, James O.
Wilder (Tennessee), 70–75
Williams, Aubrey, 129–30, 135, 150,
    195
Williams, Claude, 97–99
Williams, Susan, 236
Wine, Alice, 93, 179
Witness for Peace, 273–74

Founded in 1893,
UNIVERSITY OF CALIFORNIA PRESS
publishes bold, progressive books and journals
on topics in the arts, humanities, social sciences,
and natural sciences—with a focus on social
justice issues—that inspire thought and action
among readers worldwide.

The UC PRESS FOUNDATION
raises funds to uphold the press's vital role
as an independent, nonprofit publisher, and
receives philanthropic support from a wide
range of individuals and institutions—and from
committed readers like you. To learn more, visit
ucpress.edu/supportus.